Comparing Canada and the Americas

This book is part of the Peter Lang Political Science, Economics, and Law list.
Every volume is peer reviewed and meets
the highest quality standards for content and production.

PETER LANG
New York • Bern • Berlin
Brussels • Vienna • Oxford • Warsaw

Patrick Imbert

Comparing Canada and the Americas

From Roots to Transcultural Networks

Translated by Jonathan Cimon-Lambert
and Zishad Lak

PETER LANG
New York • Bern • Berlin
Brussels • Vienna • Oxford • Warsaw

Library of Congress Cataloging-in-Publication Control Number: 2019022845

Bibliographic information published by **Die Deutsche Nationalbibliothek**.
Die Deutsche Nationalbibliothek lists this publication in the "Deutsche Nationalbibliografie"; detailed bibliographic data are available on the Internet at http://dnb.d-nb.de/.

ISBN 978-1-4331-7213-7 (hardback)
ISBN 978-1-4331-7214-4 (ebook pdf)
ISBN 978-1-4331-7215-1 (epub)
ISBN 978-1-4331-7216-8 (mobi)
DOI 10.3726/b16235

29 Broadway, 18th floor, New York, NY 10006
www.peterlang.com

Canada… is a receptive ground for other people's fantasies.[1]

The Japanese consul had put it best when he said: "America's great and lasting significance is its existence in the mind."[2]

The concept [of culture] is characterized by three elements: by social homogenization, ethnic consolidation and intercultural delimitation… All three elements of this traditional concept have become untenable today.[3]

Les cultures ne sont pas des entités autonomes ou statiques. […] Comme les personnes humaines, les cultures n'existent qu'en relation les unes avec les autres.[4]

Contrairement à toi, je me sens à ma place partout.[5]

Notes

1. Pico Iyer, *Imagining Canada: An Outsider's Hope for a Global Future* (Toronto, The Hart House Lecture, 2001), 19.
2. Pico Iyer, *The Global Soul* (New York, Vintage, 2000), 229.
3. Wolfgang Welsch, "Transculturality: The Puzzling form of Cultures Today," in *Space of Culture: City, Nation, World*, eds. Mike Featherstone and Scott Lash (London: Sage, 1999), 194–195.
4. UNESCO, *Investir dans la diversité culturelle et le dialogue interculturel*, Paris, Rapport mondial de l'UNESCO (unabridged report), 2009, p. 9. We translate: "Cultures are not static or autonomous entities. [...] Like human beings, cultures exist only in relationship with each other." (In French in the text)
5. Kim Thúy et Pascal Janovjak, *À toi* (Montréal, Libre expression, 2011), 63. We translate: "Unlike you, I feel I am in my place everywhere." (In French in the text)

Bibliography

Iyer, Pico. *Imagining Canada: An Outsider's Hope for a Global Future*. Toronto: The Hart House Lecture, 2001.

Iyer, Pico. *The Global Soul*. New York: Vintage, 2000.

Thúy, Kim et Pascal Janovjak. *À toi*. Montréal: Libre Expression, 2011.

UNESCO, *Investir dans la diversité culturelle et le dialogue interculturel*, Paris, Rapport mondial de l'UNESCO (unabridged report), 2009.

Welsch, Wolfgang. "Transculturality: The Puzzling form of Cultures Today." In *Space of Culture: City, Nation, World*. Eds. Mike Featherstone and Scott Lash. London: Sage, 1999.

TABLE OF CONTENTS

ACKNOWLEDGMENTS

This comparative research on the Americas was made possible through the support of The Social Sciences and Humanities Research Council of Canada. This book, the result of this research, meets the objectives of University of Ottawa Research Chair directed by Patrick Imbert, "Canada: Social and Cultural Challenges in a Knowledge-Based Society."

INTRODUCTION

How can we compare the Americas according to cultural perspectives? Certainly not within the framework of a historical discourse that has tended to base itself on differences. After all, any historical discourse is controlled by its allegiance to the nation-state and tends to impose canonical points of view which serve the interests of a culture and of a society presented as homogeneous (Paquin 1999). As evidenced by the textbooks used in schools, few states would agree to legitimize several concurrent histories. Canada, which is a multinational and multiethnic state, as mentioned by Will Kymlicka in *Multicultural Odysseys* (2007), is one of the rare countries to develop a multicultural perspective that is to live its identity primarily on the ambitious idea of an economic, cultural and civic federation rather than on one simply based on territory. All historical discourses also tend to disseminate narratives legitimizing borders as a result of often arbitrary or deadly military conflicts.

The method based on historical comparisons embodies the methodological nationalism criticized by Andreas Wimmer and Nina Glick Schiller (2002) and, by others after them under different contexts and purposes; most notably by Will Kymlicka in 2007 and Carlos Sandoval García in 2007. Yet, the Americas are built on coincidences rather than on causalities[1], on encounters to develop in the present or in short-term future rather than on long-term established relationships like in Asia or in Europe. It should, however, be understood that the democratic culture in most countries in Europe and in Asia—in contradistinction with the practice of long-term European or Asian cultures of erecting grandiose historical monuments related to aristocratic or dictatorial systems—has been in place for a short period of time. However, democratic cultures have been thriving for a long time in Canada and in the United States, unlike the newer or almost non-existent democracies in many countries of the world with authoritarian histories.

Admittedly, each state tries to invent, in the process of political independence, long cultural and economic timeframes, which combine causalities in order to generate narrative-based identities. Each state usually seeks to impose these processes dualistically in order to generate a belief in homogeneity. In the nineteenth century, these timeframes and causalities are found in the paradigm of barbarism/civilization which excludes many populations in the Americas like the Natives, the Blacks and the Métis. This paradigm is in itself a particular historical and cultural configuration of a more fundamental paradigm reproduced throughout the centuries, in societies and narratives: the exterior/interior paradigm (see section: Comparative Paradigms). It is connected to an anthropological foundation of space organization and is supported by René Girard's theory (1978) which presents the detailed mechanism of the invention of solidarity based on the exclusion of a scapegoat as a result of the struggle of all against all aiming at controlling a desired object. This struggle is rooted in the mimesis of appropriation leading everybody to try to control the object of desire produced by a model. This mimetic mechanism threatens to constantly destroy the social order. Hence, the barbarism/civilization paradigm joined a broader master narrative (Lyotard 1979), which is Eurocentric and colonialist, the ramifications of which extend throughout the world in the nineteenth century and the first part of the twentieth century. However, during the second half of the twentieth century and in the twenty-first century, the barbarism/civilization paradigm transforms itself in a series of elements eluding dualism, playing on non-dualism, fluidity and concepts such as chameleonage (see section: The Generalized Chameleonage), legitimacy of displacements and ideas of inter, multi and transculturalism (section: Transcultural Citizenship).

That is why, for the last sixty years, the barbarism/civilization paradigm legitimizing narratives of exclusion has been questioned. It should be noted that in 1991 Colombia changed its constitution of 1886 for a multicultural one by removing the assertion that all Colombians were descendants from

Castille in Spain. It was this assertion that led to violent exclusions, because it did not correspond to any constructive dynamic in the daily socio-economic practices. In Quebec, the misleading side of history is underlined by Éric Dupont in his novel *La Logeuse* (2006). In this novel, he criticizes Joan of Arc's myth and Catholic nationalism. He also rejects the murderous disinformation of the orthodox ideologies such as Marxism and their dictatorial political regulations while promoting open, successful and ethical meetings between groups and individuals (section: The Variegated Land). As opposed to the domination by a national state history that wants to be homogenous and aims to establish a long-term perspective, Will Kymlicka, particularly in *Multicultural Odysseys*, sees Canada as a country where individuals and groups from all over the world can flourish with their different pasts. Thanks to its parabolic dimension, Yann Martel's *Life of Pi* (2001) explores the possibilities of living together in a present to be invented for the survivors (the tiger and Piscine) sharing a raft. In their encounter, each character embodies radical otherness, yet they manage to cooperate.

Moving past the perspective wherein the national culture appears as homogeneous and controlled by the nation states' stories of legitimacy to a vision promoting the study of forgotten links and dynamic encounters within the complex coincidences and simultaneities of the present context of liberalism and globalization, we will be analyzing the changes that redefine the Americas. Clifford Geertz (1983) mentions that, often, ideas and responses to similar situations (various colonial relations) or to similar discussions (of European cultural dominance) are invented in places that are not necessarily historically linked. Even so, these responses and dynamics are based on arguments aiming at similar desired effects, such as the creation of a rooted identity leading to the invention of a nation imagined as homogeneous while the changes brought on by globalization upset society and lead to the creation of multiple and networked self-images. These changes displace the dualistic and static basic paradigms defining the national identity. They turn into more inclusive dynamics where the dualistic paradigms become complex fluidities.

Thus, from a modernist vantage point, despite the dream of stability trying to control the fear of chaos, the perspectives often focused on the exploration of change, as seen in the work of T. C. Keefer entitled *Philosophy of Railroads* (1853). Nowadays, the craving for stability and the importance of dualistic paradigms is displaced by a desire to establish and study fluid connections to develop societies based on the respect of differences within a framework fostering equality.

Hence, we aim to understand how the various regions of the Americas have invented themselves, according to the sense of the word "invent" put forth by the Palo Alto school (by Gregory Bateson (1972) for example), and how they invent and reinvent themselves daily. Nowadays, they escape from the essentialist identity stemming from the nineteenth century dualism and aim at fostering multicultural relational identities. As highlighted by Abril Trigo (1997) and Yvon Rivard (2005), the Americas still remain an unfinished project. They constantly produce new stories that support cultural mobility and multiple encounters in dynamics which are open to the unexpected. These new stories are related to the prospects offered by interculturalism, multiculturalism and transculturalism (Benessaieh/Imbert 2011; Fontille/Imbert 2012).

Note

1. Hence, it is difficult to agree with a genetic approach, which tries to establish causal links when comparing the Americas such as can be found in the articles published by Lois Parkinson Zamora, Eduardo Gonzalez, José Piedra and David T. Haberly in the book edited by Gustavo Pérez Firmat titled *Do the Americas Have a Common Literature?* (Durham, Duke University Press, 1990). The appositional approach developed by Wendy H. Faris, René Prieto and Jonathan Monroe in this book is more interesting.

Bibliography

Bateson, Gregory. *Steps to an Ecology of Mind.* New York: Ballantine, 1972.

Benessaieh, Afef, and Patrick Imbert. "De Bouchard-Taylor à l'Unesco: Ambivalences interculturelles et clarifications transculturelles." In *Canadian Studies: The State of the Art/ Études canadiennes: questions de recherche*, Canadiana 10. Eds. Klaus-Dieter Ertler, Stewart Gill, Susan Hodgett, and Patrick James. Frankfurt: Peter Lang, 2011. 393–413.

Dupont, Éric. *La logeuse.* Montréal: Marchand de feuilles, 2006.

Fontille, Brigitte, and Patrick Imbert (eds.). *Trans, multi, interculturalité, trans, multi, interdisciplinarité.* Québec: Presses de l'Université Laval, 2012.

Girard, René. *Des choses cachées depuis la fondation du monde.* Paris: Livre de poche, 1978.

Geertz, Clifford. *Local Knowledge: Further Essays in Interpretive Anthropology.* New York: Basic Book, 1983.

Keefer, Thomas C. *Philosophy of the Railroads.* Montréal: Lovell, 1853.

Kymlicka, Will. *Multicultural Odysseys: Navigating the New International politics of Diversity.* Oxford: Oxford University Press, 2007.

Lyotard, Jean-François. *La condition postmoderne: rapport sur le savoir.* Paris: Éditions de Minuit, 1979.

Martel, Yann. *Life of Pi.* Toronto: Vintage, 2001.

Paquin, Stéphane. "Les théories explicatives de l'apparition des nations et du nationalisme." *Bulletin d'histoire politique*, 1999, vol. 8, no. 1 (1999): 102–14.

Pérez Firmat, Gustavo. *Do the Americas Have a Common Literature?* Durham: Duke University Press, 1990.

Rivard, Yvon. *Le siècle de Jeanne*. Montréal: Boréal, 2005.

Sandoval García, Carlos. *El mito roto: Inmigración y emigración en Costa Rica.* San Jose : Editorial Universidad de Costa Rica, 2007.

Trigo, Abril. *¿Cultura uruguaya, culturas linyeras?* Montevideo: Vintén, 1997.

Wimmer, Andreas, and Nina Glick Schiller. "Methodological Nationalism and Beyond: Nation-State Building, Migration and the Social Sciences." *Global Networks* vol. 2, no. 4 (2002): 301–34.

· 1 ·

THE INVENTION OF NATION-STATES AND FOUNDING PARADIGMS

Exterior/Interior as a Synonym for Barbarism/Civilization

Canada and Its Inter-American Ties

> Indeed, were I to engage in a genuine comparative study of cultures, it would not be the United States and Canada, or Canada and Australia, or Québec and the Transvaal that I would examine most closely: it would be Canada and Argentina.[1]

Despite previous assertions, the historical ties that have developed over the centuries between the Americas[2] should not be overlooked; in particular the connections between Canada and Latin America long perceived as insignificant. In fact, the vast majority of research on the Americas is devoted to relations with Europe: relationships emerging from rejection and withdrawal or else from continuity and imitation. Naturally, these perspectives will not be dismissed. It is important to note, however, that the study of inter-American ties (therefore excluding Europe) is still fairly new from a historical point of view, except for that of the relationship between Canada and the United States. This situation is evident in *Continental Divide*[3] by Seymour Martin Lipset and in *The Canadian Identity* by W.L. Morton, in which the four chapters are entitled "Canada in America," "Canada in the Commonwealth," "Canada and the United States" and "The Relevance of Canadian History."[4] However, there are several historical avenues helping to explore the relationship between English Canada, French Canada and the Americas because of England's strong economic, financial and technological presence in Latin American countries following their independence. For instance, a colonial thinker, Manning, claimed, "The deed is done, the nail is driven. Spanish America is free; and if we do not mismanage our affairs sadly, she is English."[5]

First, we can consider Canadian references to South America and vice versa in the context of promoting the struggle to gain independence from Europe. Take Papineau's example when he states: "En commun avec les diverses nations de l'Amérique du Nord et du Sud qui ont adopté les principes contenus dans cette Déclaration, nous regardons les doctrines qu'elle renferme comme sacrées et évidentes: que Dieu ne créa aucunes distinctions artificielles entre l'homme et l'homme; que le gouvernement n'est qu'une simple institution humaine…"[6] Correspondingly, in Venezuela—during the Revolt of the Patriots of 1837–1838 in Québec—Fermin Toro quotes a text from the "Déclaration d'indépendance du Bas-Canada" from a write-up in the *Times*, December 7, 1838: "Desde hoy el pueblo del Bajo Canada queda libre de toda obedencia a Gran Bretaña."[7] Based on this misinterpretation (considering the eventual failure of the Patriots' revolt), Toro castigates the English political and economic domination. Furthermore, he criticizes colonialism in the broader context of dismantling the European discourse relating to a socioeconomic practice he considers disastrous for the people. He affirms that it is independence that leads to economic progress. Nevertheless, consider the slightly different perspective of José Antonio Saco from Cuba. In 1838, faced with the tyranny of the Spanish colonization and the inability to gain independence from the colonial power through the use of force, he draws economic, educational, cultural and political comparisons with England's colonization of Canada. In his conclusion, Saco points to the well-being of an Upper and Lower Canada governed by a Parliament with financial control, and to a colonial power amenable to semi-autonomy. He shows Canadians' capacity to develop the local economy, knowledge, communications, and democratic institutions: "[…] que de 17 periodicos que habia en 1827, su número paso de 50 en 1835, publicandose 12 en solo la ciudad de Montreal. Bajo de ciertas consideraciones, bien puede afirmarse que la imprenta es allí mas libre que en la misma Inglaterra."[8] In his very well documented study, he points out that Canada attracts numerous immigrants while Cuba still depends on the importation of slaves. We should also bear in mind Adolfo Francisco Sauvalle's[9] 1869 translation of the Canadian Confederation text, in which he shows the necessity of following a Canadian approach to maintaining the ties with the motherland while benefiting from a freedom based on parliamentary democracy. For Canada, the implementation of this approach included a bilingual parliament: "Podrá emplearse indistintamente el idioma francés o el inglés, en el Parlamento General y en sus procedimientos, así como en la Legislatura Local del Bajo Canadá y en los Tribunales federales y Provinciales del mismo."[10] For Toro and Sauvalle, a slow evolution towards independence in legislature leads to the possibility of becoming gradually independent without armed conflicts. It is true that this slow evolution in achieving sovereignty deviates from the progressive ways of democracy, as shown in many countries of Latin America ruled by dictators. However, it would allow for Cuba to be on the right track instead of being caught within the colonial domination of Spain.[11]

In the process of exploring inter-American ties, the importance of travelers should not be overlooked; not just the clergy, like the francophone Sisters of Providence sent to Chile by Monseigneur Bourget, but all active supporters of the French in Mexico from 1864 to 1866[12] who opposed independence-oriented revolutionary movements based on the separation of church and state. These anti-revolutionary allies include French Canadians like Faucher de Saint-Maurice, author of *Deux ans au Mexique* (1881) and *Notes pour servir à l'histoire de l'empereur Maximilien* (1889), Honoré Beaugrand (*Anita* (1879)),[13] Arthur Taschereau, Alphonse Têtu and Robert d'Ailleboust d'Estimeauville de Beaumouchel.[14] They went to Mexico and fought with French troops against Juarez and the Mexican people. It is worth mentioning that some of these active partisans travelled from the American Civil War in the United States. Prince Felix zu Salm Salm, for example, fought on the side of pro-slavery Southerners, and then went to help Maximilian in Mexico. Even more liberal figures like Beaugrand would support Napoleon III in Mexico. The defense of Latin European values and the support brought by the French-Canadian middle-class to the anti-revolutionary Mexican middle-class trumped democratic ideals associated with an appreciation of continental values praised in Canada by red liberals or pragmatic liberals like Étienne Parent. Equally important were the Mexican reforms of 1857, which followed years of conflict between dictatorial factions and revolutionary groups whose exploits were presented in newspapers like *The Quebec Gazette* and *Le Castor*.[15] A liberal constitution was enacted, together with the Reform Laws of Juarez, ending the Catholic Church's privileges and compelling the Church to submit to civil laws. These changes were unacceptable for the French-Canadian ultramontane Church and especially for Monseigneur Bourget, the Bishop of Montreal, who considered the revolutionaries barbarians (vice versa for the revolutionaries).

A noteworthy example, from a different frame of reference, is Onderdonk of the Canadian Pacific who was committed to the Buenos Aires/Rosario railway when Sarmiento became president of the Republic of Argentina and called upon English funds to modernize the country. Engineers such as William Perkins are also worth mentioning: born in 1827 (possibly in Saint-Eustache, QC), he moved to California in 1849, to Chile in 1852 and in 1863 to Rosario, Argentina, where he became editor of *El Ferrocaril* and contributed to the construction of the Rosario-Buenos Aires[16] railway. Sarmiento, the opponent of the dictator Rosas in Argentina, is also an important figure. Before becoming the President of the Republic of Argentina, Sarmiento travelled to Europe, and then to the United States and Canada in 1847. He published a travel journal which showed the superiority of the United States' civilization over Europe's, while noting technological advances in Canadian development. However, he was critical of colonization by England and of the clergy's influence in Lower Canada.[17]

Various inter-latitudinal influences and collaborations can still be traced. For instance, the translation of Louis Riel's texts in Brazil concerning Métis issues in Canada,[18] the promotion between the two world wars of ties with Latin America by Paul Bouchard and Dostaler O'Leary, and the numerous writings and reprints in Quebec of French Canadians' texts including those of Robert de Roquebrune originally published in France in *La Revue de l'Amérique latine*.[19] In the latter, de Roquebrune's discourse alternates between a fascination for Mussolini's triumphant Latin fascism and a more democratic outlook articulating the struggle between Latin and Anglo-Saxon spheres. Significantly, a Union of Latin American countries was promoted in 1949, by Dostaler O'Leary, who proposed that French Canada establish cultural and other ties with Latin American countries in order to escape English domination and the influence of the United States: "Car, Latins, nous le sommes aussi intensément qu'eux par notre culture française qui nous fait communier à leur façon de penser et de sentir, et notre foi catholique qui est précisément demeurée une des caractéristiques de ce monde latin, dont la philosophie, établie avec clarté et construite avec logique, a toujours répugné aux formules empiriques."[20] This perspective is still presented as valid in 1984 in an issue of the Journal *Possibles* published in Montreal: "… il y a entre les Québécois et les Américains de l'hémisphère sud, un air de parenté: un caractère latin…"[21] Comparing the Americas along these lines is to impose the perspectives established by those who projected a colonial gaze on the Americas and forgot all the other very important cultures of the Americas as well as the dynamics of hybridity.

Changing perspective from eurocentrism to transamerican issues, consider more recently the new multicultural constitution of Colombia from 1991 that replaces the previous one dating from 1886 in which all Colombians were said to be of Castilian origin. The new Constitution is strongly influenced by Canadian thinkers such as Will Kymlicka and Charles Taylor and by Canadian governmental policies. This is made clear by Daniel Bonilla-Maldonado[22] and Héctor Alonso Moreno Parra and his colleagues[23] in their assessment of the new Constitution's contribution to the well-being of Colombian cultural groups and its links to the theoretical perspectives of the Canadian authors. Mexican and Costa Rican deliberations affirming the legitimacy of diversities not from the rather problematic European models[24] defining the nation as a coincidence more or less perfect between a State and a culture,[25] but from Canadian and Latin American examples are also relevant, as seen in the books of Pablo Lazo,[26] Carlos Sandoval García,[27] Zilá Bernd[28] or in the texts of Gabriela Chavarria Alfaro.[29] From the beginning of the nineteenth century to the early twenty-first century, there is more research encompassing, for example, the activities of engineering firms such as SNC-Lavalin, mining companies, Canadian banks (in particular Scotiabank and Royal Bank), in the Caribbean and in various Latin American countries, literary and scientific exchanges along with the impact of Canadian Studies Associations, in Argentina, Colombia, Mexico and particularly in Brazil.[30] Direct relations between Canada and Latin America are more numerous than we think and deserve further study.

Comparative Paradigms for the Americas

Although a comprehensive study of these historical ties is not the aim here, an overview of the background is useful in assessing the paradigms that underlie the effectiveness of interhemispheric socio-cultural comparisons, from the North to the South Pole. Essayists, writers, artists and thinkers in the Americas explicitly or implicitly allude to most of these paradigms,[31] from *Facundo* by Sarmiento to *Imagining Canada* by Pico Iyer; from the *American Scholar* by Emerson to *Le Siècle de Jeanne* by Yvon Rivard; and from *Philosophy of Railroads* by Keefer to *La Globalización imaginada* by García Canclini or *Do the Americas Have a Common Literature?* by Gustavo Pérez Firmat.

Consequently, as a point of departure, the basic interior / exterior paradigm synonymous with self / other (and until recently with civilization / barbarism), will be retained here, as well as Inclusion / Exclusion, Unique Otherness Linked to Europe / Multiple Otherness of the Americas; Long Time-Frame / Short Time-Frame / Momentary; Past / Future; Coincidence / Causal Inference; Roots / Family Tree / Animal metaphors; Simultaneity / Historicity; Racial Purity / Interbreeding / Hybridity / Creoleness; Frontier / Border[32]; Protection / Encounter ; Zero-Sum Game / Nonzero-Sum Game[33]; Fact / Promise; Continuous / Discontinuous; Territorial Logic / Knowledge Society Logic; Belonging / Belonging To Oneself; Solved / Unsolved contradictions; Stable Identity / Multiple Self-Images; Settled/ Nomadic; Creation / Generation; Orphan / Bastard; and Homogeneity / Relationality concepts. These paradigms are not fixed and will progressively change. They switch from the pursuit of permanence to a mastery of dynamic relationships with each other. These changes reveal an overshadowed European influence and a repudiation of the causality defining the works of the national master narratives that justify exclusion processes conjointly through Mimesis of appropriation and the Scapegoat, as analyzed by René Girard in *Things Hidden since the Foundation of the World.*[34] These changes result in paradigmatic displacements associated with series of texts, metaphors, arguments, and narratives. Moreover, differences can be discerned through contextualization within the dynamics of "glocalization"[35] and through inter, multi and trans-cultural attempts to manage new globalized encounters, which exist in permanent states of uncertainty and transition. Consequently, it is through synthesis and generalization[36] that the benchmarks, dynamics and trends outlined and detailed within various regions of the Americas in different eras and from diverse contexts can be best understood.

From Dualistic Essence of Identity to Legitimacy of Travel

In the Americas of the late 18th and early 19th century, new societies were developing in almost all regions on a new continent where, named as such (the New World), the development of human and material wealth was to be initiated. Those rooted in the territory, the Creoles, and other newcomers, debated the foundations of modernity (the term first appears in 1849), pertaining to self-government as a principle of individual and collective structuring based both on generation and creation. The debates taking place in the Americas were based on new principles founded neither on a divine order nor on pre-established territories but on the idea of the people's sovereignty. There is much talk pertaining to "the people" in the 19th century; however, the people themselves are rarely heard, like in Argentina where discussions on the subject were held by the romantic intellectuals of the School of 1837. "The people" tend to be defined by enlightened leaders in mainly nebulous ways. This ambiguity was integrated into early attempts at drafting Constitutions, where universality was sought within a dynamic in which uncertainty as a democratic principle aimed to establish an identity—often temporary and at times inadequate for much of the population. This is reminiscent of the Costa Rican perception of identity. Until 1948 the Government denied citizenship to Black Anglo-Protestants from the Caribbean coast despite the fact that they had been established in the country for generations. There were multiple difficulties, hesitations and fundamental differences in the approach to legitimizing the discussion around independence and the generation of a progressive autonomy. Indeed, the passage from basic constitutional principles to questions about the foundation of civil society proves difficult at times. Issues such as domestic markets, technological development, school curricula, the administration of justice, and the development of communications and social organization[37] trigger political and cultural debates that continue to rage. These conflicts in turn pose challenges to principles and territorial boundaries instead of determining ways to implement these principles into practice.

In this context, between an essentialism geared towards stability through the imposition of sometimes conflicting values regarding settlements and economic development, and a poorly conceived vision for the future as emphasized by Noah Jitrik,[38] the configuration of identity and relational behaviors drift into a (sometimes) rigid attribution process[39] managed by groups that tend to occupy the centre. This process is primarily related to control, seduction or exclusion. It can be described by the following R. D. Laing quotation: "To get someone to *be* what one wants him to be [...] is another matter. The best way is, within a hypnotic (or similar) context, not to tell him what to *be*, but to tell him what he is. Such *attributions*, in context, are many times more powerful than orders."[40] The process is exemplified in John Cheever's short story "The Chaste Clarisse," as a variation on the "dumb beauty" stereotype: "He heard people say that she was beautiful and stupid."[41] Baxter, the protagonist, attempts to seduce the married woman, eventually succeeding by telling her repeatedly that she is intelligent. She considered herself to be rather stupid, an opinion shared by a number of her acquaintances: "Baxter listened patiently for he knew by then that she merely wanted to be taken for something she was not- that the poor girl was lost. 'You're very intelligent,' he said now and then. 'You're so intelligent.' It was as simple as that."[42] Often identities are forcibly imposed on people although their own sense of self is much more ambiguous.

Moreover, the power of attribution is heightened by feelings of desire or rejection, as in the case illustrated by John Cheever in which sociocultural dynamics are tied to the invention of homogeneous groups. In the case at hand, the goal was to invent principles based on exclusion in the Americas; particularly for the Indigenous peoples and Afro-descendants classified as barbarians. Along with the Métis nations, as W. L. Morton[43] underlines, these peoples provide a link beyond the United States, to Latin America. To this end, the Indigenous meanings and their linkage to the territory are removed as they belong to what are considered dead civilizations while their monuments and languages are systematically destroyed (except in Paraguay where Guarani is spoken by the general population along with Spanish thanks to the influence of the Jesuits). In an integrated approach, the Nations in gestation establish close relationships with the territory itself as a legitimate ground for declaring independence, and subsequently between territory and Constitution. For example, the preamble of to the Constitution of Argentina states at one point: "[…] para nosotros, para nuestra posteridad y para todos los hombres del mundo que quieran habitar en el suelo argentino […]."[44] In Article 14 concerning the role of Congress, the Constitution further states: "Arreglar definitivamente los límites del territorio de la Nación, fijar los de las provincias, crear otras nuevas […]."[45] Hence, thinkers and politicians in the Americas imported the concept of the nation as it was understood and implemented by Europe in the 19th century as a result of a Westphalian idea of political and economic relations. It is basically positivist and essentialist, and, as Noah Jitrik underlines, the idea continues to this day:

> I believe that here lie the roots of a continuing debate, one that at present has serious political overtones; a debate between those who think in terms of national essences and those who think in term of constructions. For the latter, a "being" would not be a Hegelian point of departure to which one must inevitably return, but rather a kind of objective whose contours can only be defined from the projects dictated by necessity and history.[46]

Jitrik emphasizes that these constructed identities (he will not go as far as to say "invented"), are linked to a permanent future and not to the preservation of a status quo. Thus, towards the end of the 20th century, Jitrik calls into question the guiding principles of the Scholastic-influenced Latin American elites who often held sway until the rise of the dictatorships of the 1970s.

Compared to these forms of essentialist thinking, United-States essayist Randolph Bourne's remarks from 1916 evoking the evolution of immigration in the United States, indicate a socio-philosophical approach that is much more fluid than that of the abovementioned thinkers: "We are not dealing with static factors, but with fluid and dynamic generations."[47] As we shall see later, at the time of postmodernity and postcoloniality, the valorization of essences and stability are recontextualized by emphasizing the Legitimacy of Travel, Chameleonage and Multiple Self-Images. Many contemporary thinkers and artists like Pico Iyer[48] and Carlos Monsivais[49] have recently emphasized their fluid identities. The evolution from a static process of attribution to a valorization of changing and dynamic relations is clearly apparent in Mark Kingwell's *The World We Want*. He attempts to redefine the concept of citizenship; observing that it was no longer linked to the historical model based on blood, faith or law, but rather that it could be thought of as "the act of participation itself."[50] Mark Kingwell emphasizes that being the citizen of a country graced by the attribute of Canadian, Chilean or Mexican is just one role among others. He says: "We are (1) inquirers… (2) moral agents… (3) house holders and consumers… (4) workers or economic agents… (5) cultural beings… (6) intimates."[51] He continues by underlining that the role of a citizen is deemed to be the most important of all. However, the role varies greatly according to local conditions and risks losing its prominent position either because of consumer fetishism, cultural separatism or individual isolation. These trends fascinate Pico Iyer in *The Global Soul*. He infuses this idea with humor when he says, for example: "Lacking a binding sense of 'we', he (the contemporary citizen) might nonetheless remain fiercely loyal to a single airline."[52]

Comparisons: From the Americas to the Nation-State

The goal then is to first consider a few binary operating paradigms established since the creation of nations by thinkers adhering to the essentialist positivism and metaphysical realism of the 19th and 20th centuries, much criticized recently by North American pragmatists such as Cornel West.[53] Secondly, it is important to understand the recontextualization of these paradigms by contemporary thinkers. These thinkers favor a complex approach by adopting a dynamic triangulation. In the passage from dualism to the ternary or to the multiple, cross-cultural, interdisciplinary and trans-American comparisons emerge. The dualistic paradigms produced by 19th and 20th century thinkers in the Americas transcend national borders even though, like the barbarism / civilization paradigm, they are assessed differently by competing political groups inside and outside every country. Thus, for progressives like Sarmiento inclined towards the port cities and Europe, barbarism[54] is the hinterland, and the city represents civilization; so is the case with Étienne Parent in French Canada, despite the prominence of ultramontanism. For proponents of ultramontane Catholicism in Quebec (like Patrice Lacombe in *La terre paternelle* in 1845[55]), "the city" and Europe are sinful places and "civilization" is rooted in the heart of the village, a perspective with which a novelist like Albert Laberge in *La Scouine*[56] disagrees. However, these divergent valuations merely endorse the modus operandi of the barbarism / civilization paradigm, commonly used because it allows groups to be considered as homogeneous. From this point of view, it is clear who should be excluded. Consequently, large sociocultural configurations transgress borders. This does not delegitimize the contextualization of these paradigms according to their corresponding national dynamics. However, the point of departure in most research on the Americas, such as that of Yvan Lamonde, Jesus Martín Barbero, Winfried Siemerling and Sarah Casteel, is the national—leading then to comparisons that highlight certain aspects of the Americas at the expense of elements pointing to its convergent dynamics. Moreover, as alleged by Winfried Siemerling and Sarah Casteel,[57] the concern sometimes is that even comparisons may dilute the Canadian national characteristics for which thinkers, artists, politicians and intellectuals fought in the sixties and the seventies. As shown by Margaret Atwood in *Survival*,[58] the Canadian national identity had to be defined and defended against a colonial discourse. The goal there was to depart from the overbearing U.S. and English colonial cultural holds and their social and aesthetic codes, as parodied by Stephen Leacock in "Gertrude the Governess or Simple Seventeen."[59] These fears and approaches are legitimate, but in our glocalized world, in our Americas in motion, it is also very useful to reflect on the Americas, from the broadest to the narrowest aspects, as does researcher Néstor García Canclini in *La Globalización imaginada*.[60] Canclini, however, tends to forget Canada. Endangering national identity is the criticism that Cynthia Sugars, Winfried Siemerling and Sarah Casteel[61] have offered regarding much of the comparative research on the Americas. They point out that several studies focus on the relationship between the United States and Mexico or parts of Latin America, but that Canada is forgotten, and appears at times to not exist outside Canadian research circles. Our perspective starts from the large configurations covering the continent in order to study local dynamics in Nation States and in specific regions (without forgetting Canada and Quebec), to subsequently observe the paradigms that connect with the features of regions or countries, in keeping with broader dynamics linked to the Americas.

Roots and Determinism

In the 19th century, thinkers attempted to disseminate universalistic assumptions from within an optimistic interpretation of history based on the ideology of progress[62] whose linearity imposed clear choices or radical rejections. For ideologists like Destutt de Tracy and theorists such as Ampère and Jean-Baptiste Say, progress was a unidirectional vector, binding the universality of humanity to a dichotomy between the local colonial (leaning towards barbarism) and the civilized values seen as very rarely present in the Americas from a 19th century European perspective. Henry Thomas Buckle captures this perspective in his highly influential research demonstrating the influence of soil and climate on civilizations. He noted that wealth is extracted from the soil only "by virtue of a mere physical relation between the character of the soil and the quality or value of the produce that it almost spontaneously affords."[63] However, "the agency of climate, which gives wealth by stimulating his labour, is more favorable to his ultimate progress than the agency of the soil."[64] From this determinism, Buckle constructs a hierarchy of men, at the top of which stand those who can achieve progress and at the bottom, barbarians. The builders of pre-Columbian cities are included in this last category, but are deemed less barbaric than the others who are "ignorant, and therefore brutal, practicing no restraint, and recognizing no law" and continuing "to live on in their old and inveterate barbarism."[65] Furthermore, he maintains that the entire population of Brazil is barbaric and idle: "For even at present, with all the improvements constantly introduced from Europe, there are no signs of real progress; while notwithstanding the frequency of colonial settlements, less than one-fifteenth of the land is cultivated. The habits of the people are as barbarous as ever."[66] Thereby, even though Europe had created a historical continuity, a "long term," it never really takes root in the Americas. According to Buckle, the Creoles are nearly as barbaric as the Indigenous people because they are not able to develop the region economically and technically, an inherent continental limitation stemming from climatic conditions. There is no escape from such a tenacious determinism which refuses to relinquish the established order and condemns the people, according to Buckle, to vegetate in a state of underdevelopment. From these precedents, an entire system of marginalization takes shape in economic, aesthetic and literary terms; as Angel Rama recalls: "El sistema literario europeo, adaptándose a la división internacional del trabajo, había fijado para el centro el derecho omnímodo a tratar asuntos proprios, internos, o indistintamente asuntos exoticos, externos, en tanto relegaba a la periferia a proveedora de exotismos para el eventual consumo de las metrópolis, del mismo modo que el sistema económico la relegaba a proveedora de materias primas que serian elaboradas industrialmente en el centro."[67]

Despite these negative perspectives, the Creoles consider themselves civilized compared to the Indigenous people or to Blacks, while appearing insecure in the eyes of Europeans. Creoles transform stereotypes about Indigenous people into a *pecking order*, a system of hierarchic dominance. This dynamic is specified by the Brazilian thinker Darcy Ribeiro as follows:

> [...] the ruling classes tended to define themselves as the agents of Western and Christian civilization, considering themselves more perfect, prudent, and pious, so much advanced over savagery that their destiny was to impose themselves as the natural rule of the good over the bad, of the wise over the ignorant... In their view the rulers were simply forcing those inactive Indians to live a destiny more in conformity with the will of God and the nature of man. The colonist became rich and the workers were saved for their eternal life.[68]

In Ribeiro, we see the play between long term and short term in its very movement. The Creoles are living within a short-term temporal frame but are linked to the European long term that is manifested in identity stories linking causality and temporality (see section: Causality and Narrative) and in their building of a tradition. Therefore, they can focus on the benefits of the present. However, the Indigenous people are not included in the long vector of progress and are considered to be savages. They are seen as depending on the emotion of the moment instead of being rational persons. The long term planification eludes them and they are given a future—a long term—only from a metaphysical and otherworldly perspective. Redemption awaits them, but much later; that is, in heaven. This scenario parallels attempts at literary redemption offered by Bibaud in his *Biographie des Sagamos illustres de l'Amérique septentrionale*[69] where he compares the Canadian Indigenous Peoples to Homeric heroes.

Our theoretical outlook is far removed from the European universalist historic approach linked to colonization and centered on the predominance of a homogeneous nation-state. Our outlook allows to better take into account the similarities and the meeting points within the Americas. The limitations of the European perspective become clear once the meeting points of the diverse cultures of the Americas are taken into consideration. Rather than being causally linked, they are causally independent (see section: Chance, Causality). In order to control this element of randomness (a source of anxiety in the 19th century in particular), and to turn it into a causality related to values and attribution processes which help define identities, dualistic paradigms were used in the 19th and 20th centuries. These rationalizations linked to dualistic paradigms were recontextualized into ternary dynamics towards the end of the 20th century.

Ancestors and Descendants: Generate and Create

The thinkers of the Americas wanted to found strong and legitimate nations. From their perspective, to achieve this goal, these nations had to be generated. They had to have a point of origin and a connection to a lineage, retaining a long line of continuity, rather than embracing new creations. Thus, the drive to self-generate which was a source of strength for Europe was not tenable in the Americas due to a lack of stable historical, cultural and architectural bases from which to assert this potential for self-generation. The people of the Americas had to accept their European genesis and explore filiations. The United States declared that they wanted to invent something radically new after the revolution, promoting industry and knowledge, and not just bucolic farmers rediscovering nature or the Garden of Eden. This would then position them as potential models with respect to the invention of the American democracy and its aim to realize the concept of Manifest Destiny.[70] Along with the Creoles, seeking to develop their lives from within uncertain self-images, it is necessary to add examples of those who valued productivity through work. A source of middle-class wealth stemming from a Protestant work ethic was familiar to Sarmiento in Argentina through his exposure to English Freemasonry, which shaped his thoughts and those of many Latin American architects of independence. Thus, the inhabitants of European-influenced ports were those civilized by work. Étienne Parent in Canada shared the same perspective: it was, he claims, necessary to escape idleness and focus on work: "Le sauvage d'Amérique a pris nos vices et laissé de côté nos vertus, il a pris ce qui fait notre faiblesse et négligé ce qui fait notre force, le travail et les idées de la civilisation. Le sauvage pense comme nos nobles au sujet du travail et le tient en mépris."[71] Joining Parent is Boucher de Boucherville who thought that Blacks were not in line with the prescribed work ethic; as slaves, they produced less as they did not share responsibility: "Par de sages et justes lois de police, les nègres seront obligés de travailler, comme les serviteurs blancs sont obligés de le faire dans les autres pays."[72]

The struggle for legitimacy was thus seen in terms of lineage, that is to say, from ancestral ties offering diverging visions of continuity; this was true for the Río de la Plata, Venezuela and Canada. However, the struggle for legitimacy was contested in Latin America. Some, like Briceño Iragorry,[73] favored Spain as a worthy model. For Iragorry, Spain lived on in New Spain. Others, like Sarmiento[74] and Parent, proposed a progressive and civilized Europe without the barbarity of Spain. Others suggested a return to the *Bible*, evoking the Garden of Eden, which distorted the original goals for the development of the Americas; Canada, as W.L. Morton reminds us, was established through commercial and port connections with Europe, particularly with England: "Canadian history was metropolitan from its beginning."[75] This was also true for the Río de la Plata, Brazil, and the United States, where it all started with ports and continued through land settlement and the invention of the *frontier* (section: From the Frontier).

Still, others wanted the nation to be created without any direct ties with Europe or the colonial country. To this end, they sought to reclaim the biblical theme associated with the Garden of Eden. However, they never managed to assert their new identity without referring to Europe. They then returned to a Biblical Europe. Anne Hébert thus describes the invention of the French-Canadian nation in *Le premier jardin*: "The first man was named Louis Hébert and the first woman, Marie Rollet. They planted the first garden with seeds from France. They designed the garden based on this idea of garden, this memory of garden, kept in their head, and it looked very much like a garden of France, thrown in the woods of the New World."[76] This is also a recurring fantasy for some early 20th century immigrants. Gabrielle Roy presents a similar picture in *Un jardin au bout du monde*,[77] and particularly in the short story of the same title where Martha thinks about her little corner of European garden and tries to create a flower garden in the Prairies with flowers that grow just as well in Canada as in Europe.

Compared to this parentage that ensures the durability of civilization in the long term, Bagehot's research in 1873 about the notions of context, adjustment to the environment, progress and originality (that is, variations *beyond* a Platonic essence and the stabilities defined by dualism), was concerned with what was created and what was generated. He stressed that what was created had as much validity as what was generated; however there was a tendency to promote a discourse favoring generation when it came to inventing the Nation-States in the most legitimate way possible: "Primitive nations [...] made believe that new persons were descended from the old stock, though everybody knew that in flesh and blood they were not. They made an artificial unity in default of a real unity [...] what was made did as well as what was born."[78] It is remarkable that this reflection was articulated within a Darwinian scientific framework, since the book was subtitled "Thoughts on the Application of the Principles of 'Natural Selection' and 'Inheritance' to Political Society." Indeed, Bagehot was interested in the struggle to invent nations and he used examples from South and North America. In 1873, Bagehot tried to synthesize the obsessions of the century, i.e. movement, change, exchange, adaptation, progress, variation and the mixing of groups, targeting the stable if not the inertial. He tried to find solutions to this potential chaos, the great fear of modernity. He noted that in this will to present the nation as generated, the struggles between discourse and options were strong and that the various discourses manifested the Darwinian conceptions of social relations played by power struggles between those who considered themselves "civilized" and "others." The civilized always aimed to create a unity based on an essence derived from a long continuity. This did not prevent Bagehot from underlining, for example, the topic of race mixing as an engine of change. He cited M. Quatrefages, concluding that South America was an experimental laboratory for the mixing of races as were Florida and Louisiana, and that the progress of the various racially mixed groups was determined by the environment. Some, like Bagehot, hesitated between two discourses: that of creation, open to the potential recognition of interbreeding, and that of generation, based on the combination of the family tree and roots tied to Europe, leading to an exclusive dualism. Bagehot noted that the discourse about generation favored by thinkers and politicians was oriented towards inventing new nations following the European models, basing themselves on a Westphalian vision of relations between nations rather than on one that would see the invention of a new civilization.

This also fascinated Mexican thinkers who sought to break away from colonial influences. Even in 1909, Andrés Molina Enríquez,[79] a disciple of social Darwinism, claimed that the predominance of a mixed race (Mestizo in Spanish) comes from natural selection and that Mexico will therefore assert itself through its hybridity. José Vasconcelos continued this idea idealistically in the 1920s in *La raza cósmica*, translated in paintings and murals by Diego Rivera. He said that the mixed race produced in Latin America would transform humanity and that it would rise in power, while slowly being whitened by the mixing of people. He continued by asserting that:

> [T]his mandate from History is first noticed in the abundance of love that allowed the Spaniard to create a new race with the Indian and the Black, profusely spreading white ancestry through the soldier who begat an indigenous family, and Occidental culture through the doctrine and example of the missionaries who placed the Indians in condition to enter into the new stage, the stage of world One.[80]

In this genetic and cultural intermingling, the superiority of the European cultural origin would assert itself and open onto a new age very different from the past conquests of the "Reds" or the "Whites" that destroyed one another:

> The purpose of the new and ancient continent is much more important. Its predestination obeys the design of constituting the cradle of a fifth race into which all nations will fuse with each other to replace the four races that have been forging History apart from each other. This dispersion will come to an end on American soil; unity will be consummated there by the triumph of fecund love[81] and the improvement of all the human races.[82]

It is clear that for Vasconcelos, Latin America had a fundamental civilizing manifest destiny, like the United States, as it was predestined to regenerate mankind, following God's plan. This mission was conferred by Providence. It is remarkable to see that Vasconcelos, when he used these concepts of plan and predestination, was very close to U.S. Protestant ethics professing that Latin America, like the United States, would carry out God's plan. However, in the United States the plan was to spread the idea of democratic civilization in which everyone would live freely and morally with the ability to realize one's own potential for individual development far from oppression. The fact remains that all of Vasconcelos's reasoning was still caught in a vision of the nation as generated and homogeneous; he said that nations would merge, without making clear that inwardly they were still highly heterogeneous. Moreover, he aimed at a universalism which claimed to be homogenizing in the process of miscegenation: "In this fashion, the synthetic race that shall gather all the treasures of History in order to give expression to universal desire shall be created."[83]

The universalism associated with these concepts stemmed from the idea of a "civilizing" whitening, a form of eugenics; it did not lead to recognizing that diversity generates diversity, as it is mentioned by Gregory Bateson (1972) and is expressed by political documents such as Canada's multicultural Constitution. Finally, this goal of mixing races lead to Vasconcelos' clear exclusions: "We recognize that it is not fair that people like the Chinese, who, under the saintly guidance of Confucian morality multiply like mice, should come to degrade the human condition precisely at the moment when we begin to understand that intelligence serves to refrain and regulate the lower zoological instincts which are contrary to a truly religious conception of life."[84] These contradictions inherent in an interbreeding orchestrated under the guidance of a fusional universalism were questioned in 1999 in Isabel Allende's *Hija de la fortuna*. In the book, the heroine, who migrates from Chile to the United States in the nineteenth century, eventually marries the Chinese Tao Chien. Within Vasconcelos' grandiose vision lies a social, economic and genetic Darwinism, controlled by a culture of European origin escaping from what he sees as zoological instincts: "This infinite quietude is stirred with the drop put in our blood by the Black, eager for sensual joy, intoxicated with dances and unbridled lust."[85]

From Sarmiento to Vasconcelos emerged an attempt to solve life situations experienced as contradictory based on the belief that the soil and climate determine the character of individuals and societies. Ideally, these societies would be as modern, industrious and productive as possible. These contradictions were thus temporarily solved by the myth[86] of the empty land (there has never been any Indigenous peoples or Blacks in Río de la Plata), and by the invention of people of non-civilizable barbaric essence (such as Indigenous peoples), who therefore deserved exclusion and annihilation.

The Nation: Between Darwin and Sustainability: Targeting the Filiation Oriented Towards a Long-Term Future

In addition to his thoughts on the created and the generated nation, Bagehot pointed out that a dual discourse on time is linked to national space and its story: "*Nation-making* is the occupation of man in these ages, and it is war that makes nations… The idea of an indestructible nation is a modern idea."[87] The war in the Darwinian sense of the term makes and breaks nations yet, at the same time, we dream of an indestructible nation. Tellingly, in his epilogue to *La terre paternelle*, a novel that promotes an Edenic life in the village organized around the church in French Canada (the new Garden of Eden of newcomers' dreams), Patrice Lacombe portrays Europe and its wars as the height of barbarism. Lacombe dreams of an eternal French-Canadian nation united around God.[88] Indeed, the Americas were caught in Darwinian arguments, but they also dreamt of a continuity that would escape these wars in order to rebuild an ideal world related to the ideas of the founding fathers in the United States and the City on the Hill. Thus, even if these thinkers sought to re-establish a continuity with the distant past (which is a rather European way of thinking), they aimed at the same time for a future that was beyond the temporary imposed by the confrontational and the stability-oriented tropes. That was true for Francisco Bilbao who certainly recognized the opposition barbarism/civilization but who suggested, in *El Evangelio Americano* in 1864, the creation of an association of the South American republics to counterbalance the union of the United States of North America. It included the "universal ciudadania. Todo repúblicano puede ser como considerado Ciudadano en cualquier República que habite."[89] However, this universalism that would make the inhabitants of Latin America citizens of any republic was based on a civilization defined by republican attributes and hence excluded Blacks and Indigenous people who were not considered to be rational human beings.[90] This conception of society, defined as progressive in the 19th century when compared to the conception held by traditional elites, is based on racial exclusion. This racial exclusion was criticized by José Marti Martí in "Letter to Antonio Maceo" in 1882.[91] Recently, José Saldívar[92] underscores that racial exclusion emerges from the colonial apparatus, whose logic infiltrated modern nation-states after independence and is present in the new dynamics of globalization. However, Saldívar focuses almost exclusively on subaltern writers whose epistemological ground may produce a "coherent version of the world."[93] Moreover, he does not underscore that racial exclusion, although an important issue until now, has been displaced by the implementation of laws and constitutions fostering multiculturalism in many countries of the Americas. This new dynamic integrating the recognition of cultural diversity into the workings of nation-states in the Americas (which were thought to be homogeneous), leads to conceiving of the nation-state as being in a process of permanent reinvention, open to a social mobility connected with the knowledge-based society as shown by Doug Saunders in *Arrival City*[94] (section: From the Frontier).

Even José Vasconcelos, the Mexican apostle of interbreeding, who leant towards a synthesis of races that would generate a new cosmic race out of the Americas, was apprehensive when considering otherness. This in turn led him to choose a form of ancestral Hispanicity totally rejected by Sarmiento, for whom Spain represented the height of obscurantism. Vasconcelos wished to assert a strong Latin identity that rejected Anglo-Saxon culture. He then divorced the people of Spanish America from their indigenous and Black ancestors:

> Por ponernos encima de los prejuicios, a la altura de la humanidad mas ilustre, renunciamos desde la emancipación nuestro abolengo. Pero, ahora, las generaciones desenraizadas, desprovistas de herencia, se acogen a la bastardia. Y las vemos rotulando el producto nacional con el marbete extranjero o poniendo en la prosa las asperezas de quien, por sentirse intimamente un sajonizante, ya no le basta el humilde castellano nativo.[95]

In this text, we find both the loss of ancestry (bastardy being thus always close to barbarism), the rejection of the other superior—the Anglo-Saxon—and the desire to preserve the humble Castilian. A whole relationship of power and exclusion manifests itself here, preventing any effective consideration of the dynamics of encounter with otherness and supposing therefore that the self could not be defined as a multiplicity of elements.

In Venezuela, Mario Briceño-Iragorry's work also reflected this perspective. He helped advance a dualistic conception of the world when he stressed that the origins of the population of Venezuela were closer to Spain than to that of the indigenous people or the Blacks: "And if I esteem my Hispanic ancestry far more than I do the part of me I inherited from the colonized Indians and the enslaved Africans, it is because my Hispanic ancestors are not only numerically greater but have also been the culturally dominant element in the history of our nation. My case is typical of most Venezuelans."[96] The rejection of the hybrid, of the mixed, is everywhere at all times. This was often the case until the 1960s, as shown in René Depestre's amusing short story "Noces à Tiscornia,"[97] in which a mixed couple arrives in Cuba in 1952. The couple consists of a white woman and a mulatto, of Haitian origins. They were confined before being sent back where they came from (Europe), because "in our Republic the mixed couple has no place."[98] This perspective had spread across the continent. For instance, Anyelick Campos Zamora and Larissa Tristán Jiménez highlight the very powerful myth of the European origin in Costa Rica: "[...] se asoció ese pretendido origen español con la 'blancura' que caracteriza a la población costaricense... una vinculación entre etnia y democracia, al atribuir el progreso de Costa Rica a dos factores pricipales: la expansión escolar y la 'raza especial' de la 'estirpe española' de la cual descenderian todos los costaricenses."[99] As shown by the two authors, this has led until very recently to a perception of Nicaraguan immigrants as barbarians. Understandably, claims such as those made by an author like Silviano Santiago, are not always obvious: "The major contribution of Latin America to Western culture is to be found in its systematic destruction of the concepts of unity and purity..."[100] Therefore, the mythification of Bolivar[101] and Columbus or the promotion of a single inheritance opened the way for the construction of an authenticity that generated exclusion and racism, as underlined by Étienne Balibar: "Since there is no way to find racial-national purity or to guarantee its source in the origins of the people, it must be fabricated after the idea of a (super) national Superman."[102] This was the program imposed by dictators stuck in the past and preoccupied by order and tradition, as in Chile under Pinochet's rule: "Dramatic broadcasts and other fiction programs must contain moral concepts, which do not damage morality and high principles and which do not exalt morbidity. They must not be based on the situation the country is living through... The remainder of programs must be concerned fundamentally with transmitting the culture of our people and emphasizing the values of nationality. The transmission of good Chilean music is especially recommended."[103] That resonates with a passage in *Nikolski* by Nicolas Dickner where the narrator, Noah, a Métis born from of a mixture between a French-Canadian and a Chippeyan, meets a beautiful Venezuelan woman with whom he has a child. But she asserts that "'Simon is 100% Venezuelan' [...]; Arizona hung onto this strange independence which he had to respect, at least if he wanted to avoid deportation on some distant island of the Aleutian Islands."[104] This connects well with Iragorry's claim: "Our origins are rather to be found by retracing the remote past of the Spanish navigators and by accepting as our own that unique history which is already in danger of becoming extinct."[105]

Otherness

The barbarism/civilization opposition is one of the foundations of the organization of any society that arises through opposition, as Michael Shapiro reminds us. And what society, especially in the context of modernity, does not arise through opposition? This researcher points out that the subject knows him/herself through others while at the same time ignoring this dependency and imagining himself fully independent.[106] This desire for self-generation by avoiding confrontation with the other, coupled with a connection to the earth, is already present in the story of Adam: a man is created from the earth by a male God and not from a womb. This is combined with the attribution process which, through the normal grammatical structure (subject/verb to be/attribute) specific to Indo-European languages, makes essential a quality that positively determines identity because, as highlighted by Edward Sapir[107] and Benjamin Lee Whorf,[108] there is no marker of temporal or situational relativity. In this context, the purpose of the Nation-State is to increase this ontological desire through discursive meanings, hiding the fact that this impulse against alterity is, in part, a way to replace an absent or vague internal consistency. Thus, people imagine themselves as having been generated over the long term by European ancestors who thought themselves self-generated from the earth; or else people dream of having been created, new, original and able to break with the attachments to the motherland, as exemplified by Kim Thúy's characters. They dream of being new in the New World: "Je sais seulement que, un matin très tôt, j'ai ouvert les yeux et vu un monde si parfait que j'en ai eu le vertige."[109] It is only recently that we have dared to see ourselves as the product of various relationships; this is made evident through multiculturalism and through theoretical developments like Glissant's concept of creolity (1990) or its definition by Jean Bernabé, Patrick Chamoiseau and Raphaël Confiant: "La Créolité est l'agrégat interactionnel ou transactionnel des éléments culturels caraïbes, européens, africains, asiatiques et levantins, que le joug de l'Histoire a réunis sur le même sol."[110] As emphasized by Vévé A. Clark, this new awareness leads to a new conception of literacy defined as the reader's ability to be familiar with more than one language and "to comprehend the literatures of Africa, Afro-America, and the Caribbean from an informed indigenous perspective."[111]

Otherness in Europe and in the Americas

It is important to appreciate that the barbarism/civilization opposition did not have the same meaning in the Americas as it did in Europe. Colonial Europe generalized the political and aesthetic discourse on barbarism. According to these discourses, barbarism was similar in Africa, Asia and the Americas. Fermin Toro in "Europa y América"[112] reminds us that the Europeans considered the people of the Americas to be semi-barbarians. This point of view was based on the perceptions of English merchants, for example, who would broadcast in Europe, which was still rampant with massacres and horrors from the Napoleonic wars, "un general concepto de nuestra barbarie,"[113] as Mariano Moreno (a theoretician of free trade quoted by Irazusta) writes in 1809. This coincided with what colonialists like E.G. Wakefield said in 1834. For Wakefield, the Anglo-Saxon world was civilized while the others, including the Creoles, the descendants of Europeans born in the Antipodes, were wild:

> If they (the Dutch Colonies of South-Africa) had not obtained some slaves, that is, some combination of labour in the particular works of their farms, they would, being so scattered, and prevented from combining their own labour, have degenerated into the state of those savage descendants of Spaniards, who inhabit the plains of Buenos Ayres[114]... What country, in which land is cheap, is most fit... to provide the English with cheap corn?...not Buenos-Ayres, because the people of this colony (*sic*) are barbarously unskillful and have no desire for English goods; [...] but the United States, Canada, and the English settlements in South Africa and Australia; because in all of those countries, corn might be raised on cheap land, with English skill, by people anxious to buy English goods.[115]

For Wakefield, the Creoles were savages and barbarians, which as Bourinot reminds us, resonated with the stereotypes conveyed by the British press about Canadians: "Thanks to the English illustrated papers, the average native is generally represented as a white man in a blanket coat, with sash and capote, travelling on snow shoes; and we may consider it fortunate that he has risen so far in the scale of civilization as not to be pictured in complete Indian costume of paint and feathers."[116] But for Sarmiento in *Facundo*, there was a nuance; the Indigenous people, the Blacks and the Creoles of the hinterland were barbarians because they were no good for work, sinking into idleness; however, the Creoles in the port cities like Buenos Aires were civilized, having ties with Europe:

> L'incorporation des indigènes pratiquée par les colonisateurs doit avoir contribué grandement à produire ce résultat malheureux (l'oisiveté, l'inaptitude à l'industrie). Les races américaines vivent dans l'oisiveté et se maintiennent incapables de se livrer à un travail pénible et suivi même par la contrainte. C'est ce qui a suggéré l'idée d'introduire des nègres en Amérique, idée qui a produit de si fatals résultats. Mais la race espagnole ne s'est pas montrée mieux douée pour l'action quand elle s'est vue dans les déserts d'Amérique abandonnée à ses propres instincts.[117]

Thus, the European discourse invented an undifferentiated barbarian across the planet, because only Europe represented access to progress. The way forward was clear and founded on dualism. On the other hand, for the people of the Americas, the Creoles, the settlers and the white immigrants, there were at least two categories of other. The first category was positive, superior, civilized Europe; and, subsequently, the United States. Tellingly, this is what Sarmiento said about North America in 1847 after his visit to Europe, where he observed the appalling conditions of the workers and the peasants: "The people of North America have no literature [...] but [...] they have [...] the most complete civilization"[118] Obviously, there was a difference between dormant Canada, or even French Canada under the rule of the clergy, and the United States. Nevertheless, he saw Montreal as technically advanced:

> In this respect, Montréal is the most highly civilized city on the planet; but because of an interesting moral aspect, it is also a fossil curiosity.[119] "But if you want to turn back the pages of history and see it as it was at the end of the Middle Ages, go to Montréal and there you will find it in all of its primitive simplicity, full of passion and force and concentrating in itself, as in Spain in the times of Queen Isabella, patriotism, power and heroism."[120] "The priest, as in the olden days, is the parish's schoolteacher... the children are indoctrinated with fervor in their beliefs and fortified against all dangerous innovations [...]."[121]

He concluded by praising the United States: "Still, after examining the chief nations of Christendom, I have come to the conclusion that the Americans are the only really cultured people that exist on this earth and the last word in modern civilization."[122] That outlook endorsed the idea of Manifest Destiny with regards to the United States' duty to enlighten the world and spread republicanism and democracy throughout the planet. However, Sarmiento later understood the domineering ambitions of the United States and moderated his views. The second category was negative and inferior, consisting of the Indigenous, the black slave and the various Métis that did not fit into the new work logic, wherein according to Parent and contrary to the Bible, work is freedom, "le travail, c'est la liberté."[123] The barbarism/civilization paradigm synonymous with idleness/work was thereby used by the thinkers of the Americas, who were emulating the Europeans. However, it was difficult to invent identities that were not problematic because the simplistic binary dualism (i.e. Europe positive/the others negative) was applied to complex relationships. Indeed, where could the Creoles locate themselves between European superiority (asserted by the imposition of its literature, for example) and the inferiority of the Indigenous people and the Blacks? They were caught in between, surrendering to European dominance. Moreover, the children of the soil often rubbed shoulders with the Indigenous people and the Blacks with whom they had children. What became of the children then? This was the whole problem with the invention of nations and identities that were constructed from a dualistic paradigm providing inadequate support for the relationships that were and are not only economic and ethnic, but also cultural, sexual and emotional. Indeed, as Darcy Ribeiro points out about *Mamelucos* in Brazil, hundreds of thousands of children of the soil are born from mixtures between populations with very diverse cultural and genetic histories. The dualistic paradigm merely succeeded in avoiding the complexity of interbreeding and the genetic but also socio-cultural ways to manage encounters: "The Indian's concept was that a woman is simply the sack into which the male deposits his seed. The one who is born is the child of the father and not of the mother."[124] The problem was that these children, usually of white fathers and Indigenous mothers, were rejected by their fathers who considered them unclean. What Darcy Ribeiro calls *cunhadismo* led to Métis children being recognized neither by the Indigenous peoples nor by the Whites. These *Mamelucos*, Darcy Ribeiro further explains, colonized[125] not only Brazil but the entire Río de la Plata region. They were considered barbarians by Sarmiento and were until recently called *Cabecitas negras* (small black heads) by the Argentines who are often not aware of their origins.

Let us go back for a moment to the attempts by Las Casas to redeem the savages by acknowledging Indigenous peoples as sons of God; keeping in mind that the Jesuits and Franciscans were aiming to rebuild a more spiritual humanity in the New World.[126] This task was entrusted to the Franciscans, who converted the remains of the pre-Columbian pyramids into churches and dreamt of organizing "indigenous life according to the rules of Sir Thomas More's Utopia, inspired anachronistically by the original Indian cultures."[127] In other words, they wanted to embody Christianity in indigenous bodies in order to achieve a form of happiness on earth. It was indeed a form of reincarnation, a rebuilding of the world on this new continent. Meanwhile, Bibaud's book showed a distinctly different perspective from that of Thomas More. Bibaud presents, framed in ethical and redemptive aesthetics, Indigenous people as Homeric heroes, just as the Renaissance honoured rediscovered ancient Greece. But comparing literary Indigenous peoples to ancient heroes would hardly help their plight. The real problem for Indigenous peoples was that their differences were never accepted and recognized, neither by those who rejected them as barbaric, nor by those who glorified them by elevating them to the level of Homeric heroes! Obviously, attempts have been made since then to find various solutions to establish equality, but these attempts have mainly resulted in disasters. In order for Indigenous people to reach full equality, they are expected to submit to their persecutors, who must "help" them to achieve this civilized equality. We know of the damage this caused when we think of the reform schools in Canada and the United States. Equality is only a way of denying their differences; this is exactly what Kymlicka recalls in his theorizations on multiculturalism.[128]

What does Ribeiro propose for the recognition of Indigenous people? Something rather controversial. Darcy Ribeiro notes: "What was called for was setting the norms of a compensatory right by which Indians would have the same rights as Brazilians—voting and performing military service, for example—but those rights should not be imposed on them as if they were duties."[129] Revealingly, in Ribeiro's statement above, the term "Brazilians" seems to suggest that the "Indians" are not Brazilian. Moreover, in the homogenizing logic of the nation-state, compulsory military service subjects the individual to hierarchical constraints. Asserting that this is a right that should not be decreed as if it were a duty, points to a discontent with regards to a state narrative according to which equality and difference have no place and the Indigenous, having always been oppressed by the government and the army, should take part in their own oppression. Ribeiro thereby shows that the question of belonging is not defined directly by the nation but by the regiment to which the individual may belong, as was the case until the First World War in Europe. This case is ironically evoked by Pico Iyer in *The Global Soul*: "'Where do you come from?' is coming to seem as antiquated an inquiry as 'What regiment do you belong to?'"[130] It is perceived as something outdated, notwithstanding that for some very poor people in Brazil, doing military service may certainly provide economic benefits as well as relieve concerns related to identity.

In other words, in this case too, a significant portion of the population is rejected, as René Depestre clearly highlights: "Tu n'as pas idée de prendre un Noir comme professeur. As-tu pensé aux voisins? Aux domestiques? Que fais-tu du décorum qui est le nôtre dans ce pays (le Brésil)?"[131] To establish effective and productive relationships, people must escape the European colonial perspective; a dynamic the Americas will only create by reflexive policies that implement multicultural and cross-cultural designs of social, economic and cultural relations. As José Vasconcelos pointed out, these strategies lead to the understanding that the children of the soil in the Americas are born from interethnic and intercultural encounters resulting from coincidence more than from the effects of long temporalities and established relationships. His hybrid eugenics assessed the potential of Latin America in *La raza cósmica*. However, the racist aspects of his thinking must be recognized, because the mixture—though positive in his case—leads nevertheless to racial laundering and whitening. It was only in 1928, with Oswald de Andrade in Brazil and his essay, *Manifesto Antropófago*,[132] that we see a profound reconfiguration of the barbarism/civilization paradigm and its link to dominant European dualistic essentialism with an aim to open up to a third state. Oswald de Andrade displaces the balance of power: "Nous voulons la révolution caraïbe. Plus grande que la Révolution française. Unifier toutes les révoltes efficaces convergeant vers l'homme. Sans nous, l'Europe n'aurait même pas sa pauvre Déclaration des droits de l'homme."[133] Oswald de Andrade, in a bold reversal, stated that the Americas, somehow, invented Europe. Indeed, through their distinct differences, the Indigenous people contributed to Europe's break with Augustinian dictates that condemned as heretical the idea of remote, undiscovered or uninhabited areas. Thus, he reviewed the approach of philosophers that questioned the Christian philosophies based on a reflection on identity as something changeable. If Native Americans, radically other, did not exist, could the philosophers of the Enlightenment like La Hontan, Helvetius or Voltaire, who closed their eyes to the slave trade[134] (when they themselves did not invest in such trafficking), have engaged in the reflection leading to a philosophical-historical discourse threatening the unity and the centralism of a European discourse excluding others and fixed on the eternal? This is doubtful. The work of Oswald de Andrade led to the integration of cultures through interbreeding, multiplying the possibilities of simultaneity and contiguity. He rejected both the dualistic European colonial domination and the eugenicist attempts to improve the race, lauded by José Vasconcelos, that relied on Hegelian dynamics, going from the barbarism/civilization opposition to a higher synthesis where Indigenous peoples and Blacks dissolved into white.

However, this barbarism/civilization paradigm was recontextualized according to political fluctuations and sociocultural contexts, particularly in the production of stereotypical themes, as seen in numerous 20th century texts. Stereotypes are always efficient vehicles of exclusive classifications. Let's consider the story "Back to Kentucky" in *Contes anglais* by Jacques Ferron. It is about a "Yank" who fights in Europe in order to restore democracy in the face of the nazi, fascist and stalinist horrors; which ones, Ferron does not specify, sticking instead with a generalized impression of raging war. This Yank meets, seduces and marries a Belgian francophone. Note the description of the encounter: "L'Amerloque, lui, avait joué au sauvage toute son enfance, puis était allé au cinéma apprendre son monde à deux dimensions puis rien."[135] To start with, calling someone a "Yank" categorizes the person as inadequate, which is further confirmed by a list of activities that designate him as a savage: he neither knows the world, nor literature, only Hollywood. This depiction is all the more surprising because a soldier at the front would certainly not have experienced the war like a movie, given the horror of injuries, death and shelling! What comes next, however, is the most interesting part of the narrative: the character does not want to learn French, and his wife, caught in the French/Flemish linguistic struggle, is unable to learn English. They choose to settle in Canada, in the suburbs of Montreal, because this is a place that accommodates "nos déficiences linguistiques."[136] Thus, because the place is accommodating (meaning, in this context, non-homogenous and with a weak identity), in its vagueness it tolerates all inadequacies. Parents are also referred to as "loony."[137] As for the children, we learn that: "Ce sont eux qui vous apprendront l'anglais, ma chère!"[138] Thus, as seen with Ribeiro in Brazil, speaking of the heterogeneity of encounters in undefined space, the hybrid children are practically orphans and must fend for themselves.[139] Ferron's children from different cultures will thus begin anew, based on the dominant language of the Anglophone father. For Ferron, the enemy is found within the barbaric homogeneity of the citizens of the United States[140]; for Ribeiro, the homogeneous excludes the *Mamelucos*. Ferron, however, has another point, "Que sommes-nous sinon une marche de l'Europe en Amérique. L'Europe a été perdante. Il était assez naturel qu'un soldat américain vint achever chez nous sa victoire."[141]

The barbarism/civilization dualism is thereby differently contextualized by Ribeiro and Ferron. For Ribeiro, who speaks of the 19th and early 20th century in Brazil, Europe is civilized whereas the Métis are barbarians. Ferron, speaking after the Second World War, affirms the victory of the barbarians born in the United States who threaten the tradition and civilization of European French Canada. In Ferron's text, as in that of Ribeiro's, the Americas' contribution is negative (especially that of the Métis), although Ribeiro suggests opportunities for encounters in his 1995 work, in a country made up of many cultures which slowly opens up to the recognition of otherness. Ferron considers the Americas to be negative, since he mistakes the popular culture of the United States with the only cultural foundations of the Americas. This is a trend that occasionally develops in the analyses of contemporary research wherein a partial vision of the United States, a global leader of sophisticated cultures as evidenced by its numerous and sophisticated research centres, leads to confusions between Americanism and Americanization. In 1964, Ferron, like many Quebecois elites, still sees Quebec as being a continuation of

Europe. In his research on Americanism (which, however, comes later[142]), Yvan Lamonde illustrates a contrary point of view. In this tale, Ferron voices the perspective of a cultural discourse based on the idea of a homogeneous community tied to a Europe which is seen as the most important socio-cultural reference for French Canada. The separation of groups is therefore unavoidable, as there are no encounters between the immigrants and the "old-stock" Quebecker. The immigrants appear to be stronger agents of colonization than the English Canadians, as they are related to the United States.[143] Here, Quebec is threatened by an English language that triumphs and by immigrants who, contrary to the prevailing stereotypes in the literature of English Canada, are not failures or victims like in English Canada. This point is emphasized by Margaret Atwood in her analysis of "Last Spring They Came Over" by Morley Callaghan: "Canada does pretend to offer a promise: she seems to offer newcomers a chance to exploit her; but this promise is seldom kept, at least in fiction. The would-be exploiters become the exploited, as they join the swelling ranks of Canadian victims."[144] Jean-Claude Lenormand also highlighted the conditions leading to failure in his work, *Québec-Immigration: zéro*,[145] published in Quebec in 1971.

Overall, it is important to have a clear idea of what can be proven by these repeated observations of failure that appear to be very different from the positive dynamics of Dany Laferrière and Kim Thúy's *self-making man* and *self-making woman* (section: From Generations). With regard to Lenormand, should the emphasis be placed on stopping immigration, or on the fact that immigrants do not have what it takes to be successful, as their abilities do not match what is demanded? Or is it more important to find solutions to improve immigration and avoid xenophobic exclusions? In other words, is there a permanent sense of resentment towards others, as Marc Angenot suggested in his book *Les idéologies du ressentiment* ?[146] Or is there a tendency towards rethinking relations with others, as shown in Kymlicka's theories on multiculturalism in 2007 and on the interculturalism of reasonable accommodation developed by Gérard Bouchard and Charles Taylor in 2008? Though Lenormand's work had already started the process of rethinking power relations in the seventies, it was still a dualistic world governed by strong resentments. Quebec in the sixties was caught between two "others," like most parts of the Americas: on the one hand, civilized Europe, and on the other, the barbaric United States and Americanization as the disseminator of a destructive popular culture. In 1964, Ferron noted that Quebec was successful only in defining itself as a victim striving to achieve uniformity through a common language and fighting against the others, while threatening those who did not integrate. It did not consider itself yet an entity that was part of the Americas; this would come later through research by Gérard Bouchard, Yvan Lamonde, Jean-François Côté and many others, and again in the democratic process of Reasonable Accommodations led by Gérard Bouchard and Charles Taylor,[147] and next in Gérard Bouchard's book, *L'interculturalisme: Un point de vue Québécois*.[148] Yet in 1965, in the novel *La Nuit*, also by Ferron,[149] Frank/François kills his threatening English-Canadian alter ego. It is only after this act that he is able to get in touch with the Italian taxi driver, and the black woman, Barbara, whose name can be easily associated with barbary. He then sees his own multiple identity, as a bank manager, a Buddhist and a communist; this multiplicity adds contradictory attributes to his personality instead of leading to a new identity formation stemming from a process of slowly solving his contradictions. Muliplicity is similarly characterized in Yann Martel's *L'histoire de Pi*.[150] However, in *Contes anglais*[151] Ferron continues with the left-wing French European rejection of the United States' culture, confining the two cultures to dualistic stereotypes that do not reflect Québec's status as a meeting place for Whites, Blacks, Indigenous people and recent immigrants. The same outlook is evident in a text written by Pierre Vallières,[152] one of the apostles of Quebec Marxist and pro-independence revolution, that was considered progressive at the time of its publication. In his book, *Nègres blancs d'Amérique*, Pierre Vallières compares Quebeckers to white Negroes, first exploited by British imperialism and then by American capitalism. We will not deny, as shown by many authors from Gabrielle Roy in *Bonheur d'occasion* to Paul Chamberland in *Terre Québec* and *L'afficheur hurle*, that the French-Canadian minority had been relegated to the margins of the Canadian state. However, it is important to remember what Vallières said about the Blacks in Quebec: "Au Québec, les Canadiens français ne connaissent pas ce racisme irrationnel qui a causé tant de tort aux travailleurs blancs et aux travailleurs noirs des États-Unis. Ils n'ont aucun mérite à cela, puisqu'il n'y a pas, au Québec, de 'problème noir.'"[153] The workings of a dichotomous perspective are thus apparent.[154] The people of the United States are the barbarians, because of their fierce racism that led to the Civil Rights movement. For Pierre Vallières, the barbarians are the capitalist bourgeois who must be eliminated. The civilized are the common people who are exploited. However, as seen in his book, dualism prevents the disenfranchised Blacks from gaining visibility in Quebec, many of whom were, as Marcel Trudel[155] has shown, born in Canada since the arrival of the slaves who worked for French Canadians. Moreover, George Elliott Clarke[156] and Yves Antoine,[157] also point out that many Blacks arrived in Canada in the 19th century after fleeing the United States, settling in Southern Ontario or in Halifax (Nova Scotia). There is no black problem because the Black population in Quebec is small and for the most part without a voice. It is only in the 1980s that Dany Laferrière—attentive to differences, racism, immigration, multiculturalism, interculturalism and negative stereotypes—humorously discusses the problem in a new light in *Comment faire l'amour avec un Nègre sans se fatiguer*.[158]

Garrison Mentality, West and Frontier: Different Forms of Exclusion and Inclusion

> "Son rêve était plus excitant que sa mémoire, voilà le grand principe sur lequel s'est édifiée l'Amérique," dit l'assistant de recherche de Martin quand il cherche à savoir ce qu'est devenu Dubois, un Canadien français parti dans l'ouest.[159]

Thinking of the immense hinterland as barbaric has important implications for the initiation of relationships with others as well as for oneself: this perspective conceives of an internal border that cuts the country in two, constructing a threatening space which leads people in the Americas to take refuge in the city turned towards Europe. Europe is not only seen as civilized but is also thought of as a source of cultural innovation for the whole continent, a point of view which cannot explain what it means to live in the Americas. Consider the garrison mentality referred to by Margaret Atwood, proposing that individually Canadians often fail while collectively, as seen in Pierre Berton's *The National Dream* and *The Last Spike*,[160] they succeed. In the words of Margaret Atwood: "The collective hero can be an expression of a closed and ingrown garrison mentality or of a living community; collective action has been necessary for survival but it may also stifle individual growth."[161] W.L. Morton, an advocate of the importance of a history of the North for Canada, has a comparable outlook: "The North makes necessary an absolute dependence on one's fellows on co-operative skills, on communal capital."[162] Thus, the garrison mentality is an expression of a need for protection against a barbaric space that slows expansion. This protection against the vastness of nature and against the threatening otherness of the Indigenous peoples is re-contextualized through stereotyped conversations about the menace of the cold, creating a starting point for possible cooperation. This is highlighted by the narrator of *Tres lotos en un mar de fuego* by Camila Reimers: "Conversación ideal en ascensores, fiestas de diplomáticos y comienzo de reuniones de negocios. Mientras más frio mejor, nos sentimos unidos por una naturaleza inhóspita, héroes compartiendo un destino congelado. "[163]

The frontier, on the other hand, does not rely on the dualism of territorial logic. Its paradoxical creation is extensively detailed in stories of the *Wild West* in the United States. Indeed, the frontier is presented as empty, open, and above all, endless. This is never true of a geographical space, which is always limited contrary to knowledge, which can always be expanded, open to new discoveries and hence perceived as limitless.[164] This paradoxical narrative related to the frontier is at the root of the break from a European imaginary based on borders—particularly since the Treaty of Westphalia and the consequent will to create stable and delimited nation-states (i.e. restricted, insular spaces). The expansion of nation-states is possible only through war because, in the face of this finite sum of wealth that any territory represents, one's victory entails another's defeat in a constant reactivation of the belief that life is a zero-sum game. From this point of view, the concept of frontier in Canada is ambiguous, particularly in the work of W.L. Morton, who was fascinated by the North. In a passage in his paper entitled "The North in Canadian Historiography," the term frontier signifies a limit: "As the agricultural frontier moved westward, it left an open flank to the north. This became a permanent frontier, an enduring demarcation line between wilderness and farmland, between North and South."[165] However, at the end of his text, the frontier becomes an unfinished space: "Finally, the North… as a source of treasure… the unfolding of the permanent frontier."[166] Therein, according to Morton, lies the future of Canada; from its wealth and the power of the federal government. Thus, a discursive syncretism can be seen at work between the European conception of territory: the North as a limit to cereal agriculture and, at the same time, the new continent perception of the North as a place open to a practically unlimited development of riches through mining, knowledge and technology.

This frontier is an important category when comparing the Americas, because, as is evident in Brazilian literature, it can be metaphysical; or economically ordered as in Canada or economically anarchistic as in the United States. More importantly, it demarcates the two cultures' respective approach to self-invention and to others. The frontier is first conceived as an empty space, the expulsion and the massacre of the Indigenous peoples thus erased. Jean-Paul Lacasse notes, however, that the notion of an open space is linked to indigenous cultures. Lacasse studied the Innu cultures of Canada and noticed that their relationship with the territory was different from that of the

Europeans, because for the Innu hunter "le territoire était partout."[167] The Innu writer points out that the idea of the territory as frontier, as open space, is contrary to European anxieties that have led to the construction of borders everywhere and to the division of the territory.

From this perspective, it is interesting to note how the Copper Inuit[168] were represented in two versions of the same book, one in English and the other one in French, by the Museum of Civilization in Ottawa (now the Museum of History). There were significant differences in how Anglophones and Francophones represented the Copper Inuit, especially in their respective projections of a European perspective and of the minority Quebec conception of threatening distant spaces belonging to others. In the English version of the book, the group was organized around the independence of families and individuals. They were related to regional groups exploring vast territories: "Inuit communities were real communities not merely groups of people who happened to be living near one another."[169] In the French version, the Inuit "évoluent à l'intérieur d'une terre d'errance que la tradition et d'ancestrales querelles ou de vieilles peurs ont vaguement délimitée [...] au-delà d'une certaine limite [...] Danger."[170] The Quebec writer projected his perception of territory and of the threat represented by the other from a minority perspective within the Anglophone majority. Yet, the Inuit like the Innu or other Indigenous groups see the territory as a vast open space. Innu culture, according to Jean-Paul Lacasse, sees the territory as a frontier that is not a threat to the inner self. For Quebeckers, on the other hand, what lies beyond the provincial boundary represents the Anglophone world, which assimilates Francophones, reducing them to a minority. The beyond is thus a culturally and even economically threatening space. The Francophone commentator favoured an interpretation of the societal workings of the Copper Inuit as being similar to his own *a priori*, thinking both in terms of limited space and of the long-term in reference to Europe.

The frontier, conceived in all the expansive force of its paradoxical logic offered a rich land presented as having infinite potential for the millions of immigrants who dreamt of becoming successful settlers; self-made men and land-owners. The frontier was a place, in the United States and in Western Canada, of individual freedom greater than that found in Europe or in the East of the continent, as it allowed for development through expansion. It had the feel of a practical democracy coupled with capitalism that measured and registered the vastness of the land, granting land titles, which ultimately lead to a space, which filled up and became delimited, as did all other spaces.

The power of the creative contradiction—that of the frontier's limitlessness—is strong in the Americas, seeing as they do not seek to solve contradictions but rather to accumulate elements as they appear. For example, François, a character in *La Nuit* by Ferron, proclaims himself communist, Buddhist and bank manager. But the creative power of the frontier had a limited lifespan and subsided into the dominant property logic. This is what the vast majority of the immigrants sought even if discursively the aim was, as Frederik Jackson Turner states, to establish a new civilization and initiate economic development: "The West opened a refuge from the rule of established classes, from the subordination of youth to age, from the sway of established and revered institutions."[171] This space also often welcomed different or rejected individuals, not just Mormons who, persecuted, settled in the Utah desert. There were also Blacks who, originally slaves in the South, became owners. This is the narrative that Oscar Micheaux's *The Conquest: The Story of a Negro Pioneer*[172] relates. Hence, the West had an impact on identity building. Individuals did not only belong to a place, they belonged to themselves (which was revolutionary in the 19th century). Moreover, owning a property was then used as a guarantee, allowing people to obtain credit and develop trade. After his trips to Europe, Canada and the United States, Sarmiento, now President of the Republic, did everything possible to bring immigrants to Argentina. However, only the more "civilized" ones, i.e. settlers from Northern Europe, Germany, Switzerland and England, were granted land recorded in the land registry.[173] The open pampas (frontier of the Southern Cone) became as civilized as the province of Entre Rios, for example. It turned into a place of development and integration where people from everywhere converged on a new territory,[174] inventing new socioeconomic relationships from which the Blacks and the Indigenous continued to be excluded.

If the Brazilian sertão was primarily a metaphysical space which was not linked to legal and democratic economic development (as Brazil, led by an emperor, only outlawed slavery in 1883), the frontier of the United States was a democratic and economic space that was part of a larger narrative—that of Manifest Destiny.[175] John O'Sullivan promoted the idea of Manifest Destiny in 1845, but it had already been conceived in 1818 when President Andrew Jackson defeated the combined Spanish and Seminole forces established in Florida. His goal was to free this territory from Spanish colonization in order to open it to democracy, thereby realizing God's plan. Consequently, the citizens of the United States were rewarded by God for their desire to universalize democracy and eliminate barbarism.

This plan can be understood through a nature conceived from literature (as in Argentina and Canada) and through descriptions borrowed from Europe. Hence, nature was often seen through the lens of European literary rhetoric more than through an observation, which could have created a new esthetic stemming from the Americas. Alsop spoke of Maryland as a new earthly paradise where fruits and flowers were like the hieroglyphs of our Adamic situation.[176] This vision is consistent with Protestant views and those of the deistic Freemason State-Unions who saw the source of a natural religion in the map of the universe. In William Paley's 1804 *Natural Theology*,[177] the universe is governed by a great architect who placed the Americas, and the United States in particular, at the heart of a civilizing mission. As stated by President Jackson: "Providence has showered on this favoured land blessings without number and has chosen you as the guardians of freedom to preserve it for the benefit of the human race."[178] We see once again that the *you* was turned towards the future, like the frontier, because it concerned what could be developed. *You* referred to future immigrants plus the whole of humanity aspiring to freedom. The frontier thus becomes a garden, a village and then a space where the values of urban modernity will be established, extending to the suburban bungalow (section: From the Frontier): knowledge, industry, technology, all that is produced in the United-States, Canada, Argentina, etc. For President Jackson, the geographical frontier was combined with a human frontier linked to the infinity of future humanity and the expansion not only of economic knowledge but also of cultural and ethical-democratic knowledge.

The brutal and savage frontier, often represented in Europe and even in Canada by a cowboy who defends himself without the assistance of the police or of the army, is actually economically and culturally civilized. It is a brutal but open meeting place where various communities live together and cooperate and where each individual has decided to become his own master, as seen in *Hija de la fortuna* by Isabel Allende[179] (about the California gold rush), or even in *Klondyke* by Jacques Languirand.[180] In the latter, the author develops a dual reflection regarding two strong tendencies in Quebec—nomadism versus the sedentary lifestyle: the seeds of an ambitious and dynamic middle class are placed within a configuration that displaces the barbarism/civilization paradigm to give way to a third element, that of the frontier. This dynamic is intended to be inclusive, as highlighted by Isabel Allende and Jacques Languirand, because it favours escaping a world-view that considers life a zero-sum game, that is life tied to a finite amount of wealth and exacerbating rivalries. This can be seen in the farmers' situation in the West during the 1929 crisis, as Sharon Butala demonstrates in her book, *The Perfection of the Morning* : "This is how it was that my sisters and I grew up with the notion of the farm as a mythic paradise from which we had been expelled, by drought and bankers, and could never return."[181] The frontier tends to multiply objects of desire, to favour access to these objects and to control violence, except of course with respect to Indigenous peoples and often to women.[182] The paradigm thus becomes ternary, barbarism/civilization/*frontier*, clearing a cooperative space for encounters between people from all over the planet, exploring the opportunities provided by spatial coincidence.

The Hybridization of Spaces: Property and Liberalism

When Creoles, who were open to modernity, moved to the frontier, the frontier became open to a potential hybridization of spaces. This led to the combining of the spirituality of the infinite with that of the Garden of Eden. This was shown in José Marti's discourse:

> De la charrue est née l'Amérique du Nord, tandis que l'Espagnole est issue du limier. Une guerre ordonnée par le fanatisme avait chassé du poétique univers de ses palais aériens le Maure efféminé par l'opulence, et la soldatesque désormais sans emploi, abreuvée de gros vin et de haine envers l'hérétique se rua, de fer bardée et l'arquebuse au poing, sur l'Indien au plastron de coton.[183]

This operates differently in the agriculturalist discourse that is found in *Jean Rivard défricheur* and *Jean Rivard économiste* by Antoine Gérin-Lajoie,[184] which sees the village as a Garden of Eden, but also as a place for economic advancement complemented by knowledge. But this discourse is often based on both a tautology and a contradiction; for example, in *Le véritable petit Albert*, J. N. Duquet says: "L'agriculture! Quelle mine inépuisable à exploiter!"[185] In this popular book, the confusion between the dominance of solar energy and fossil fuel is symptomatic of a country that exports both its mining and agricultural resources, in a world where fossil fuel supports burgeoning industrialization but where the farmer is not overlooked. This is further affirmed in the following excerpt: "Le fumier est *le capital du cultivateur*."[186] In this world wavering between the vast availability of natural resources and growing knowledge, contradictory expressions abound. These include propositions such as: "Les rives du Saint-Laurent bordées de riches villes habitées *par des cultivateurs*."[187] Building cities in the countryside is indeed Antoine Gérin-Lajoie's dream.

The civil servant turned writer encourages people to clear land and build cities (which have all the characteristics of a village), thus developing local industry and aiming at self-sufficiency.[188] This dream doesn't lack ecological appeal, concurring partly with an aspect of the North-American pioneering tradition found in Thoreau's *Walden*.[189] The Creole, the settler and the man of the New World were in a process of constant transformation in the 19th century, even if they were simultaneously constrained by the dualistic barbarism/civilization paradigm.

It is important to bear in mind the nuanced remarks of various thinkers and the fact of these hybridizations, even if they were merely theoretical at the time. An example can be found in Étienne Parent's speeches at the Canadian Institute. An apostle of economic liberalism (as opposed to red liberalism), Parent knew how to reconcile economic and Church discourses, arguing against both the *Bible* and the legitimacy of ultramontanist views, promoting their perception of the *Bible*: "Tu travailleras à la sueur de ton front." However, for him, "le travail c'est la liberté."[190] Parent avoided the easy antitheses which Sarmiento and the Canadian clergy subscribed to, assigning opposing values to spaces (pampa = barbarism / city = civilization for Sarmiento, and village = civilization / city = barbarism for the Canadian clergy). His speeches represented an approach that took into account the past and the future by creating transitional links that allowed for reflection as part of a continuity of thought, leading to qualitative dynamic leaps: "[L'industriel] est le père de l'Amérique civilisée […] Ce sont des cités sans nombre et des empires que l'industriel a conquis sur la nature sauvage, non plus avec l'épée et le sang d'autres hommes mais bien avec la hache et les sueurs de son propre front."[191] The industrialist was armed with an axe and the sweat of his brow! He was thus still a very primitive industrialist, very close to the biblical picture while eliminating all elements of wilderness. Nevertheless, Parent's art was to present the man who arrives, the *settler*, as an individual using techniques, like an industrialist and not like a village parishioner repeating the same gestures from century to century. By this process of attribution, he transformed the farmer into a motor of progress who built cities based on the model of the United States, like we see in *Jean-Rivard économiste* by Antoine Gérin-Lajoie. However, Parent did not go so far as to affirm, like W. L. Morton, that urbanity had preceded colonization, citing the fact that Quebec, Montreal, and Halifax were ports reserved for the trade of fur, timber and mining resources from the North; for import/export in already globalized trade routes. Sarmiento[192] said the same thing about Buenos Aires and Río de la Plata, whose rivers were given in concession to English merchants in the 19th century. Despite all that, Parent's portrait of the French-Canadian changed radically, as space was no longer divided between the country and the city. At the same time, he continued to reject the Indigenous people's space, that is to say, the forests and those who pass through them; the *coureurs des bois*. The city arose from the territory and from its logic, to which were added business, technical, and financial knowledge. The city arose out of pre-capitalist era development and fit into an evolutionary dynamic where identity transformed from territorial logic to an industrialist logic. Thus, a knowledge-based society was constituted in which education became another available resource that transformed the territory into networks.

The impact of these networks can be measured in the *Philosophy of the Railroads*, published in 1853 by English Canadian T. C. Keefer. He brought important social issues to light to demonstrate that trains would completely change Canadians' lifestyle by reducing distances which would henceforth be measured in time. Time gained importance as the importance of space faded; this is evidenced by the fact that people in different regions of Canada, and eventually everywhere in the Americas, learned to live according to time zones and not local time. As a corollary, in 1885, universal time was established in Greenwich, England, under the leadership of Canadian Sanford Fleming. Continental networking was operational, pending that of the planet. Keefer's thoughts on combining philosophy, sociology, rationalism and cultural identity were tailored to the vastness of the continent. They joined the willingness of the Argentinian Juan Bautista Alberdi to link philosophy and cultural identity. Hence, philosophy would become both social and political, working in unison with America,[193] rather than being trapped and rehashed either by the fathers of the Church, or by Greco-Latin classicists and their traditions. In the 19th century, the influence of these traditions was weakening in some European countries, such as England and Germany, in the process of advanced industrialization. In any case, the farmer himself would be able to send his products to remote towns, if not in even more distant markets that already required "speed, economy, regularity, safety."[194] World trade was in motion at the end of the 19th century and the Anglo-Canadian municipalities paid taxes for the railway which connected them to rail networks. Thus, it marked a profound and rapid change which also caught the attention of Sarmiento, president of the Republic of Argentina, who dreamt of canals and railways such as those built by the Canadian William Perkins between Buenos Aires and Rosario.

However, this industrial progress, coupled with education and exploitation of the continent—requiring a massive influx of immigrants—was not considered, before Randolph Bourne in the United States in 1916, as a potential encounter between different ethnic groups, as suggested by Bagehot in 1873. It was monopolized by European descendants. The only change of perspective was the one already initiated by Étienne Parent, who saw no division between town and country, as confirmed by the establishment of the railway which allowed the marketing of local perishable products. Little by little, the barbarism/civilization dichotomy was displaced in favour of opening up to the continent and to its wealth, as Randolph Bourne shows in his text, "Transnational America": "What we have achieved has been rather a cosmopolitan federation of national colonies, of foreign cultures, from whom the sting of competition has been removed. America is already the world federation in miniature, the continent where for the first time in history has been achieved that miracle of hope, the peaceful living side by side, with character substantially preserved, of the most heterogeneous peoples under the sun. Nowhere else has such contiguity been anything but the breeder of misery."[195]

The break between barbarism/civilization synonymous with countryside/city or city/countryside, according to different political optics, was rejected by Parent, Bourne, and others. Nevertheless, it would persist with regards to minoritized groups such as the Indigenous and Black peoples for a long time, at least until after World War II.

The Frontier and Eden

Even if it has different significations for different groups, the frontier is an important category when comparing the Americas because it integrates the unfinished into its operational culture. The unfinished is always linked to spirituality-related thinking. Unique to particular immigrant groups such as the Doukhobors, sometimes it is directly metaphysical. As Gabrielle Roy points out in "La vallée Houdou": "Ils savent ou à peu près, rapportera l'interprète, que la montagne et la rivière ne sont qu'illusion, mais ils disent: peu importe, puisque nous les voyons… Mais les Doukhobors ne voulaient rien entendre… assurés d'être les seuls à comprendre le mystère du monde…"[196] The spirituality of the unfinished is now philosophical for Yvon Rivard who compares the frontier to the ocean: "En effet, quand on marche dans la prairie, on a l'impression d'être à la surface, au milieu et au fond de quelque chose qui n'est ni la terre ni le ciel mais un mélange des deux, une sorte d'océan à cause du ciel si haut qui pèse sur nous et de la lumière si pure qui gonfle le sol et allège notre pas."[197] This physical and metaphysical frontier is also explored through baseball.[198] Played in a green space which is simultaneously closed and open to the infinite, the ball can be hit over the fence, getting lost in an imaginary frontier that evokes paradise. In the novel *Shoeless Joe Jackson comes to Iowa* by Canadian writer W. P. Kinsella,[199] Shoeless Joe Jackson says, "This must be heaven," referring to the field of dreams. The narrator, Ray Kinsella, replies: "No. It's Iowa."[200] In other words, in opening its wealth to immigrants, the frontier of baseball is heavenly, like a new Garden of Eden.[201] It is an expression of providence far from Europe. It is this providence that Georges Desmeules evokes in *Le projet Syracuse*: "Le baseball joue la mise à mort de l'Européen qui sommeille encore dans chaque Américain."[202] Providence in the New World, as it is understood in the United States, is associated with the discourse of rebirth; far from conflicts, scarcity, and a territorial logic which require not only very hard work (according to zero-sum game logic) but participation in the removal of wealth from others in order to survive. This brings us to the Jesuit Acosta who four centuries earlier was so dazzled by the beauty and wealth of the Americas that he ardently, lyrically, and quasi-heretically compared them to paradise: "Ceux qui pensent que le paradis terrestre est situé sous la zone équinoxiale, il semble que ce soit avec quelque raison. Non que je veuille décider par moi-même que le Jardin des Délices dont parle l'Écriture s'y trouve… mais parce que si l'on peut dire qu'il existe un paradis sur terre, c'est là où l'on jouit d'une température aussi suave et agréable."[203] This also brings to mind Vespucci, quoted by Delumeau: "Si le paradis terrestre subsiste en quelque endroit de la terre, j'estime… qu'il ne doit pas être très éloigné de ces régions."[204] But if the thread of colonized open space is followed, brought into relief by the creolized newcomers who were proud of themselves on this frontier, it leads to a recycled, urban 20th century garden, that of the suburbs dotted with flower-filled bungalows, as Jacques Ferron describes in *L'Amélanchier*.[205]

From the Frontier to the Bungalow

Little by little, as large geographical areas were filled, the frontier changed into an industrial and urban world through the intermediary of a vision of indeterminate exploitable wealth; namely, knowledge of exploiting natural resources. This application appears in *La Flore laurentienne* by Brother Marie-Victorin.[206]

In exploring the meanings in flora, he establishes a new understanding of the environment in Quebec, appropriating the territory and its identity implications through the creation of new knowledge. Following Brother Marie-Victorin, *L'hiver de force* by Réjean Ducharme[207] attempts to advance knowledge at the margins of an urban culture which is dominated by access to a world caught up in media stereotypes. His intertext proposes reimagining the garden into a livable urban space where privacy regulates the melancholy of overgoverned urban existence. Through this perspective, Ducharme's work at times recalls Ferron's *L'Amélanchier*,[208] where the protagonist creates an Edenic garden in his backyard.[209] In some respects, this garden resembles the intimacy offered by the Latin-American patio. The backyard in contrast with the façade and the hectic pace of the street and adjacent industrial parks, provides a substitute for an Edenic place. But this backyard is still restricted and doesn't always circumvent the deepest longings:

> Every blade of grass, every trill from a red-winged blackbird, every sparkle of sun on the Frenchman River that trickled past our house at the hay farm seemed more precious… In the city for short visits now I studied people's houses, or the rows of condominiums or the new apartment buildings, assessing how close they were to each other, how big their yards were, what their occupants had for views, trying to imagine how I would live again in the city and what arrangement might be acceptable should something happen to Peter or the ranch… I tried to imagine life without this space, this welcome, close presence of grass and sky.[210]

In addition to the backyard, the longings which often obsess urban populations recall calendar art and the dream of having access to an unspoiled and esthetic nature. Here the kitsch of Norman Rockwell comes into play: the idyllic and stereotypical landscapes of the middle-class[211] recycle romantic scenes from the 19th century, like the little red-roofed house lost near the woods, found in paintings from Uruguay to Canada.

At any rate, it is within the imaginations of the middle-class that the bungalow and the expansion of the suburbs seem to provide an agreeable solution for the in-between civilized nature/city, especially seeing as the backyard of the bungalow is large enough to be transformed into a baseball field by children. It is usually close to the real brand new neighbourhood baseball field, which is an important part of the spatial organization of new urban dreams built in what was up until recently the countryside.[212] Furthermore, it allows an escape from slums or from confined downtown spaces. The suburb seems endless, nestled between the city and the countryside, inspiring dreams in immigrants of Indian origin who leave various regions in India or Africa to settle in Mississauga instead of Toronto. For instance, this is the suburb alluded to by Arundhati Roy in *The God of Small Things*[213]; it has become well-known throughout the planet among aspiring immigrants originating from India. The dream of limitless expansion rests in a space no longer based on city/countryside or civilization/barbarism dualism. They are combined, in the hope of working within the logic of a new frontier; that of polyculturalism and the capitalization of knowledge and technologies. In fact, contrary to Alejo Carpentier's *Los pasos perdidos*,[214] there is no longer any question of getting lost in the woods which are now traversed by the trans-Amazonian highway and inhabited by Indigenous people who are delegated from various NGOs[215] to go back in time up the Orinoco while effectively managing an infinite number of connections in multiple global networks, as demonstrated by Néstor García Canclini in *La globalización imaginada*.

However, all is not Edenic in this urban recycled garden. This is what Jerzy Kosinski points at in his parody of the expulsion from the Garden of Eden. In *Being There*,[216] Kosinski playfully reformulates the idyllic, enclosed garden. He plays humorously with the intertext of literary works devoted to the garden. *Being There*, translated in Spanish as *Desde el Jardín*, tells the story of a young man completely disconnected from society who lives with his guardian in a house with a beautiful garden. He is responsible for the garden's maintenance. His only other activity is watching television. When his guardian dies, the young man, alone with the fantasies rooted in his limited existence and surrounded by the garden and media discourse, is evicted from the house. It is then that he discovers the city for the first time but speaks only in terms of gardening. People interpret his simplistic comments regarding seasons and gardening as metaphors for their stereotypes of modernity, urban life and the importance of the economy. In the hero's words, the crises will go away: after a hard winter, spring will flourish. Worn out metaphors, also referring to the circular structuring of the *roman du terroir* in Canada, the United States and Brazil,[217] are similarly used to show the change in discourse connecting the countryside to the city, where the Edenic garden remains present as the hope of America. Kosinski's character manages to make his way in this new society and become a media celebrity and then a financial advisor to the President of the United States, when his sentences are read as sage metaphors for a better economic future, and thus seen as related to the renewed expansion of the economic frontier.

Jerzy Kosinski clearly proposes a version of the Garden of Eden different from that of its origins, not as an enclosed and protected space, but as an exploration of the new frontier which, in the 20th and the 21st centuries, is no longer territorial, but rather based on economic exchange, media communication and the accumulation of knowledge in a globalized urban expansion. In this frontier, discursive worlds intertwine and generate new spaces for exchanges in a competitive globalized and democratized cacophony, where power relationships are decontextualized and recontextualized.

This is also what Hernando de Soto shows in *The Other Path.* De Soto is the apostle of informal entrepreneurship and critic of Peruvian bureaucratic horrors. He shows how bureaucracy prevents the poor (generally Métis or Indigenous peoples) from creating their own businesses, by outlining the prohibitive costs (in time and money) of obtaining the necessary permits which take more than a year to get. He glorifies the spirit of free enterprise, grey market business and the dynamism of those who would otherwise remain unemployed. He devotes himself to Peru and observes the transformations of a city like Lima:

> The surrounding desert and hills have ceased to be a passive landscape and they become part of the city, and the city's European style has yielded to a noisy, tawny skinned personality. But the cities have also conferred individuality on their inhabitants. Individual effort has come to predominate over collective effort.[218]

The landscape is changing, as the authorities have finally decided to give ownership titles to migrants who built their houses "favela style" by occupying land (whether private or municipal) which did not belong to them. De Soto points out how the property titles are then used to provide guarantees on the basis of recognized capital to obtain loans or microloans, allowing for the development of rational business plans which are no longer dependent on money lenders:

> Under the guidance of De Sotos' think-tank, 300,000 titles were registered in urban Lima from 1991 through 1995. The results were soon palpable. By 1998, the value of the registered urban typically doubled; previously non-existent private mortgage and consumer credit markets had begun to develop.[219]

In the 19th century, this dynamic attracted immigrants to the Americas, the place where the *revolution was based on giving property titles to the poor.* This is highlighted by Bharati Mukherjee in *Jasmine* through a character named Du, a Vietnamese adolescent adopted by a family in Iowa after the conquest of South Vietnam by communists and the collectivization of life in a harsh dictatorship: "Owning is rebellion, it means not sharing, it means survival. He ate bugs and worms and rodents. He lived."[220] Certainly, Du does not criticize property, consumer society or technology, as the lack thereof caused the death of his family. In North America, he is able to start a new life. This new beginning is also the subject of Doug Saunders' analyses in his book entitled *Arrival City*, where he devotes himself to various slums and suburbs created by migrants and immigrants who create similar urban spaces everywhere in the world, particularly in Canada, the United States, Brazil and Venezuela, but also in India, China, Germany and England. Saunders shows the vitality and dynamism of poor and migrant workers, whose slums are not an affliction to be remedied but the very future of contemporary cities: "These transitional spaces—arrival cities—are the places where the next great economic and cultural boom will be born, or where the next great explosion of violence will occur. The difference depends on our ability to notice, and our willingness to engage."[221]

This dynamic, which signals a desire to enhance the value of proprietorship, shows that the barbarism/civilization paradigm is coupled with profound structures of cultural rejection that come from the educated elites, landowners, and bureaucrats towards the Métis, other Indigenous peoples, all migrants, and the poor from within and without the country. The poor eventually penetrate socioeconomic functioning and drastically change the landscape of cities and sometimes even the historical centers controlled by the elites.[222] Thus, with universal participation in knowledge capitalization, free trade, and property ownership, and sometimes in systems tied to corruption (as seen in *The White Tiger* by Aravind Adiga (2008)), countries become more competitive in the context of glocalization. We also see that integration happens efficiently through cultural recognition, as well as access to employment and to the economy. These different means of integration are among some of the fundamental points of *Arrival City* by Doug Saunders. They are not sufficiently highlighted by the theorists of multiculturalism, such as Will Kymlicka (2007). They do point out, however, that cultural rights cannot be recognized effectively without acknowledging civil, social, and political rights. As for Saunders' book, it is necessary to emphasize that, in the context of migration where lives are transformed, where the struggle for economic advancement is intense and community relations are distended, it remains unclear how cultural rights can be recognized and applied to citizenship rights while the priority is the ambition to succeed and to migrate to a richer and more comfortable environment.

These dreams leading to migration is also what infuses the dynamics of reasonable accommodation in Quebec. In the eyes of those born in Quebec, what do the immigrants want? Certainly not to share the canonical historical consensus and the established point of view, or the common representational structures, since they do not share the same past. That is why, at the Bouchard-Taylor Commission for "reasonable accommodation" (2008), the majority of participants born in Quebec stressed, session after session, the dividing differences (which include religion and appearance, the veil, the kirpan, etc.), which in turn led to the formation of a Charter of values (ultimately not applied). Principally, the lack of shared passed or shared values was emphasized during these sessions. Hence, people born in Quebec hardly heard what the majority of immigrants were discussing. For them, the important thing was that their academic and professional abilities be recognized in order to find employment. In other words, they wanted a chance—based on democratic merit—to compete for and to participate in the creation of wealth. Different people want to share a space for economic exchange and the development of the community, participate wholly in this development and share access to wealth, while sharing a territory and common reference points. To do this, it is necessary for those who are in a position of authority in Quebec to think not in terms of territorial logics that define wealth as finite and where competition engenders the potential for loss, but according to the logic of a knowledge-based society which offers the possibility of creating new collective wealth from the perspective that life is not a zero-sum game. In this case, we move from a Darwinian perspective to a perspective of social ecology,[223] which allows universal access to competition through intrinsic recognition in a liberal capitalist society: recognition of diplomas, degrees and professional capabilities, access to credit, ownership, etc.

Multiple encounters can happen anywhere, through the internet (Facebook and Twitter, for example), in an expanding urbanity which can even transform an isolated home into a bright household component of the global brain, as mentioned by Pierre Lévy.[224] These meetings are no longer controlled by social constraints specific to places established long ago, much less by a fate dependent on gods, as in Sophocles' *Antigone*, but by chance that is related to coincidences. New perspectives open to capable individuals who perceive new realities. This expression is taken from Michael Delisle's novella, which features an immigrant from the rural interior of his country. He emigrates from his village to the city because "[l]a rencontre opère bel et bien une rupture temporelle et un retour de soi à soi par l'intermédiaire de l'autre."[225] However, the encounter also permits a renewed relationship with the past, with the mother figure; a dimension that can also be observed in *La logeuse* by Éric

Dupont (2006), in the journeys of Rosa Ost who sends letters from Montreal to the community she left in Gaspé. There is no loss of contact or identity in the encounter, but rather learning from new relationships in the context of the accumulation of knowledge.

Rethinking Relations With the Founding Peoples

For a long time, multiracial people, Indigenous peoples and Blacks were not recognized as founders. The founders were the "civilized" Whites. This tendency persists because decisions to recognize the founding peoples go through exclusionary processes, which are sometimes almost complete historical deletions. We have to bear in mind that there were Black slaves in English Canada and in French Canada. Let's consider then Angélique's story retold by Lorena Gale in a play by the same name[226]: based solely on rumours, this black slave was hanged after being accused of burning down a part of Montreal. Gale presents a Canada at variance with its usual historical representation as the last station on the Underground Railroad (a haven for Blacks fleeing slavery in the United States). Angélique wants to leave Canada for New England, which she sees as a refuge, but she is caught before crossing the border. Slaves contributed to Canada's development, but they left neither archives nor literature; they remained a very small minority and because of their status as slaves they were not considered important. Thus, they are not part of the founding peoples of Canada. Although multicultural policies have contributed to the recognition of others, Laura Rizzà notes that they have jeopardized the recognition of long-established Black Canadians. In "Dismantling Canadian Multiculturalism in African-Canadian Fiction," particularly in her analysis of Lawrence Hill's *Any Known Blood* (2007),[227] Rizzà writes that the long history of Black Canadians is engulfed within the accommodations extended to newcomers. In fact, the narrative of multiculturalism argues that different people (including Black people) have been in Canada for only a short time, as they all tend to be perceived as immigrants, making the long presence of Blacks invisible. A similar perspective is evident in the recent work of Mathieu d'Avignon and Camil Girard[228] about the celebrations for the 400th anniversary of the founding of the city of Quebec. The authors discuss the place of others in the daily life of Quebec. In Mathieu d'Avignon's interview with Marcel Trudel,[229] Trudel emphasizes that French Quebec was also built with the participation of the Indigenous people and the English, to name only these two. Trudel notes that, in the genealogical trees, there are plenty of Scottish, German, and Indigenous people, while successful foundation of Quebec City is credited to Pierre Dugua du Mons, lieutenant general of New France from 1603 to 1612. If the latter has been forgotten to Champlain's benefit, it is because he was Protestant. The tone of the reinterpretation of official historical formulations, based on misinformation and criticism, are a given. It helps to understand that the choice of the two founding peoples, English Canadians and French Canadians, stems from decisions that ignore the acknowledgement of a past that is often deliberately overlooked.[230] Consider also Silvio Marcus de Souza Correa and Camil Girard's text[231] comparing the French colonies of the New France with those of coastal Brazil: Rio de Janeiro (1555–1560) and Maranhao (1612–1615). It appears that the smooth operation and expansion of the colony took place through the movement of people. This means that the French were often integrated with the Indigenous populations (in Brazil as well as in Quebec), to the point of interbreeding, which was not viewed favourably by the elites who banned these practices. Furthermore, many Indigenous people went to France to be shown to the French, some eventually studying and starting careers. This movement of people was based on travel, adoption, marriage and cohabitation, which produced enough bilingual and Métis people to maintain a useful and lucrative trade between various communities, whether in New France or Brazil.

Thus, it is very useful to make trans-American comparisons (as opposed to sticking to narratives limited by borders) in order to understand the dynamics that lead to the invention of the nations and communities of the Americas, and to be cognizant of the omissions that have occurred. We can then understand how the people live and how to judiciously and effectively reinvent the Americas. From this point of view, consider Ghislain Picard and Mathieu d'Avignon's conclusion[232]: it is necessary to review history in order to accept that the Indigenous peoples are at the origin of New France, as they are in Brazil, as Oswald de Andrade points out in his 1928 *Manifeste anthropophage*. This implies that the history of Quebec is not five hundred years old, but rather several thousand years old. In other words, these researchers place the New World in a specific context, one not limited to that of Europe transported to the continent. As we can see, the long term analyzed by Gérard Bouchard switches from Europe to indigenous pre-colonial times. These perspectives aim to provide a point of entry, allowing the Indigenous peoples and the Blacks of the Americas to assert themselves and develop within nations and within wider transnational and transcultural contexts open to their recognition.

The rethinking of power relations in historical domains as well as in economics and culture is just beginning and is still a challenge to date; d'Avignon and Camil Girard's ideas are very recent. Rejection has been continuously reinforced, resulting in a literary and historical canon, which has produced and reproduced stereotypes that are difficult to counter.

Notes

1. Robin W. Winks, "Canada and the Three Americas," in *Friends so Different*, eds. L. Lamont and J. D. Edmonds (Ottawa: University of Ottawa Press for the Americas Society, 1989), 156.
2. Our goal is not to discuss the different perspectives between national association and international ones. However, it is worth noting that there is still a certain fear of the comparative dimension among certain groups of researchers due to the fact that, for instance, like in Canada, national identities and cultural difference have taken a long time to be recognized (section: Comparisons). There are also national legitimations, which prevent researchers from going beyond borders. One can compare the website of the International American Studies Association (www.iasaweb.org), whose founding president is Djelal Kadir, and that of the American Studies Association (theasa.net), which goal is to promote the research dealing with the United States. The goal of IASA is to link Americanists and foster comparisons within the Americas and their links with the world. In this case, Americanists are people dealing with the whole continent. See, for instance Djelal Kadir, (co-ed. with Theo D'haen, Paul Giles, and Lois Parkinson Zamora) *How Far Is America From Here?* (Amsterdam: Rodopi, 2005).
3. Seymour Martin Lipset, *Continental Divide: The Values and Institutions of the United States and Canada* (New York: Routledge, 1991).
4. W. L. Morton, *The Canadian Identity* (Madison/Toronto: The University of Wisconsin Press/The University of Toronto Press, 1964).
5. Manning to Lord Granville, December 17, 1824, quoted from Julio Irazusta, *Influencia económica británica en el Río de la Plata* (Buenos Aires: Eudeba, 1963), 53.
6. "Adresse de la Confédération des Six Comtés au Peuple du Canada" (1837) in *Papineau, Writings* selected and presented by Fernand Ouellet (Québec: Les Presses de l'Université Laval, 1970), 80. Our translation: "Together with the various nations of North and South America that adopted the principles contained in the Declaration, we consider that the doctrines it contains are sacred and obvious: that God created no artificial distinctions between man and man; that the government is a mere human institution … ."
7. Fermin Toro, "Europa y América," in *La doctrina conservadora: Ofrecimento por Romulo Betancourt* (Caracas: Ediciones commemorativas del sesquicentenario de la independencia, 1960), 35. Our translation: "From this day on the people of Lower Canada are exempt from all allegiance to the British."
8. José Antonio Saco, "Paralelo entre la isla de Cuba y algunas colonias inglesas escrito por Don José Antonio Saco," in José Antonio Saco, *Obras*, vol. 3, ed. Eduardo Torres-Cuevas

(La Habana: Editorial Imagen Contemporanea, 2002), 135. Our translation: "The number of newspapers increased from 17 in 1827 to 50 in 1850 with 12 published only in Montréal. Under certain conditions, we can say that there, the press is freer than in England itself."

9. Francisco Adolfo Sauvalle, *Constitución del Canada: Notas relativas a la confederación de las provincias británicas de la América del Norte* (Habana: Imp. La Antilla, 1869), 14.
10. *Ibid.*, 18. We translate: "French or English can be used indiscriminately in parliament and procedures as well as in the legislature of Lower Canada and in the federal and provincial courts of Lower Canada."
11. This did not happen. José Martí was obliged to fight for independence and he was killed during the war May 19, 1895.
12. See also the links between Mexico and the French Canada in the 20th century: Maurice Demers, *Connected Struggles: Catholics, Nationalists, and Transnational Relations between Mexico and Québec, 1917–1945* (Montréal/ Kingston: McGill Queen's University Press, 2014).
13. Published in *La Patrie*, no. 2, 3, 4, February 1879.
14. On this topic: Roger Le Moine, "L'Aventure mexicaine de quelques Québécois: 1864–1867," and also "'De Québec à Mexico' de Faucher de Saint-Maurice: entre la fidélité à une tradition de lecture et la recherche d'originalité," in *Les discours du Nouveau Monde au Canada français et en Amérique latine au XIXe siècle/Los discursos del Nuevo Mundo en el Canadá francófono y en América latina en el siglo XIX*, eds. Marie Couillard and Patrick Imbert (Ottawa: Legas, 1995), 253–62 and 263–75, respectively.
15. February 27 1845, March 10 1845.
16. Silvia Docola, "William Perkins, un Canadiense proyectando ciudad/ región, Rosario 1858–1874," in *Les discours du Nouveau Monde au Canada français et en Amérique latine au XIXe siècle/Los discursos del Nuevo Mundo en el Canadá francófono y en América latina en el siglo XIX*, eds. Marie Couillard and Patrick Imbert (Ottawa: Legas, 1995), 192–211.
17. Domingo Faustino Sarmiento, *Sarmiento's Travels in The United States in 1847*, translated into English by M.A. Rockland (Princeton: Princeton University Press, 1970).
18. Mathias Carvalho, *Louis Riel, poèmes Amériquains* (Trois-Pistoles, Québec: Éditions Trois-Pistoles, 1997).
19. On this topic: Michel Lacroix, "Lien social, idéologie et cercles d'appartenance: Le réseau 'latin' des Québécois en France (1923–1939)," *Études littéraires*, "Réseaux littéraires France-Québec (1900–1940)," ed. Denis Saint-Jacques 36. 2 (2004), 51–70.
20. Dostaler O'Leary, *Introduction à l'histoire de l'Amérique latine* (Montréal: Éditions latines, 1949), 25. Our translation: "For we too are Latin, as deeply as they are, through our French culture, which makes us communicate to their way of thinking and feeling, and through our Catholic faith which precisely remained a feature of this Latin world, whose philosophy, clearly established and logically constructed, has always repelled the empirical formulae."
21. Marcel Fournier, Éditorial, *Possibles*, vol. 8, no. 4: 7. Our translation: "…between Quebeckers and Americans of the southern hemisphere, there is a similarity: a 'latin' character…."
22. Daniel Bonilla Maldonado, *La Constitución multicultural* (Bogotá: Siglo del hombre editores, 2006).

23. Héctor Alonso Moreno Parra, Alejandra Machado Maturana and Adolfo Léón Rodríguez Sánchez, *El multiculturalismo en la Constitución de 1991: en el marco del bicentenario* (Cali: Universidad del Valle, 2010).
24. Even though European interculturalism was recently compared to Quebec interculturalism, multiculturalism is criticized in *L'Interculturalisme: dialogue Québec-Europe. Actes du Symposium international sur l'interculturalisme* (Montréal, 25–27 May 2011) under the direction of Gérard Bouchard *et al*. Multiculturalism, however, has very different meanings in England and in Germany. In fact, there is no multiculturalism in Germany, as the immigrants, mainly Turks and Kurds, have never been considered as permanent citizens but more as workers who would eventually return to their home countries. This has nothing to do with the situation in Canada, the United States or Australia. Like Canadian multiculturalism, Quebec interculturalism considers that immigrants would become established in Quebec and in Canada; this basis helped develop the theories, laws, procedures and regulations that had already been in place for a very long time. Contrastingly, in Europe where two world wars, the Shoah, and the recent wars in former Yugoslavia have shown an inability to appreciate cultural differences and to grant equality to different cultures, those from different cultures are not encouraged to actively participate in society. This exclusion is apparent in countries like France, Germany, Spain and Belgium.
25. Tzvetan Todorov, *Nous et les autres. La réflexion française sur la diversité humaine* (Paris: Seuil, 1989), 422.
26. Pablo Lazo Briones, *Crítica del multiculturalismo* (México: Universidad Iberoamericana, 2010).
27. Carlos Sandoval García, *El mito roto: Inmigración y emigración en Costa Rica* (San Jose: Editorial Universidad de Costa Rica, 2007), XV.
28. Zila Bernd, (org.), *Dicionário de Figuras e Mitos Literários das Américas* (Porto Alegre, Brasil: Tomo editorial/UFRGS editora, 2007).
29. Gabriela Chavarria Alfaro, "El papel de los inmigrantes en las nuevas cartografías literarias de América Central," Conference at IX Jornadas de Literatura Comparada, Universidad del Litoral, Santa Fe, Argentina. Conference organised by the Association of comparative literature of Argentina (2012).
30. See: Zila Bernd, "Les études canadiennes: perspectives transaméricaines," in *Trans, multi, interculturalité, trans, multi, interdisciplinarité*, eds. P. Imbert and Brigitte Fontille (Québec: Les Presses de l'Université Laval, 2012), 155–63.
31. For the last fifteen years, many researchers like Gérard Bouchard, Marie Couillard, Patrick Imbert, Yvan Lamonde, Djelal Kadir, Licia Soares de Souza, Zila Bernd, Winfried Siemerling, Jean-François Côté, Nestor García Canclini, Gustavo Pérez Firmat, Jean Morency, Annette Paatz, Barbara Buchenau, Maximilien Laroche, Hortense Spillers, José David Saldívar and Seymour Martin Lipset have compared the political, media and literary discourse in the Americas without necessarily drawing comparisons with Europe. However, most of these researchers dedicate their research predominantly to one particular area of the Americas: Nestor García Canclini focuses on South America ignoring Canada almost completely, Licia Soares de Souza focuses on Canada-Brazil relations, Yvan Lamonde on Quebec and the United States, Hortense Spillers concentrates on problems with race, gender and sexuality in a fragmented perspective, Gustavo Pérez Firmat's research leads

to interesting insights into the valorization of historical consciousness by Lois Parkinson Zamora or racial and cultural miscegenation by Eduardo Gonzalez; however the book does not lead to a set of characteristics that would define American literary traditions.

32. It should be noted that in English the frontier is an endless open space and that its meaning is the opposite of the French border (frontière). It is in the English sense that frontier is used in some Latin American countries: "Históricamente, la tenancia de la tierra era más amplia en Costa Rica y hasta hace poco una frontera agricola daba la posibilidad de colonizar nuevas tierras." Bridget Hayden, *Salvadoreños en Costa Rico: Vidas desplazadas* (San José: Universidad de Costa Rica, 2005), 130. Our translation: "Historically, land ownership was more widespread in Costa Rica and until recently an agricultural *frontier* provided the opportunity to colonize new lands."
33. On this topic: Patrick Imbert, *Les Amériques transculturelles: les stéréotypes du jeu à somme nulle* (Québec: Les Presses de l'Université Laval, 2013).
34. René Girard, *Des choses cachées depuis la fondation du monde* (Paris: Livre de poche, 1978). René Girard, *Things Hidden since the Foundation of the World* (London: Athlone, 1987).
35. "Glocalization" mixes the global and the local.
36. In other words, we recognize the usefulness of research aimed at identifying recurring motifs such as the Lost Way, the Phantasm of the Great Novel, the Fear of the End and the Haunting Presence of the Road as explored by Jean Morency in *La littérature québécoise dans le contexte Américain* (Québec: Nota Bene, 2012) in which he studies Gabrielle Roy, Victor-Lévy Beaulieu, Edgar Poe and Alejo Carpentier. However, we focus more on the binary paradigms currently turning into ternary or multiple relationships, which allow us to give a full account of a greater number of important works, along with certain workings of media and advertising discourse. This also allows us to expand the research to the whole continent.
37. As noted by a *Times* journalist, if the French Revolution had abolished the passport system, it would have done more for freedom than the broadcasting of grand principles that may or may not be relevant in very different ways in different societies.
38. Noé Jitrik, "Between Being and Becoming: Identity, Latinity and Discourse," in *The Noé Jitrik Reader*, ed. Daniel Balderston (Durham: Duke University Press, 2005), 27–34
39. Patrick Imbert, "Le processus d'attribution," in *Les discours du Nouveau Monde au XIXe siècle au Canada français et en Amérique latine/Los discursos del Nuevo Mundo en el siglo XIX en el Canadá francófono y en América latina en el siglo XIX* (Ottawa: Legas, 1995), 43–60.
40. R. D. Laing, *The Politics of the Family* (Toronto, CBC, 1969), 11.
41. John Cheever, *The Stories of John Cheever* (New York: Knopf, 1952), 32. We find this theme somewhat modified in *Comment faire l'amour avec un Nègre sans se fatiguer* by Dany Laferrière where the Anglophone student is described as physically attractive but very naïve.
42. *Ibid.*, 34.
43. W. L. Morton, "The North in Canadian Historiography," in *Contexts of Canada's Past: Selected Essays of W. L. Morton*, ed. A. B. McKillop (Toronto/ Ottawa: Macmillan/Carleton University Press, 1980), 229–39.
44. Our translation: "… for us, for our posterity and for all the people on the planet desirous of living on Argentinian soil …."

45. Our translation: "Clearly defining the national territory, establishing the limits of the provinces, creating new ones ...."
46. Jitrik, *The Noé Jitrik Reader*, ed. Daniel Balderston, 31.
47. Randolph Bourne, "Trans-National America," *The Atlantic Monthly*, vol. 118 (1916): 88.
48. Pico Iyer, *The Global Soul* (New York: Vintage, 2000).
49. Carlos Monsivais, *Los rituales del cáos* (Mexico: Era, 1995).
50. Mark Kingwell, *The World We Want* (New York: Viking, 2000), 12.
51. *Ibid.*, 13.
52. Iyer, *The Global Soul*, 19.
53. Eduardo Mendieta, *Global Fragments: Latin-Americanisms, Globalizations, and Critical Theory* (Albany: State University of New York Press, 2007).
54. The introduction of the book by Hortense Spillers (ed.) titled *Comparative American Identities: Race, Sex, and Nationality in the Modern Text* (New York: Routledge, 1991) locates the origin of American identity in the figure of Caliban in Shakespeare's *The Tempest*. However, using the Caliban/Prospero binary leads to producing a metaphoric discourse presenting power relationships in a colonial context. It is more important to start with texts produced by thinkers such as Sarmiento, Canclini or Kymlicka, who are directly involved with dynamics originating in the 19th, 20th and 21st centuries in the Americas.
55. Patrice Lacombe, *La terre paternelle* (Québec: Côté, 1877).
56. Albert Laberge, *La Scouine* (Montréal: Imprimerie modèle, 1918).
57. Winfried Siemerling and Sarah Phillips Casteel (eds.), *Canada and Its Americas* (Montreal/Kingston: McGill Queen's University Press, 2010).
58. Margaret Atwood, *Survival: A Thematic Guide to Canadian Literature* (Toronto: Anansi, 1972).
59. Stephen Leacock, "Gertrude the Governess or, Simple Seventeen," in *Nonsense Novels* (Montréal: Publishers Press, 1911).
60. Nestor García Canclini, *La Globalización imaginada* (Buenos Aires: Paidos, 1999).
61. Cynthia Sugars (ed.), *Home-work: Postcolonialism, Pedagogy and Literature* (Ottawa: University of Ottawa Press, 2004); Siemerling and Casteel (eds.), *Canada and Its Americas*.
62. Marc Angenot, "La invención de la humanidad y el sujeto del progreso," in *Tiempo, espacio e identidades*, eds. Maria Teresa Dalmasso, Fernando Andacht, and Norma Fatala (Buenos Aires: Editorial La Crujia, "Colección DeSignis," vol.15, 2010), 153–69.
63. Henry Thomas Buckle, *History of the Civilization in England* (New York: Appleton and Company, 1861), 37.
64. *Ibid.*, 75.
65. *Ibid.*
66. *Ibid.*, 76. This perspective led to the creation of numerous human zoos in Europe. Christian Báez y Peter Mason. *Zoológicos Humanos. Fotografías de Fueguinos y Mapuche en el* Jardin d'Acclimatation *de París, Siglo XIX* (Santiago, Chili: Pehuén, 2016 [2006]).
67. Angel Rama, *Las Mascaras democraticas del Modernismo* (Montevideo: Fundación Angel Rama, 1985), 177. Our translation: "The European literary system, having adapted to the international division of labour, reserves for itself the full right to deal with its own products, domestic themes and exotica, external topics provided they are marginalized; as a purveyor of exoticism for the eventual consumption by the metropolis, in the same way

that the economic system has relegated the role of supplying raw materials to the periphery for industrial development by the centre."

68. Darcy Ribeiro, *The Brazilian People: The Formation and Meaning of Brazil*, translated by Gregory Rabassa (Gainesville: University Press of Florida, 2000), 41.
69. François-Marie Bibaud, *Biographie des Sagamos illustres de l'Amérique septentrionale* (Montréal: Lovell et Gibson, 1848).
70. Patrick Imbert, "Destino Manifesto," in *Dicionário de Figuras e Mitos Literários das Américas*, ed. Zila Bernd (Porto Alegre: Universidade Federal do Rio Grande do Sul et Tomo editorial, 2007), 178–84.
71. Étienne Parent, *Du travail chez l'homme*, 23 septembre 1847: 76. Our translation: "The savage of America took our vices and left out our virtues, he took what makes us weak and neglected what makes us strong, i.e., work and the ideas of civilization. The savage thinks about work like our nobles do and holds it in contempt."
72. Georges Boucher de Boucherville, *Une de perdue, deux de trouvées* (Montréal: Sénécal, 1974), 293. Our translation: "Through wise and fair policies, Negroes will be forced to work, as white servants are forced to do in the other countries."
73. Mario Briceño-Iragorry, *A People Crisis/Mensaje sin destino* (Caracas: Monte Avila, 1994).
74. Clarice Lispector's flamenco allegory comes to mind here (*Selected Cronicas* [New York: New Directions Paperbooks, 1991], 99). She underlines the deadly fight between the two dancers: "They have never thought of understanding each other. They have each brought themselves as their banner."
75. W. L. Morton, *Contexts of Canada's Past: Selected Essays of W. L. Morton*, ed. A. B. McKillop (Toronto/Ottawa: Macmillan/Carleton University Press, 1980).
76. Anne Hébert, *Le premier jardin* (Paris: Éditions du Seuil, 1988), 76.
77. Gabrielle Roy, *Un jardin au bout du monde* (Montréal: Boréal, 1994).
78. Walter Bagehot, *Physics and Politics* (London: Kegan Paul, 1873), 68.
79. Andrés Molina Enríquez, *Los grandes problemas nacionales* (Mexico, Editorial Era, 1978 [1st ed., 1909]).
80. José Vasconcelos, *The Cosmic Race* (Baltimore: John Hopkins, 1997), 17.
81. It is clear that Laura Esquivel in *The Law of Love* (New York: Random House, 1996) parodies this ideal vision of blending ethnic groups.
82. Vasconcelos, *The Cosmic Race*, 18.
83. *Ibid.*
84. *Ibid.*, 19.
85. *Ibid.*, 20.
86. Zila Bernd, (org.), *Dicionário de Figuras e Mitos Literários das Américas* (Porto Alegre, Brasil: Tomo editorial/UFRGS editora, 2007).
87. Bagehot, *Physics and Politics*, 77.
88. Patrice Lacombe, *La terre paternelle* (Montréal: C.O. Beauchemin et Valois, 1871). This tendency linking nation and eternity was apparent recently at Yves Blais' funeral. The Parti Québécois candidate for the Masson riding was a nationalist militant for Québec's independence: "I hope that in heaven sovereignty has been already reached, said a mourner [...] Otherwise you will work there for a good part of your eternity [...] And we are confident that together, you will ask God to push this small nation to attain your ideal."

Le Devoir, Tuesday, November 24th, 1998. According to the mourner, all are gathered in heaven in a distinct sovereign state, whereas down here, there are marked divisions among Francophones.

89. Francisco Bilbao, *El Evangelio Americano y paginas selectas* (Barcelona: Mauci, 1920 [1864]), 113. Our translation: "… the universal citizenship. Every republican may be considered to be a citizen of any republic he lives in."
90. A situation that José Vasconcelos in *La raza cósmica* seeks to correct by proposing an inter-breeding eugenics, where the Whites improve the mixing of races through genetic dominance. As for Oswald de Andrade, he suggests in his 1928 *Manifeste anthropophage* that cannibalism as a cultural mix combines the contributions of Europeans, Indigenous people and Blacks and allows a rejection of what is unsuitable for the Americas; especially the frozen codes of colonialist Platonic dualism.
91. José Martí, "Letter to Antonio Maceo, 20 July 1882," in *Obras Completas* (Havana: Editorial Nacional de Cuba, 1963), 172–73.
92. José David Saldívar, *Trans-Americanity. Subaltern Modernities, Global Coloniality, and the Cultures of Greater Mexico* (Durham: Duke University Press, 2012).
93. *Ibid.*, xx.
94. Doug Saunders, *Arrival City* (Toronto: Knopf, 2010).
95. José Vasconcelos, *Obras completas* (México: Libreros Mexicanos Unidos, 1957), 1364. Our translation: "Because we are placing ourselves above the prejudices and on par with the most illustrious humanity, we have renounced our ancestors since emancipation. But now uprooted generations, without ancestry, are coupling with the illegitimate. And we see it as making the most of the national product with foreign resources or putting in prose aspirations of those who are not concerned with the humble Castilian in the corner in order to feel intimately Saxon."
96. Briceño-Iragorry, *A People Crisis/Mensaje sin destino*, 43.
97. René Depestre, "Noces à Tiscornia," in *Alléluia pour une femme-jardin* (Paris: Folio, 1981), 149–81.
98. *Ibid.*, 156.
99. Anyelick Campos Zamora and Larissa Tristán Jiménez, *Nicaragüenses en las noticias* (San José, Costa Rica: Universidad de Costa Rica, 2010), 35. Our translation: "This alleged Spanish origin was associated with the whiteness that characterizes the Costa Rican population … a link between ethnicity and democracy assigns Costa Rican progress to two main factors: the development of education and the 'special race' specific to the Spanish origin from which all Costa Ricans would descend."
100. Silviano Santiago, *Space In-Between: Essays on Latin American Culture* (Durham: Duke University Press, 2001), 30.
101. This mythification is radically altered in Gabriel Garcia-Marquez' *El general en su laberinto* (Buenos Aires: Planeta, 1995).
102. Étienne Balibar, "Paradoxes of Universality," in *Anatomy of Racism*, ed. D. T. Goldbert (Minneapolis: University of Minnesota Press, 1990), 285.
103. Armand Mattelart, *De l'image des médias en temps de crise* (Paris: Moreau, 1979), 182.
104. Nicolas Dickner, *Nikolski* (Québec: Alto, 2007), 221.
105. Briceño-Iragorry, 55.

106. Michael J. Shapiro, *Violent Cartographies: Mapping Cultures of War* (Minneapolis: University of Minnesota Press, 1997), 32.
107. Edward Sapir, *Anthropologie* (Paris: Seuil, 1967).
108. Benjamin Lee Whorf, *Linguistique et anthropologie* (Paris: Denoël, 1969).
109. Kim Thúy, *Män* (Montréal: Libre expression, 2013), 74. Our translation: "I only know that, very early one morning, I opened my eyes and saw a world so perfect that I felt dizzy."
110. Jean Bernabé, Patrick Chamoiseau, and Raphaël Confiant, *Éloge de la créolité* (Paris: Gallimard, 1989), 26. Our translation: "Creolity is the interactional or transactional aggregation of the different Caribbean, European, African, Asian and Levantine cultural elements that the yoke of History has gathered on the same soil."
111. Vévé A. Clark, "Developing Diaspora Literacy and *Marasa* Consciousness" in *Comparative American Identities: Race, Sex and Nationality in the Modern Text*, ed. Hortense J. Spillers (New York: Routledge, 1991), 40–61.
112. Fermin Toro, "Europa y América," in *La doctrina conservadora: Ofrecimento por Romulo Betancourt*, 89.
113. Cited by Julio Irazusta, *Influencia económica británica en el Rio de la Plata*, 23. Our translation: "a general conception of our barbarity."
114. Edward Gibbon Wakefield, *England and America* (New York: A. M. Kelley, 1967 [1st ed. 1834]), 264.
115. *Ibid.*, 246.
116. John George Bourinot, *Canada as a Home*, reprinted from *The Westminster Review* for July 1882, Toronto, J.S. William Printer: 22.
117. D. F. Sarmiento, *Facundo* (Paris: Stock, 1934), 37. Our translation: "The integration of the indigenous people practised by the colonizers must have contributed greatly to produce this unfortunate outcome (idleness, inability to industry). The American races live in idleness and remain unable to engage in a strenuous and steady work even by constraint. This is what led to the idea of introducing Negroes in America, an idea that has produced such fatal results. But the Spanish race has not proved itself better endowed for action when abandoned to its own instincts in the American deserts." This idea is shared by all of the thinkers of the time. "Et les sauvages restent des sauvages parce qu'ils n'ont pas développé les lois de la propriété." (Our translation: "And the savages remain savages because they have not developed property law." Lamartine, *Le conseiller du peuple*, 1849–1851, vol. 1: 26. This is a typical example of disinformation in good conscience; the territories of the Indigenous peoples were taken by the Whites or bought for almost nothing.
118. *El Mercurio*, 18 juin 1842.
119. Domingo Faustino Sarmiento, *Sarmiento's Travels*, 233.
120. *Ibid.*, 235.
121. *Ibid.*, 237.
122. *Ibid.*, 151.
123. Étienne Parent, *Du travail chez l'homme*, 75. Our translation: "work is freedom."
124. Darcy Ribeiro, *The Brazilian People: The Formation and Meaning of Brazil*, 70.
125. In *La mémoire du feu* (Montréal: Lux, 2013), Eduardo Galeano emphasizes that *Mamelucos* often fought against Black slaves who tried to live a free life in *Palmeras*, that is territories they were able to control.

126. *Ibid.*, 33.
127. *Ibid.*, 34.
128. Will Kymlicka, *Multicultural Citizenship: A Liberal Theory of Minority Rights* (Oxford: Clarendon Press, 1995).
129. Ribeiro, 99.
130. Iyer, *The Global Soul*, 11.
131. René Depestre, "Samba pour Cristina de Melo Pessoa," *Éros dans un train chinois* (Paris: Gallimard, 1990), 32. Our translation: "You have no idea what it means to take in a Black as a teacher. Have you thought about the neighbours? About the servants? What are you doing to our decorum in this country (Brazil)?"
132. Oswald de Andrade, "Manifesto Antropófago," in *Obras completas* (Sao Paulo: Editora Globo, 2000). For quotations, we will use: Oswald de Andrade, *Anthropophagies* (Paris: Flammarion, 1982, [1st ed. 1928]).
133. *Ibid.*, 269. Our translation: "We want the Caraíba Revolution. Bigger than the French Revolution. Unify all effective revolts converging towards man. Without us, Europe would not even have its pathetic Declaration of the Human Rights."
134. See Louis Sala-Molins, *Le code noir ou le calvaire de Canaan* (Paris: PUF, 1987).
135. Jacques Ferron, *Contes* (Montréal: Hurtubise HMH, 1985), 165. Our translation: "The Yank had played the savage throughout his childhood, then went to the cinema to learn about his two-dimensional world, in which, lacking the third dimension, everything was illusory."
136. *Ibid.*, 166. Our translation: "our linguistic shortcomings."
137. *Ibid.*
138. *Ibid.* Our translation: "It is they who will teach you English, my dear."
139. We observe an interesting variant in the film *Starbuck* by Ken Scott (2011), where the main character donates his sperm, fathering several hundred Quebec children looking for their father, who finally acknowledges them as a real and active community while becoming head of the family with a newborn baby.
140. However, this barbarian fought to save Europe from the nazi and fascist barbarism, subsequently fighting with Europeans against Stalinist barbarism and communist gulags.
141. Ferron, *Contes*, 166. "What are we if not a stepping stone from Europe to America. Europe was losing. It was quite natural that an American soldier came here to achieve his victory." Europe lost the battle against Nazis but won the war thanks to the Canadians, the Americans and the English as well as to the small armies in exile and the resistance fighters inside. At the same time, it lost its world power in face of the power of the United States and through decolonization. Therefore, here too, the imprecision with which the word "lost" is applied generates interesting anxieties expressed in an elliptical literary discourse that allows for an understanding of the conditions of the "uncertain" identities mentioned by Ferron.
142. Yvan Lamonde, *Ni avec eux ni sans eux: le Québec et les États-Unis* (Montréal: Nuit blanche, 1996).
143. Sometimes, the term English Canadian applies to immigrants, i.e., Italian immigrants studying in the Anglophone schools in Montréal.
144. Margaret Atwood, *Survival: A Thematic Guide to Canadian Literature*, 151.

145. Jean-Claude Lenormand, *Québec-immigration: zéro* (Montréal: Parti Pris, 1971).
146. Marc Angenot, *Les idéologies du ressentiment* (Montréal: XYZ, 1996).
147. *Fonder l'avenir, le temps de la conciliation: Commission de consultation sur les pratiques d'accommodement reliées aux différences culturelles*, Report by Gérard Bouchard and Charles Taylor (Saint-Lazare, Québec, 2008).
148. Gérard Bouchard, *L'interculturalisme: un point de vue québécois* (Montréal: Boréal, 2012).
149. Jacques Ferron, *La nuit* (Montréal: Parti Pris, 1965).
150. Yann Martel, *L'histoire de Pi* (Montréal: XYZ, 2003).
151. Jacques Ferron, *Contes anglais et autres* (Montréal: Orphée, 1964).
152. Pierrre Vallières, *Nègres blancs d'Amérique* (Montréal: Parti Pris, 1979).
153. *Ibid.*, 26. Our translation: "In Quebec, the irrational racism that has hurt white and black workers so much in the United States is unknown to French Canadians. There would be no point to it, as there is no 'black problem.'"
154. Contrary to the European left-wing, the Quebec left keeps quiet about the Indigenous peoples. As Madeleine Ouellette-Michalska underlines in the chapter entitled "Du côté de l'Éden" in her volume of essays *L'Amour de la carte postale* (Montréal: Québec/Amérique, 1987), the left-wingers claim "le statut de 'nègres blancs' d'Amérique" (Our translation: "the status of 'white negroes' of the Americas") for Francophone Quebeckers, yet "il ne vient à personne l'idée de se dire Indien" (149) (Our translation: "nobody wants to call themselves Indian"). It is only later, mainly in the counter-culture left-wing essays of Patrick Straram, a French immigrant to Canada, that the Indigenous peoples would get a fairer representation (Patrick Straram, *Le bison ravi* [Montréal: l'hexagone/l'obscène nyctalope, 1972]).
155. Marcel Trudel, *L'esclavage au Canada français* (Montréal: Éditions de l'Horizon, 1963).
156. George Elliott Clarke, *Execution Poems: The Black Acadian Tragedy of "George and Rue"* (Wolfville, Nova Scotia: Gaspereau Press, 2001).
157. Yves Antoine, *Inventeurs et savants noirs* (Paris: L'Harmattan, 1998).
158. Dany Laferrière, *Comment faire l'amour avec un Nègre sans se fatiguer* (Montréal: VLB, 1985).
159. Roch Carrier, *Petit homme tornade* (Montréal: Stanké, 1996), 207. Our translation: "'His dream was more exciting than his memory, this is the great principle upon which America was built,' says Martin's research assistant when he tries to find out what has happened to Dubois, a French Canadian who left for the West."
160. Pierre Berton, *The National Dream: The Great Railway, 1871–1881* (Toronto: McClelland and Stewart, 1970); *The Last Spike: The Great Railway 1881–1885* (Toronto: McClelland and Stewart, 1971).
161. Margaret Atwood, 172.
162. W. L. Morton, 239.
163. Camila Reimers, *Tres lotos en un mar de fuego* (Ottawa: Mapalé Publishing, 2006), 97. Our translation: "Ideal for elevator conversation, diplomatic parties and the beginning of business meetings. The colder it is, the better it is; we are heroes sharing a frozen destiny."
164. Clearly, even there the space is, as Sharon Butala shows in *Wild Stone Heart* (Toronto, Canada: HarperPerennial, 2000), 121, invented through discourse: "The more I think about the Sasquatch as non-Amerindians understand him, the more I think of him as

an inevitable construct for a people arriving on a new continent about which they knew nothing, refusing to learn from its inhabitants, continuing to declare the continent as 'empty' and 'untouched,' despite the evidence of its far-flung population whose ancient ability to survive on the land's resources should have been obvious to the new arrivals."

165. W. L. Morton, 234.
166. *Ibid.*, 239.
167. Jean-Paul Lacasse, *Les Innus et le territoire: Innu tipenitamun* (Sillery, Québec: Septentrion, 2004), 153. Our translation: "the land was everywhere."
168. Inuits are Indigenous people of the Arctic and Innu are a group of Indigenous peoples linked to Crees, etc.
169. David Morrison and Georges-Hébert Germain, *Inuit: Glimpses of an Arctic Past* (Ottawa: Canadian Museum of Civilization, 1995), 32.
170. Georges-Hébert Germain (under the scientific direction of David Morrison), *Inuit: Les peuples du froid* (Ottawa: Musée canadien des civilisations, 1995), 32. Our translation: "evolve within a wandering land that tradition and ancestral feuds or old fears vaguely delineated [...] beyond a certain limit [...] Danger."
171. Frederick Jackson Turner, "The Significance of the Frontier in American History, 1893," in *Rereading Frederick Jackson Turner*, ed. John Mack Faragher (New York: Holt, 1994), 37.
172. Oscar Micheaux, *The Conquest: The Story of a Negro Pioneer* (Lincoln, Nebraska: The Woodruff Press, 1913).
173. Adriana Rizzo, "Exclusion sociale et exclusion de l'immigrant en Argentine aux temps de la mondialisation. Leurs traces dans les discours médiatiques," (Our translation: "Social exclusion of immigrants in Argentina in the era of globalization. Their visibility in media dialogue.") in *L'interculturel au cœur des Amériques*, Collection des Amériques/The Americas Series/Colección de las Américas, eds. Daniel Castillo Durante and Patrick Imbert (Université d'Ottawa/Université du Manitoba: Legas, 2003), 143–66. Moreover, in Argentina in 1876, a law inspired by the *Homestead Act* of the United States allowed the distribution of lots from 25 to 50 hectares to immigrants. However, huge surfaces of the "desert" were granted to the ruling class individuals so that by 1890 there was no more land to give. See Guy Bourdé, *Urbanisation et immigration en Amérique latine* (Paris: Aubier, 1974), 151.
174. The same thing happened to the Italians, colonizing the regions around Porto Alegre in the South of Brazil 50 years after the Germans, where the Italians transformed the region into a center for wine production.
175. Patrick Imbert, "Destino Manifesto," 179.
176. Jean Delumeau, *Une histoire du paradis* (Paris: Fayard, 1992), 153. Our translation: "hieroglyphics from our primitive, Adamic situation."
177. William Paley, *Natural Theology or Evidences of the Existence and Attributes of the Deity* (London: J. Faulder, 1809).
178. Kris Fresonke, *West of Emerson: The Design of Manifest Destiny* (Berkeley: University of California Press, 1999), 6.
179. Isabel Allende, *Hija de la fortuna* (Buenos Aires: Editorial Sudamericana, 1999).
180. Jacques Languirand, *Klondyke* followed by *Le Québec et l'Américanité* (Montréal: Cercle du livre de France, 1971).

181. Sharon Butala, *The Perfection of the Morning: An Apprenticeship in Nature* (Toronto, Canada: HarperCollins, 1994), 5.
182. Sarah Carter, *The Importance of Being Monogamous: Marriage and Nation Building in Western Canada to 1915* (Athabaska/Edmonton: Athabaska University Press/University of Alberta Press, 2008).
183. José Marti, *Notre Amérique* (Paris: Maspero, 1968), 189. Our translation: "North America was born from the plough; Spain, from the bloodhound. A war ordained by fanaticism had driven the Moor, effeminated by opulence, from the poetic world of his aerial palaces; unemployed soldiers, now watered on house wine and on hatred for heretics, rushed at the cotton-clad Indian, with branding irons and muskets in hand."
184. Antoine Gérin-Lajoie, *Jean Rivard économiste* (Montréal: Rolland, 1876); *Jean Rivard le défricheur canadien* (Montréal: Rolland, 1874).
185. Joseph Norbert Duquet, *Le véritable petit Albert* (Québec: Darveau, 1881), p. 125. Our translation: "Agriculture! What an inexhaustible mine to exploit!" Clearly, the interpretation of this book varies with the era and the place. For example, in *The Serpent and the Rainbow*, Wade Davis mentions that his instructor in voodoo cites *Le Petit Albert*, the very inspiring medieval witchcraft book.
186. *Ibid.*, 122. Our translation: "Manure is the capital of the cultivator."
187. *Ibid.*, 164. Our translation: "The shores of the Saint-Laurent lined with rich cities inhabited *by farmers*."
188. Gérin-Lajoie, *Jean Rivard économiste*.
189. See Eugene P. Moehring, *Urban America and the Foreign Traveler, 1815–1855* (New York: Arno Press, 1979).
190. Étienne Parent, 75. Our translation: "You will succeed by the sweat of your brow" and "work is freedom."
191. *Ibid.*, 76. Our translation: "[The industrialist] is the father of civilized America [...] These are cities without number and empires that the industrialist has conquered over wilderness, not with the sword and the blood of other people but with the axe and the sweat of his own brow."
192. Domingo Faustino Sarmiento, *Facundo* (Paris: Stock, 1934 [1st ed. 1845]).
193. J. Gracia and I. Jaksic, "The Problem of Philosophical Identity in Latin America," *Revista Interamericana de Filosofia*, vol. XXXIV, no. 1 (1984): 59.
194. *Ibid.*, 11.
195. Randolph S. Bourne, "Trans-National America," *The Atlantic Monthly*, vol. 118 (1916): 93.
196. Gabrielle Roy, "La vallée Houdou," in *Un jardin au bout du monde* (Montréal: Beauchemin, 1975), 147. Our translation: "They know or guess, said the interpreter, that the mountain and the river are illusions, but they say: it doesn't matter because we can see them...Yet the Doukhobors would not listen... sure of being the only ones to grasp the mystery of the world..."
197. Yvon Rivard, *Le siècle de Jeanne* (Montréal: Boréal, 2005), 303. Our translation: "Indeed, when you walk in the prairie, you have the feeling of being on the surface, in the middle and at the bottom of something that is neither earth nor sky, but a mixture of the two; a kind of ocean, because of a sky so high that it weighs on you and a light so pure that it swells the earth and lightens your step."

198. In order to realize the important presence of this game in literature see Michel Narceau, *Double jeu: baseball et littératures américaines* (Montréal: Le Quartanier, 2012).
199. W. P. Kinsella, *Shoeless Joe Jackson comes to Iowa* (Dallas, Texas: Southern Methodist University Press, 1993).
200. *Ibid.*, 43.
201. Marc-André Towner, "Le jardin de baseball des Amériques," in *Les jardins des Amériques: éden, home et maison*, ed. Patrick Imbert (Ottawa: chaire de recherche: "Canada: enjeux sociaux et culturels dans une société du savoir," 2007), 205–37.
202. Georges Desmeules, *Le projet Syracuse* (Québec: L'Instant même, 2008), 218. Our translation: "Baseball plays out the death of the European who sleeps in every American."
203. Réal Ouellet, *Locus amoenus, âge d'or et paradis terrestre dans les textes français du XVIIIe siècle sur les Antilles* [Online] [www.sociocritique.mcgill. ca/mythamerique.htm] [Consulted in 2005]. Our translation: "Those who say that terrestrial paradise is located in the equinoxial zone seem to be justified in their opinion. Not that I want to be the one to decide that the Garden of Delights is found there ... but if there were a paradise on the earth, it would have a climate just as sweet and delectable."
204. Jean Delumeau, *Une histoire du paradis* (Paris: Fayard, 1992), 146. Our translation: "If heaven on earth still survives somewhere, I think ... it could not be far from these regions."
205. Jacques Ferron, *L'Amélanchier* (Montréal: Éditions du Jour, 1970).
206. Frère Marie-Victorin, *La Flore laurentienne* (Montréal: La Salle, 1935).
207. Réjean Ducharme, *L'hiver de force* (Paris: Gallimard, 1973).
208. Ferron, *L'Amélanchier*.
209. Heather Cullen, *L'herbier de force: l'intertextualité botanique chez Jacques Ferron et Réjean Ducharme*, Master's thesis, Département des lettres françaises: Université d'Ottawa, 2004.
210. Sharon Butala, *The Perfection of the Morning: An Apprenticeship in Nature* (Toronto, Canada: HarperCollins, 1994), 183.
211. Carlos Monsiváis, *Los rituales del caos* (México: Era, 1995), 67.
212. See Marc-André Towner, "Le jardin de baseball des Amériques."
213. Arundhati Roy, *The God of Small Things* (Toronto: Random House of Canada, 1997).
214. Alejo Carpentier, *Los pasos perdidos* (Barcelona: Bruguera, 1979).
215. Daniel Mato, "Sobre la fetichización de la globalización y las dificultades que plantea para el estudio de las transformaciones sociales contemporaneas," *Revista venezolana de analísis de coyuntura*, vol. 5, no. 1 (janvier-juin 1999): 129–47.
216. Jerzy Kosinski, *Being There* (New York: Harcourt Brace Jovanovich, 1971).
217. They are also based on an Indigenous causality that exists in parallel with the temporal linearity of the Catholic Church's image of going to the Garden of Eden in paradise.
218. Hernando de Soto, *The Other Path* (New York: Harper & Row, 1989), 3.
219. *Forbes* (15 mai 2000): 106. This proves retrograde colonialists and members of the Creole elite wrong: "A passion for owning land prevents the existence of a class of labourers for hire ...." Edward Gibbon Wakefield, *England and America*, 1834, 36.
220. Bharati Mukherjee, *Jasmine* (New York: Grove and Weidenfeld, 1989), 30.
221. Doug Saunders, *Arrival City*, 3. In his novel, *The White Tiger* (New Delhi, India: HarperCollins, 2008), Aravind Adiga suggests: "It may turn out to be a decent city, where hu-

mans can live like humans and animals can live like animals. A new Bangalore for a new India. And then I can say that, in my own way, I helped to make New Bangalore."

222. We see similar situations produced by globalization and the influence of the recognition of entrepreneurial values in Aravind Adiga's *The White Tiger*. These situations also appear in numerous articles published in *Wired* magazine showing the evolution of culture in India influenced by access to education and the opening to the world. P. Imbert, "Cultural Changes and Economic Liberalism in Canada and in the Americas," in *Converging Disensus? Cultural Transformations and Corporate Cultures: Canada and the Americas* (Ottawa: University of Ottawa Research Chair: "Canada: Social and Cultural Challenges in a Knowledge-Based Society," 2006), 15–77.
223. We could speak of a domestic mimesis of appropriation as a function of the multiplication of the objects of desire, if we follow a Girardian approach.
224. Pierre Lévy, "Société du savoir et développement humain," in *Le Canada et la société des savoirs: Le Canada et les Amériques*, ed. Patrick Imbert (Ottawa: University of Ottawa Research Chair: "Enjeux sociaux et culturels dans une société des savoirs," 2007).
225. Michael Delisle, *Le palais de la fatigue* (Montréal: Boréal, 2017), 9. Our translation: "the encounter does indeed bring on a temporal shift and a return to oneself through the other."
226. Lorena Gale, *Angélique* (Toronto: Playwrights Canada Press, 2000).
227. Laura Rizzà, "Dismantling Canadian Multiculturalism in African-Canadian Fiction," in *Cultural Challenges of Migration in Canada/Les défis culturels de la migration au Canada*, eds. Klaus Dieter Ertler and Patrick Imbert (Frankfurt: Peter Lang, 2013).
228. *A-t-on oublié que jadis nous étions "frères"?: Alliances fondatrices et reconnaissance des peuples autochtones dans l'histoire du Québec*, eds. Mathieu d'Avignon et Camil Girard (Québec: Les Presses de l'Université Laval, 2009), 180.
229. "La place des 'autres' dans l'histoire du Québec: entrevue avec Marcel Trudel réalisée par Mathieu D'Avignon, le 21 août 2007," in *A-t-on oublié que jadis nous étions "frères"?* eds. Mathieu d'Avignon and Camil Girard, 9–29
230. In literature in Québec, there was almost no main indigenous characters before 1960. See, however, Yves Thériault, *Ashini* (Montréal: Fides, 1961).
231. Silvio Marcus de Souza and Camil Girard, "Métissage culturel lors des alliances franco-amérindiennes au Nouveau Monde au XVIe et au début du XVIIe siècle (Brésil-Canada-Nouvelle-France)," in *A-t-on oublié que jadis nous étions "frères"?* 40.
232. Ghislain Picard and Mathieu d'Avignon, "Conclusion. A-t-on oublié que jadis nous étions 'frères'?" in *A-t-on oublié que jadis nous étions "frères"?* 163–79.

Bibliography

Adiga, Aravind. *The White Tiger*. New Delhi, India: HarperCollins, 2008.
Allende, Isabel. *Hija de la fortuna*. Buenos Aires: Editorial Sudamericana, 1999.
Andrade, Oswald de. *Anthropophagie*. Paris: Flammarion, 1982 (1st ed., 1928).
Angenot, Marc. "La invención de la humanidad y el sujeto del progreso." In *Tiempo, espacio e identidades*. Eds. Maria Teresa Dalmasso, Fernando Andacht, and Norma Fatala. Buenos Aires: Editorial La Crujia, "Colección DeSignis," vol. 15, 2010. 153–69.

———. *Les idéologies du ressentiment*. Montréal: XYZ, 1996.

Antoine, Yves. *Inventeurs et savants noirs*. Paris: L'Harmattan, 1998.

Atwood, Margaret. *Survival: A Thematic Guide to Canadian Literature*. Toronto: Anansi, 1972.

Bagehot, Walter. *Physics and Politics*. London: Kegan Paul, 1873.

Balderston, Daniel. (ed.). *The Noé Jitrik Reader*. Durham: Duke University Press, 2005.

Balibar, Étienne. "Paradoxes of Universality." In *Anatomy of Racism*. Ed. David Theo Goldberg. Minneapolis: University of Minnesota Press, 1990.

Beaugrand, Honoré. *Anita*, in *La Patrie*, no 2/3/4, février 1879.

Bernabé, Jean, Patrick Chamoiseau, and Raphaël Confiant. *Éloge de la créolité*. Paris: Gallimard, 1989.

Bernd, Zilá. (org.). *Dicionário de Figuras e Mitos Literários das Américas*. Porto Alegre (Brasil): Tomo editorial/UFRGS editora, 2007.

Berton, Pierre. *The National Dream: The Great Railway, 1871–1881*. Toronto: McClelland and Stewart, 1970.

———. *The Last Spike: The Great Railway 1881–1885*. Toronto: McClelland and Stewart, 1971.

Bibaud, François-Marie. *Biographie des Sagamos illustres de l'Amérique septentrionale*. Montréal: Lovell et Gibson, 1848.

Bilbao, Francisco. *El Evangelio Americano y páginas selectas*. Barcelona: Mauci, 1920(1864).

Bouchard, Gérard. *L'interculturalisme: un point de vue québécois*. Montréal: Boréal, 2012.

Bouchard, Gérard *et al*. *L'interculturalisme: Dialogue Québec-Europe, Actes du Symposium international sur l'interculturalisme*. Montréal, 25–27 mai 2011.

Bouchard, Gérard, and Charles Taylor. *Fonder l'avenir, le temps de la conciliation: Commission de consultation sur les pratiques d'accommodement reliées aux différences culturelles*. Saint-Lazare, Québec, 2008.

Boucherville, Georges Boucher de. *Une de perdue, deux de trouvées*. Montréal: Sénécal, 1974.

Bourdé, Guy. *Urbanisation et immigration en Amérique latine*. Paris: Aubier, 1974.

Bourinot, John George. *Canada as a Home*, reprinted from *The Westminster Review*. Toronto: J.S. William Printer (July 1882): 22.

Bourne, Randolph. "Trans-National America." *Atlantic Monthly*, vol. 118 (1916): 86–97. https://www.theatlantic.com/magazine/archive/1916/07/trans-national-america/304838/

Briceño-Iragorry, Mario. *A People Crisis/Mensaje sin destino*. Caracas: Monte Avila, 1994.

Buckle, Henry Thomas. *History of the Civilization in England*. New York: Appleton and Company, 1861.

Butala, Sharon. *The Perfection of the Morning: An Apprenticeship in Nature*. Toronto, Canada: HarperCollins, 1994.

———. *Wild Stone Heart*. Toronto, Canada: Harper Perennial, 2000.

Campos Zamora, Anyelick, and Larissa Tristán Jiménez. *Nicaragüenses en las noticias*. San José, Costa Rica: Universidad de Costa Rica, 2010.

Canclini, Nestor García. *La Globalización imaginada*. Buenos Aires: Paidos, 1999.

Carpentier, Alejo. *Los pasos perdidos*. Barcelona: Bruguera, 1979.

Carrier, Roch. *Petit homme tornade*. Montréal: Stanké, 1996.

Carter, Sarah. *The Importance of Being Monogamous: Marriage and Nation Building in Western Canada to 1915*. Athabaska, Edmonton: Athabaska University Press/University of Alberta Press, 2008.

Carvalho, Mathias. *Louis Riel, poèmes Amériquains*. Trois-Pistoles, Québec: Éditions Trois-Pistoles, 1997.

Chavarria Alfaro, Gabriela. "El papel de los inmigrantes en las nuevas cartografías literarias de América Central." Conference at IX Jornadas de Literatura Comparada, University El Litoral, Santa Fe, Argentina. Congress organized by the Comparative Literature Association of Argentina, 2000.

Cheever, John. *The Stories of John Cheever*. New York: Knopf, 1952.

Clark, Vévé A. "Developing Diaspora Literacy and *Marasa* Consciousness." In *Comparative American Identities: Race, Sex and Nationality in the Modern Text*. Ed. Hortense J. Spillers. New York: Routledge, 1991. 40–61.

Clarke, George Elliott. *Execution Poems: The Black Acadian Tragedy of "George and Rue."* Wolfville, Nova Scotia: Gaspereau Press, 2001.

Cullen, Heather. "L'herbier de force: l'intertextualité botanique chez Jacques Ferron et Réjean Ducharme." Master's thesis. Département des lettres françaises, Université d'Ottawa 2004.

D'Avignon, Mathieu, and Camil Girard. (dir.). *A-t-on oublié que jadis nous étions "frères"?: Alliances fondatrices et reconnaissance des peuples autochtones dans l'histoire du Québec*. Québec: Presses de l'Université Laval, 2009.

Delisle, Michael. *Le palais de la fatigue*. Montréal: Boréal, 2017.

Delumeau, Jean. *Une histoire du paradis*. Paris: Fayard, 1992.

Demers, Maurice. *Connected Struggles: Catholics, Nationalists, and Transnational Relations between Mexico and Québec, 1917–1945*. Montréal/Kingston: McGill-Queen's University Press, 2014.

Depestre, René. "Noces à Tiscornia." In *Alléluia pour une femme-jardin*. Paris: Folio, 1981.

———. "Samba pour Cristina de Melo Pessoa." In *Éros dans un train chinois*. Paris: Gallimard, 1990.

Desmeules, Georges. *Le projet Syracuse*. Québec: L'Instant même, 2008.

Dickner, Nicolas. *Nikolski*. Québec: Alto, 2007.

Docola, Silvia. "William Perkins, un Canadiense proyectando ciudad/region, Rosario 1858/1874." In *Les discours du Nouveau Monde au Canada français et en Amérique latine au XIXe siècle/Los discursos del Nuevo Mundo en el Canadá francófono y en América latina en el siglo XIXé*. Eds. Marie Couillard and Patrick Imbert. Ottawa: Legas, 1995. 192–211.

Ducharme, Réjean. *L'hiver de force*. Paris: Gallimard, 1973.

Duquet, Joseph Norbert. *Le véritable petit Albert*. Québec: Darveau, 1881.

El Mercurio, Domingo Faustino Sarmiento, « Dinàmicas culturales en las Américas », 18 juin 1842.

Enríquez, Andrés Molina. *Los grandes problemas nacionales*. Mexico: Editorial Era, 1978 (1st ed., 1909).

Esquivel, Laura. *The Law of Love*. New York: Random House, 1996.

Ferron, Jacques. *Contes*. Montréal: Hurtubise HMH, 1985.

———. *Contes anglais et autres*. Montréal: Orphée, 1964.

———. *L'Amélanchier*. Montréal: Éditions du Jour, 1970.

———. *La nuit*. Montréal: Parti Pris, 1965.

Fontille, Brigitte, and Patrick Imbert. (eds.). *Trans, multi, interculturalité, trans, multi, interdisciplinarité*. Québec: Presses de l'Université Laval, 2012.

Forbes, Kerry A. Dolan, 'Waking Dead Capital' (15 May 2000): 106.

Fournier, Marcel. «Éditorial». *Possibles*, vol. 8, no. 4 (été 1984): 7.

Fresonke, Kris. *West of Emerson: The Design of Manifest Destiny*. Berkeley: University of California Press, 1999.

Gale, Lorena. *Angélique*. Toronto: Playwrights Canada Press, 2000.

Galeano, Eduardo. *Mémoire du feu*. Montréal: Lux, 2013.

Garcia, J., and I. Jaksic. "The Problem of Philosophical Identity in Latin America." *Revista Interamericana de Filosofia*, vol. XXXIV, no.1 (1984).

García-Marquez, Gabriel. *El general en su laberinto*. Buenos Aires: Planeta, 1995.

Gérin-Lajoie, Antoine. *Jean Rivard économiste*. Montréal: Rolland, 1876.

———. *Jean Rivard le défricheur canadien*. Montréal: Rolland, 1874.

Germain, Georges-Hébert (under the scientific direction of David Morrison). *Inuit: Les peuples du froid*. Ottawa: Musée canadien des civilisations, 1995.

Girard, René. *Des choses cachées depuis la fondation du monde*. Paris: Livre de poche, 1978.

———. *Things Hidden since the Foundation of the World*. London: Athlone, 1987.

Morency, Jean. *La littérature québécoise dans le contexte Américain*. Montréal: Nota Bene, 2012.

Hayden, Bridget. *Salvadoreños en Costa Rica: Vidas desplazadas*. San José: Universidad de Costa Rica, 2005.

Hébert, Anne. *Le premier jardin*. Paris : Éditions du Seuil, 1988.

Imbert, Patrick. "Cultural Changes and Economic Liberalism in Canada and in the Americas." In *Converging Dissensus? Cultural Transformations and Corporate Cultures: Canada and the Americas*. Ottawa: University of Ottawa Research Chair. "Canada: Social and Cultural Challenges in a Knowledge-Based Society," 2006, 15–77.

———. "Destino Manifesto." In *Dicionário de Figuras e Mitos Literários das Américas*. Ed. Zilá Bernd. Porto Alegre: Universidade Federal do Rio Grande do Sul et Tomo editorial, 2007. 178–84.

———. "Le processus d'attribution." In *Les discours du Nouveau Monde au XIXe siècle au Canada français et en Amérique latine/Los discursos del Nuevo Mundo en el siglo XIX en el Canadá francófono y en América latina en el siglo XIX*. Ottawa: Legas, 1995. 43–60.

———. *Les Amériques transculturelles: Les stéréotypes du jeu à somme nulle*. Québec: Presses de l'Université Laval, 2013.

Irazusta, Julio. *Influencia económica británica en el Río de la Plata*. Buenos Aires: Eudeba, 1963.

Iyer, Pico. *The Global Soul*. New York: Vintage, 2000.

Kadir, Djelal, co-ed. with Theo D'haen, Paul Giles, and Lois Parkinson Zamora. *How Far Is America From Here?* Amsterdam: Rodopi, 2005.

Kingwell, Mark. *The World We Want*. New York: Viking, 2000.

Kinsella, W. P. *Shoeless Joe Jackson Comes to Iowa*. Dallas, Texas: Southern Methodist University Press, 1993.

Frère, Marie-Victorin (Conrad Kirouac). *La Flore laurentienne*. Montréal: La Salle, 1935.

Kosinski, Jerzy. *Being There*. New York: Harcourt Brace Jovanovich, 1971.

Kymlicka, Will. *Multicultural Citizenship: A Liberal Theory of Minority Rights*. Oxford: Clarendon Press, 1995.

Laberge, Albert. *La Scouine*. Montréal: Imprimerie modèle, 1918.

Lacombe, Patrice. *La terre paternelle*. Montréal: C.O. Beauchemin & Valois, 1871.

Lacroix, Michel. "Lien social, idéologie et cercles d'appartenance: Le réseau 'latin' des Québécois en France (1923–1939)." *Études littéraires*, "Réseaux littéraires France-Québec (1900–1940)," éd. Denis Saint-Jacques (Automne 2004): 51–69.

Laferrière, Dany. *Comment faire l'amour avec un Nègre sans se fatiguer*. Montréal: VLB, 1985.

Laing, R. D. *The Politics of the Family*. Toronto: CBC, 1969.

Lamartine, Alphonse de. *Le conseiller du peuple*. Paris: Lévy, 1865.

Lamonde, Yvan. *Ni avec eux ni sans eux: le Québec et les États-Unis*. Montréal: Nuit blanche, 1996.

Languirand, Jacques. *Klondyke* followed by *Le Québec et l'Américanité*. Montréal: Cercle du livre de France, 1971.

Lazo Briones, Pablo. *Crítica del multiculturalismo*. México: Universidad Iberoamericana, 2010.

Leacock, Stephen. "Gertrude the Governess or, Simple Seventeen." In *Nonsense Novels*. Montréal: Publishers Press, 1911.

Le Moine, Roger. "L'Aventure mexicaine de quelques Québécois: 1864–1867." In *Les discours du Nouveau Monde au Canada français et en Amérique latine au XIXe siècle/Los discursos del Nuevo Mundo en el Canadá francófono y en América latina en el siglo XIX*. Eds. Marie Couillard et Patrick Imbert. Ottawa: Legas, 1995. 253–62.

Lenormand, Jean-Claude. *Québec-immigration: zéro*. Montréal: Parti Pris, 1971.

Lévy, Pierre. "Société du savoir et développement humain." In *Le Canada et la société des savoirs: Le Canada et les Amériques*, Ed. Patrick Imbert. Ottawa: University of Ottawa Research Chair: "Enjeux sociaux et culturels dans une société des savoirs," 2007.

Lipset, Seymour Martin. *Continental Divide: The Values and Institutions of the United States and Canada*. New York: Routledge, 1991.

Lispector, Clarice. *Selected Cronicas*. New York: New Directions Paperbooks, 1991.

Martel, Yann. *L'histoire de Pi*. Montréal: XYZ, 2003.

Martí, José. "Letter to Antonio Maceo, 20 July 1882." In *Obras Completas*. Havana: Editorial Nacional de Cuba, 1963. 172–73.

———. *Notre Amérique*. Paris: Maspero, 1968.

Mattelart, Armand. *De l'image des médias en temps de crise*. Paris: Moreau, 1979.

Mato, Daniel. "Sobre la fetichización de la globalización y las dificultades que plantea para el estudio de las transformaciones sociales contemporaneas." *Revista venezolana de analísis de coyuntura*, vol. 5, no. 1 (janvier-juin 1999): 129–47.

McKillop, A. B. (ed.). *Contexts of Canada's Past: Selected Essays of W. L. Morton*. Toronto/Ottawa: Macmillan/Carleton University Press, 1980.

Mendieta, Eduardo. *Global Fragments: Latin-Americanisms, Globalizations, and Critical Theory*. Albany: State University of New York Press, 2007.

Micheaux, Oscar. *The Conquest: The Story of a Negro Pioneer*. Lincoln, Nebraska: The Woodruff Press, 1913.

Moehring, Eugene P. *Urban America and the Foreign Traveler, 1815–1855*. New York: Arno Press, 1979.

Monsiváis, Carlos. *Los rituales del caos*. México: Era, 1995.

Moreno Parra, Héctor Alonso, Alejandra Machado Maturana, and Adolfo Léón Rodríguez Sánchez. *El multiculturalismo en la Constitución de 1991: en el marco del bicentenario*. Cali: Universidad del Valle, 2010.

Morrison, David, and Georges-Hébert Germain. *Inuit: Glimpses of an Arctic Past*. Ottawa: Canadian Museum of Civilisation, 1995.

Narceau, Michel. *Double jeu: baseball et littératures américaines*. Montréal: Le Quartanier, 2012.

Mukherjee, Bharati. *Jasmine*. New York: Grove and Weidenfeld, 1989.

O'Leary, Dostaler. *Introduction à l'histoire de l'Amérique latine*. Montréal: Éditions latines, 1949.

Ouellet, Fernand. *Papineau*. Québec: Les Presses de l'Université Laval, 1970.

Ouellette-Michalska, Madeleine. "Du côté de l'Éden." In *L'Amour de la carte postale*. Montréal: Québec/Amérique, 1987.

Ouellet, Réal. *Locus amoenus, âge d'or et paradis terrestre dans les textes français du XVIIIe* [Consulted in 2005].

Paley, William. *Natural Theology or Evidences of the Existence and Attributes of the Deity*. London: J. Faulder, 1809.

Parent, Étienne. *Du travail chez l'homme*. 23 septembre 1847.

Rama, Angel. *Las Mascaras democráticas del Modernismo*. Montevideo: Fundación Angel Rama, 1985.

Reimers, Camila. *Tres lotos en un mar de fuego*. Ottawa: Mapalé Publishing, 2006.

Ribeiro, Darcy. *The Brazilian People: The Formation and Meaning of Brazil*. Translated by Gregory Rabassa. Gainesville: University Press of Florida, 2000.

Rivard, Yvon. *Le siècle de Jeanne*. Montréal: Boréal, 2005.

Rizzà, Laura. "Dismantling Canadian Multiculturalism in African-Canadian Fiction." In *Cultural Challenges of Migration in Canada/Les défis culturels de la migration au Canada*. Eds. Klaus Dieter Ertler and Patrick Imbert. Frankfurt: Peter Lang, 2013.

Rizzo, Adriana. "Exclusion sociale et exclusion de l'immigrant en Argentine aux temps de la mondialisation. Leurs traces dans les discours médiatiques." In *L'interculturel au cœur des Amériques*, Collection des Amériques/The Americas Series/Colección de las Américas. Eds. Daniel Castillo Durante and Patrick Imbert. Université d'Ottawa/Université du Manitoba: Legas, 2003. 143–66.

Rockland, Michael Aaron. *Sarmiento's Travels in the United States in 1847*. Princeton: Princeton University Press, 1970.

Roy, Arundhati. *The God of Small Things*. Toronto: Random House of Canada, 1997.

Roy, Gabrielle. *Un jardin au bout du monde*. Montréal: Beauchemin, 1975.

———. *Un jardin au bout du monde*. Montréal: Boréal, 1994.

Saco, José Antonio. "Paralelo entre la Isla de Cuba y algunas colonias inglesas escrito por Don José Antonio Saco." In *José Antonio Saco, Obras*. Dir. Eduardo Torres Cuevas. La Habana: Imagen contemporaneas, 2001.

Sala-Molins, Louis. *Le code noir ou le calvaire de Canaan*. Paris: PUF, 1987.

Saldívar, José David. *Trans-Americanity: Subaltern Modernities, Global Coloniality, and the Cultures of Greater Mexico*. Durham: Duke University Press, 2012.
Sandoval García, Carlos. *El mito roto: Inmigración y emigración en Costa Rica*. San Jose: Editorial Universidad de Costa Rica, 2007.
Santiago, Silviano. *Space In-Between: Essays on Latin American Culture*. Durham: Duke University Press, 2001.
Sapir, Edward. *Anthropologie*. Paris: Seuil, 1967.
Sarmiento, Domingo Faustino. *Facundo*. Paris: Stock, 1934 [1st ed. 1845].
Saunders, Doug. *Arrival City*. Toronto: Knopf, 2010.
Sauvalle, Francisco Adolfo. *Constitución del Canada: Notas relativas a la confederación de las provincias británicas de la América del Norte*. Habana: Imp. La Antilla, 1869.
Shapiro, Michael J. *Violent Cartographies: Mapping Cultures of War*. Minneapolis: University of Minnesota Press, 1997.
Siemerling, Winfried, and Sarah Phillips Casteel. (eds.). *Canada and its Americas*. Montreal/ Kingston: McGill Queen's University Press, 2010.
Soto, Hernando de. *The Other Path*. New York: Harper & Row, 1989.
Straram, Patrick. *Le bison ravi*. Montréal: l'hexagone/l'obscène nyctalope, 1972.
Sugars, Cynthia. (ed.). *Home-work: Postcolonialism, Pedagogy and Literature*. Ottawa: University of Ottawa Press, 2004.
Thériault, Yves. *Ashini*. Montréal: Fides, 1961.
Thúy, Kim. *Män*. Montréal: Libre expression, 2013.
Todorov, Tzvetan. *Nous et les autres. La réflexion française sur la diversité humaine*. Paris: Seuil, 1989.
Toro, Fermin. "Europa y America." In *La doctrina conservadora: Ofrecimento por Romulo Betancourt*. Caracas: Ediciones commemorativas del sesquicentenario de la independencia, 1960.
Towner, Marc-André. "Le jardin de baseball des Amériques." In *Les jardins des Amériques: éden, home et maison*. Ed. Patrick Imbert. Ottawa: chaire de recherche: "Canada: enjeux sociaux et culturels dans une société du savoir,"2007. 205–37.
Trudel, Marcel. *L'esclavage au Canada français*. Montréal: Éditions de l'Horizon, 1963.
Vallières, Pierre. *Nègres blancs d'Amérique*. Montréal: Parti Pris, 1979.
Turner, Frederick Jackson. "The Significance of the Frontier in American History, 1893." In *Rereading Frederick Jackson Turner*. Ed. John Mack Faragher. New York: Holt, 1994.
Vasconcelos, José. *The Cosmic Race*. Baltimore: John Hopkins, 1997.
Wakefield, Edward Gibbon. *England and America*. New York: A. M. Kelley, 1967 (1st ed. 1834).
Whorf, Benjamin Lee. *Linguistique et anthropologie*. Paris: Denoël, 1969.
Winks, Robin W. "Canada and the Three Americas." In *Friends so Different*. Eds. L. Lamont and J. D. Edmonds. Ottawa: University of Ottawa Press for the Americas Society, 1989.

· 2 ·

ESCAPING FROM NARRATIVES LEGITIMIZING EXCLUSION

Escaping From Dualism and the Legitimization of the Causes of Exclusion

In the 19th century, intellectuals in the Americas were well aware of the dualistic oppositions (such as barbarity/civilization) and of their negative impact on socioeconomic organization, even if they often ended up resorting to these oppositions or were controlled intellectually by them. For instance, Francisco Bilbao affirmed that "La América vive en el dualismo. Ese dualismo es el dogma religioso, y el principio político: el catolicismo y la república."[1] He was aware that dualism hindered the development of the Americas, which should have taken into account the concepts of new and multiple situations. However, like many other thinkers aware of this problem, Bilbao proposed the imposition of a single discourse, either that of Catholicism (with all the consequences that it would entail), or "el predominio de la libertad, como en Estados Unidos. No hay otro remedio. Quered lo uno o lo otro, pero con fé, y tendremos fuerzas cómo la Rusia o cómo los Estados Unidos."[2] In other words, Bilbao wanted dualism—which he experienced as permanent contradiction, entailing constant doubt and daily struggle—to give way to a form of monism. Bilbao did not realize that any dualism devolves into monism because, as Michel Maffesoli[3] points out, one of the principles inevitably dominates the other. Consequently, dualism generates exclusion by producing monism. Monism always excludes and does not allow thinking beyond the terms of a civilization that renders the others as barbarians. This tendency was evident in Bilbao's own proposition for the free movement of Republicans and Republican citizenship for Latin American nations, which excluded the Indigenous peoples and the Blacks, who were not part of the republican culture.

Before Oswald de Andrade's *Le manifeste anthropophage* in 1928, the recognition of diversity and equality was not evident. This led to a form of dualism and determinism creating an America cut into nation-states forced to operate homogeneously within its borders, like Europe in the 19th century. But the European nations were colonial powers which achieved their wealth through colonial domination. The nation-states of the Americas, in contrast, were colonized entities—at least from a financial and economic point of view—and were without access to colonial income. Indeed, these countries, even if they were politically independent, relied on British banks (the Baring Bank, for example, which had branches from Canada[4] to Argentina), and on English and then American expertise in order to grow. Instead, they should have tried to incorporate the strengths of the various groups and develop these strengths through knowledge and recognition of talents, in order to produce economic and sociocultural wealth that might then have been exported. It was only much later and in different areas (depending on the country) that other types of relationships would be conceived as a result of the confrontation of multiple self-images connected to glocalization movements and the influence of cultural and technological Americanization.[5] This can be seen in Sergio Kokis' *Le pavillon des miroirs*, which takes place in Brazil and in which the main character, a dynamic and progressive father of a very intelligent child, tries to achieve success from his inventions and from modern technology from the United States: "Tous les produits qu'il (le père) achète pour son travail ont des noms Anglais: Sylvania, General Electric, Westinghouse."[6] But the father fails because Brazil was at the time too focused on itself and its traditions. This type of person is presented as the new barbarian, threatening established identities. However, the dynamics of recognizing creative and technological talents and the ability to actively participate in the production of wealth are not to be confused with Americanization.

Escaping Dualism Through Complexity

Dualism is present in the contemporary world, but since the 1980s it has been brought into question through an appreciation for the ability to form complex knowledge by linking poles previously conceived as antithetical. The connection is made here by Marshall McLuhan in *Notes on the Media as Art Form*:

> North American children respond aesthetically to the powered objects in their world. Streetcars, locomotives, airplanes and motorcars are the first objects of delighted contemplation. But in the classroom the student is confronted with verbal culture in book form. For the European, on the other hand, verbal culture is as much an object and area of spontaneous delight and play as machinery for us. The conclusion is obvious. We can master verbal culture and European art only by approaching it at first as a technical problem, just as some Europeans have mastered our sports, jazz, machinery, and architecture by translating it into their verbal cultures. Once the bridge has been crossed in either direction the bridge is no longer necessary. It functions only as a grammar and crib in early stages of reading a new language.[7]

There is a progression in evidence here. Indeed, while McLuhan schematically contrasts the distinguishing paradigms of North American and European culture, the differences can be resolved, allowing the advancement of knowledge. This leads to dynamics that circumvent zero-sum games with only one winner, wherein the ally of the favoured paradigm prevails and the other always loses. It then becomes possible to capitalize on knowledge and to experience cultural and technological transformations; to live in the discursive syncretism specific to knowledge societies. These contemporary changes can also be seen in a new context in Tom Robbins' work: "We must bear in mind, however, that the central dynamic of our race has never been a conflict between good and evil but rather between enlightenment and ignorance. Ignorance makes the headlines, wins the medals… enlightenment continues to quietly sparkle… Enlightenment is its own reward."[8] There is a rejection here of religious dichotomies, of media and communications spectacles (as caricatured in Jerzy Kosinski's *Being There*[9]), permitting an acceptance of the artistic, intellectual, discursive and social creativity that embodies the beauty alluded to in Yvon Rivard's *Le siècle de Jeanne* (2005). This world of multiple creativities extends from pop art to specialized art, and is misunderstood by most of the thinkers who find inspiration exclusively in the European tradition. These traditionalists see only kitsch and popular culture in the United States. However, this is not the case for Tom Robbins, who says: "It's so interesting there. America may be the least boring country on earth…"[10]

Interestingly, there are individuals who risk presenting themselves in all the vulnerability of their difference to the point of being considered oddball[s][11], as James Baldwin says. These are, Bill Schermbrucker stresses in his novel *Chameleon*[12] (section: Chameleoning: From Negative to Positive) weird individuals "who [do] not quite fit." These creative individuals of the Americas thereby manage to escape what Esteban Echeverria criticizes in Argentina: "El mal que aqueja a la República Argentina es la extensión: el desierto la rodea por todas partes, y se le insinúa en las entrañas: la soledad, el despoblado sin una habitación humana, son, por lo general, los límites incuestionables entre unas y otras provincias."[13] They escape the fear of vast spaces and "Garrison mentality," engaging instead in proactive networking dynamics, such as the one highlighted in McLuhan's text. These distinctive individuals develop a rejection of institutional constraints. They manifest a desire to expand their singularities, encountering other singular people while recognizing the inspirational beauty of the continent and its vastness, which no longer seem threatening. This trend is described by Jocelyne Saucier in *Il pleuvait des oiseaux*: "Et de s'éclater encore d'une grande salve de rires, accompagné de Charlie qui avait abandonné toute retenue et riait d'un bon rire gras et sonore. Les deux vieillards s'amusaient comme des enfants à l'idée de ce coup asséné à toutes les travailleuses sociales de ce monde qui veulent enfermer les vieux dans des mouroirs."[14] In his book *Le siècle de Jeanne*, Yvon Rivard is also relatively close to Tom Robbins; he reflects that in the Americas one can be idle and wild, and that creativity in the Americas stems from these qualifiers. The two attributes, defined as properties of barbarism by Sarmiento, Buckle and proponents of the exclusion of difference, are now being redefined. For Yvon Rivard idleness means being in a state of receptivity to each being, to that which is different and to each landscape and situation whose beauty can be measured, because life exists at a point in time and space which could not/no longer exist. Being wild is now positive because this attribute opens up to a New World redesigned to accommodate a deepening of the otherness that is in us and in everyone:

> Et où donc, si ce n'est à Paris, peut-on conquérir ce merveilleux territoire qu'on a hérité du Nouveau Monde et qui nous permet de circuler librement parmi les autres sans vouloir rivaliser avec eux, parce qu'un sauvage, faut-il le rappeler, ce n'est pas quelqu'un qui fuit les autres mais quelqu'un qui essaie de se rapprocher de cette part de lui-même qui lui échappe et qu'il retrouve parfois dans un arbre ou un visage.[15]

The part of one who recognizes the assertion of oneself as a unique being, as suggested by James Baldwin, is receptive to the recognition of the new as a wonderful strangeness. This is evident also in George Elliott Clarke's poem, "Hinterland": "You do not recognize/aboriginal art: / fishers who are magicians, who snatch/shimmering cod/out of silver, slippery air, / Hinterland is that country/you cannot even begin/ to imagine."[16] The hinterland, like the forest of the coureurs des bois (with the village huddled around the bell tower), is a barbaric place to Sarmiento; contrastingly, it is presented in quite a positive and aesthetic way by Clarke, an African-Canadian poet from the Maritimes. For Yvon Rivard, beauty hinges on the encounter, which is a recognition of otherness, and this recognition is open to a dynamic that avoids rivalry in René Girard's sense of the word ("sans vouloir rivaliser avec eux," says Rivard). This avoids the victimization process and the scapegoating mechanism, because the other is inside one's personality as well as outside. In a contemporary understanding of the wild, a barbarism/exterior/the other synonymy is no longer valid. "D'où venaient les Indiens avant d'être sauvages?" asks Yvon Rivard's main character in *Mort et naissance de Christopher Ulric*[17] as early as 1976. The dualism of the positivist 19th century vector of progress is diluted in a combinatorial analysis where the multiple plays on dynamics of the included third. Tom Robbins brings up the idea when he says: "In America, the chronically wild, persistently haywire, strongly individualistic, and surprisingly good-humoured" are more vital than the "dullards on the religious right and the dullards on the academic left (the two faces of Yankee Puritanism)."[18] *Wild* has become a positive attribute today in the Americas. Restrictive, imported codes such as those practiced by the thinkers of Canada and Latin America have been eluded. Henceforth, the Americas, as depicted in the works of Yvon Rivard and Tom Robbins, are neither fixed on Europe, nor do they reject it. Europe no longer represents worrying domination; it no longer relegates the Americas to second place. Indeed, while staying in Paris, Alexandre, the main character of *Le siècle de Jeanne*, feels the historical weight of Europe, "car ne sont réels que les êtres, les lieux et les choses perdus et retrouvés."[19] Thus, an absence of dualism, but an accumulation of knowledge, memories, emotions and intelligence networks convert identity anchors into self-images befitting the inhabitants of the Americas, who are constantly reinventing themselves in a multicoloured capitalization of cultures in the process of recontextualization.

The wild, the creative, and the unconventional, present in Tom Robbins' work, can be found in a highly developed state among a number of artists and writers who, like Rivard, reject the ugly and industrial America which devours and destroys the environment. This same rejection is found in *Comparing* My-

thologies by Tomson Highway.[20] In it, he highlights the beauty of the continent affected and threatened by conquest and its consequences. The main character in Rivard's *Le siècle de Jeanne* talks about Montreal: "Le Nouveau Monde, c'est aussi cela, bien sûr des corps, des vitrines, des marchandises, un monde de nouveaux riches qui ne se souviennent plus de leur pauvreté, un monde de pauvres qui ne rêvent que d'être riches."[21] From this perspective, the Indigenous neither represent barbarism, nor the Homeric hero used in a redemptive anthropology (as in Bibaud's book), nor the noble savage. They personify the memory and the voice of a social ecological project which has become a discursive axis within the major currents of thought in the Americas and throughout the world. Daniel Mato explains this idea in the context of Venezuela. He shows a kind of double coding originating from specialized languages used in research and then re-exported into the creation of discourse controlled strategically by Indigenous activists. In order to succeed they used a specialized vocabulary linked to ecology aiming at convincing planetary ecologist. Mato explains that Manuel Ortega, the leader of the Emberà indigenous population of the Darién region in Panama, raised these points when requesting the support of international organizations in 1994: "Porque si nosotros dejamos eso, se van a perder muchas cosas en sectores indígenas, primero la botánica, la fauna silvestre, la biósfera, la biodiversidad, el medio ambiente [...]."[22] Mato adds pertinently that discourse is built on familiar and traditional words, yet also on the use of words like "biósfera y biodiversidad" that have a specialized use and are effective when spoken, for example, at the Festival of American Folklife organized annually by the Smithsonian Institute in Washington.

Many artists are part of the current which caricaturizes the ugliness in the world by recycling it in idiosyncratic images. Like the participants in the "American Consumer"[23] group, these artists parody business and consumer culture. This tendency is apparent in Harrod Blank's *Art cars*[24], especially in the productions of the Canadian artist Natali Leduc. These artists tend to assimilate bureaucratic economist lifestyle movements consistent with a dynamic close to surrealist tendencies expressed by Oswald de Andrade in the 1930s. They create a fantasy world where objects that inspire creativity are recycled and combined within a discursive and cultural hybridity. In other words, the purity of virgin nature, as in *Le partage des eaux* by Alejo Carpentier,[25] is dreamt of no longer. We know that being someone (*ser alguien*) is not so important and, furthermore, that we are here (*estar aqui*) and that "here" is defined not in a manner consistent with Frye's[26] anguished *Where is here?* (section: *Where is Here?*), but rather by playfully combining plural, extended and multiple spaces. The people of the Americas have aimed to "be someone," like the people of Europe, in the well-differentiated Spanish sense of the difference between the stable *ser* and the temporary *estar*. They have attempted to distinguish themselves by asserting superiority over others in a fierce battle manifestly different from Europe's, which swept the planet into two world wars, the Shoah and the genocides. But the people of the Americas have finally understood that they are all together, interests coinciding, alongside the others in a shared space. As seen above, Yvon Rivard expresses this dynamic well: "Ce merveilleux territoire qu'on a hérité du Nouveau Monde et qui nous permet de circuler librement parmi les autres sans vouloir rivaliser avec eux...."[27] "Without wanting to compete with them" is an important formulation, because in these encounters people recognize a vulnerability in each other which mirrors that of the continent and the planet. People in the Americas are trying to escape a Darwinian way of life in which the weakest are killed, in favour of a systemic one where, as Gregory Bateson (1972) says, the strong must intelligently maintain their environment or perish, because we are all interconnected.

Purity and Bastardy

> Según Kant, dijo Sophie, asesinar a un hijo bastardo es menos grave que una infidelidad... Él dice que lo lógico seria ignorar la existencia de ese hijo, porque legalmente no debería haber existido.[28]

Not everyone agrees on the lack of importance of a person's existence. Laure Conan's novel, where the focus is on an exclusive pseudo-aristocratic attribution process, affirms the sustainability of identity rooted in vertical relationships with ancestors. Marthe Robert[29] reminds us that in the Americas there is a tendency to oscillate between the orphan and the bastard, but that the bastard is generally avoided. Heather O'Neill underlines this situation in *Mademoiselle Samedi soir*: "Au Québec, on est tous des descendants d'orphelines."[30] (2019.8) The orphan continuously seeks his parents and is preoccupied with ancestors and consumed by nostalgia, aiming for creation through recognition, while the bastard wants to start over, to take on a new persona; these are two important trends in identity discourses in the Americas.

The novel *La gesta del Marrano* by Argentinean writer Marcos Aguinis illustrates the bastard's anguish at the possibility of establishing multiple horizontal relationships rather than vertical ones. Going back to the context of the Inquisition in Spanish America as it is presented by Aguinis, it is apparent that the basis of this historical situation can be easily transposed to a contemporary and partly secular context. In the novel, the Marrano Francisco Maldonado da Silva is prosecuted, imprisoned and tortured for being both Catholic in public and Jewish in private. This biculturalism is imbued with a rationality that is in opposition to faith; da Silva is a surgeon and has an extensive library, which is said to be unnecessary in the context of the small town of Ibatín: "Qué necesidad existe de enseñar historia, aritmética, geografía y gramática en este desierto de la cristianidad?[31]; Aquí no estamos en Madrid ni en Roma. Vivimos en una tierra miserable llena de infieles y de pecado. Nadie posee una biblioteca. Es una excentricidad."[32] Although at one time the book was considered an eccentricity, it is nonetheless apparent that the 19th century progressivist Americas were born out of books and seen through European literature, as Lelia Area[33] highlights in *Una biblioteca para leer la Nación*. European literary and aesthetic codes were perceived as superior, representing the only legitimate standard for literature. European writings based on the barbarism/civilization paradigm developed into writings in the Americas which developed discourses on space and its inhabitants. But let's go back to Aguinis. In order to counter this bicultural condition, the Christian Brother, confronted with biculturalism and the rise of scientific and practical rationalism, had no alternative but to return to a time before the establishment of Catholic rationality when children asked questions about hybridity. He went back to the biological in order to repudiate this satanic state of affairs. Indeed, he explained to children that mules are born of a jack and a mare or of a stallion and a jennet, yet they themselves are sterile[34]: "Son una especie intrusa, porque no aparecieron en el quinto día de la creación como las demás bestias de la naturaleza. Aparecieron mucho después, cuando un burro, en vez de aparearse con una hembra de su misma especie, lo hace con una yegua. -Está mal eso ?- Creo que está mal."[35] Moreover, when the children, seeking to quench their thirst for knowledge, asked the reason for this deviance, the Brother abandoned the truth of the scriptures, inventing a legend. A mule was upset and gave Joseph a kick during the flight to Egypt with the infant Jesus. To punish the mule, God prohibited her any progeny. In the case of statements that brought the established institutional order of the era into question and posed a potential threat to orthodoxy, the Brother cut short a form of Catholic rationality and went back to a previous argumentative position; back to invented myths that justified God's wrath and its arbitrary aspect: the mule clearly did not know who she was carrying. There too, the ante-rational was a remedy in a situation that, in an institutional context, transgressed the prohibitions based on a monosemic truth and one true God as it was understood at the time.

When one switches to the cultural and literary world in 19th century Canada, there is no recognition of otherness, because rationality and the library have been used to exclude in two ways. Firstly, Francophones in Canada were criticized for having no literature and were therefore equated with the Black and Indigenous peoples. Remember Lord Durham's famous words concerning French Canada, "Ils sont un peuple sans histoire et sans littérature."[36] In the Southern Cone, the Salon of 1837 proved that literature was already present, as Sarmiento implied. The thinking was that without literature, barbarism would prevail. The Creoles produced literature in order to gain recognition as a nation. However, literature would be also used to exclude, seeing as civilization meant gathering around the elite whose role was to invent a homogeneous nation through shared literature and language. This implied the exclusion of certain groups as well as marginalizing women; women could not be assimilated because they were perceived as irrational, much like the Black and Indigenous peoples.

Lelia Area has pointed out that this was done through projecting European aesthetic and cultural codes onto the new continent. Immense spaces were often compared to deserts, and their inhabitants to the nomadic, pagan Moors. Indeed, from the specific perspective of practical rationalism, immense spaces evoke barbarism through the symbolic image of the nomadic Bedouin. Take, for example, what French traveler Théodore Pavie said in 1838 about Montreal: "[…] (du côté du nord-ouest de Montréal) ce ne sont que des forêts sauvages, monticules noirs et bleus comme le firmament, océan de bois, de déserts, de plaines comme les steppes de l'Asie, les sables de l'Arabie, puis tout cela s'enfonce et disparaît à l'ouest pour aller se perdre dans les glaces du pôle."[37] This text shows that the description is part of a narrative constituting a working ideology of European origin. A few French-Canadian writers would use these literary references, comparing the forests near Montreal to the Arabian Desert. *L'influence d'un livre* by Philippe Aubert de Gaspé Jr. comes to mind here; his rhetoric was drawn from a set of European romantic codes: "[…] près de la Baie-Saint-Paul, le cap au Corbeau. Ce cap a quelque chose de majestueux et de lugubre. À quelque distance on le prendrait pour un de ces immenses tombeaux jetés au milieu des déserts de l'Égypte par la folle vanité de quelque chétif mortel."[38] Between the ice and the forest, the author chose to see a desert ! No Garden of Eden here. With this in mind, it is possible to establish a direct comparison with the Bible by remembering the horrors committed by pagan Egyptians when they rejected the wisdom of Moses. Moreover, one can see in these images the influence of ancient notions. Indeed, the forest is a place of paganism condemned by God[39], just as for Ibn Khaldun, the burning desert is a barbaric place where the nomads keep moving away from sedentary (and thus civilized) spaces. In this imaginary of a world derived from the Middle East, nomadism and paganism go hand in hand. In both cases, movement is rejected. Canada became a place, which valued a new form of integration based on imported 19th century European values. Towards the end of the 20th century, a rhetoric based on the desert can be seen occasionally in Canada too. However, its meaning changes, as shown by W.L. Morton's historiography glorifying the Canadian North: "The unfolding of the permanent frontier, clear as the line between the desert and the sower on the plain of Damascus[40] beyond which all conventional institution breakdown."[41] What need is there to talk about deserts and Syria in order to glorify the Canadian North, if not because of a strong intertextual influence? Here, however, the rhetoric is not centered on the static, but on the exploration of the North as a place of unfinished expansion, knowledge and resources.

In the nineteenth century, literature tries to escape to this nomadic threat by a rejection of the encounter and by overvaluing ancestry, like in any aristocratic and post-aristocratic structure. Family progeny predominates in Laure Conan's novel *Angeline de Montbrun* where an intense relationship between father and daughter (so-called "montbrunage") denotes an expression of a higher and almost aristocratic[42] civilization. In 1884, Laure Conan takes Philippe Aubert de Gaspé's obsession in *Les Anciens Canadiens* (1863) further and continues to perpetuate the idea of a lost world, complete with an idealized seigneurial system still tied to aristocratic France, where everyone knows exactly where they stand in their dealings with each other. This situation is mocked by Quebec writers in the 1960s through ironic references to clichés: "Mais 'noblesse oblige' in Jean Simard;"[43] "Elle ne manqua pas de rappeler que 'noblesse oblige' in Adrienne Choquette"[44] and "Nous … vivons avec une telle noblesse dans une telle grandeur, n'est-ce pas?" with Godbout.[45]

Literature, in Europe and the Americas, as Itamar Even-Zohar[46] points out, played an important role in the creation of nations[47] (except the United States where media icons created a sense of belonging through Hollywood and cinema). Literature was associated with school, playing a role in producing citizens defined predominantly by their secularity and disassociation with family roles (father or mother) and professional roles, and linked rather to the Nation-State[48] and its often difficult relationships with religion. The attribute of nationality now dominates, replacing identification by army regiment, while awaiting the temporary identification (specific to the 21st century), which is based on brand loyalty. Pico Iyer points this out in *The Global Soul*, referring to the fact that one can be faithful to an airline.[49] To have a recognized history as produced by the French-Canadian historian François-Xavier Garneau, confirms that the homogeneous nation exists, guaranteed by active elites' writings giving citizens an opportunity to share common a prioris masking the Struggle of All Against All for control of economic assets. Society is then ready to enter into a process of gradual or rapid decolonization (depending on relationships with the colonial power), by forming a bloc against colonizers through literary, linguistic and symbolic creations. This, in turn, enables the creation of a shared perspective, leading to the appropriation of economic and technological assets through political assertion. But a decolonization process does not mean recognition of otherness as Bill Schermbrucker[50] recently highlighted in his novel *Chameleon*, which depicts a character's journey from Kenya to Canada (see section: Chameleoning: From Negative to Positive). Once again, in the 19th century in Canada, purity is chosen over bastardy, eliminating the self-made man, with the intention of establishing a connection to a long-term temporality in order to assert a national identity oriented towards an idealized past.

Orphans and Bastards

The bastard's perspective is not often a happy one. In Quebec, Bouchard talks about the strategy of the bastard, a form of self-cannibalism: "The founding culture sustains itself not on the wealth of others, but rather, on its own poverty, on its real or imaginary lacks, through quiet and voracious subversion."[51] This process is also depicted in the portrayal of Berenice Einberg in Réjean Ducharme's *L'Avalée des avalés*.[52] Put another way, the bastard lacks access to others and the ability to lead the encounter (underlined in Oswald de Andrade's works), in order to create a dynamic that nourishes and renews social relations. Furthermore, as Bouchard points out, journalist Richard Gwynn claims that "Canadians should consider themselves a nation of 'mutts' entirely created, and autonomous from birth."[53] Here, Gwynn is moving towards a positive vision of the bastard, capable of creating a new Nation-State, which fits in with Pico Iyer's conclusion in *Imagining Canada*:

> I end now, at long last, with a confession: throughout this talk I've used the highly unlovely word "mongrel" instead of the euphonious government-approved word, "hybrid"[…] As Michael Ondaatje suggests with the use of the equally unsentimental term, "international Bastards," the process of mixing may not be pretty, but it's no bad thing if one comes without a pedigree.[54]

Pico Iyer's remarks jibe with a number of similarly oriented initiatives. In Costa Rica, for example, until recently it was difficult to adopt abandoned dogs if they were not purebred. In *Territorio de Zaguates* Adam Albright Hanna decided to emphasize the positive when advertising dogs of no definite pedigree, an angle specific to the Americas. This strategy worked and significantly increased adoptions.[55]

It is therefore clear that Marthe Robert's theory of literary creation has a special relationship with the Americas. Here we are often facing stories of children who are either orphans or bastards. It is an interesting attempt to escape dualistic barbarism/civilization paradigms (synonymous with self/others) presented from a scientifically indisputable basis in 1908 by Alfred P. Schultz in *Race or Mongrel*.[56] In a similar vein, the famous Harvard professor Louis Agassiz wrote in *A Journey in Brazil*:

> The natural result of an uninterrupted contact of half-breeds with one another is a class of men in which pure type fades away as completely as do all the good qualities, physical and moral, of the primitive races, engendering a mongrel crowd as repulsive as the mongrel dogs, which are apt to be their companions, and among which it is impossible to pick out a single specimen retaining intelligence, the nobility, or the affectionateness of nature which makes the dog of pure type the favorite companion of civilized man.[57]

This constitutes clear, scientific[58] racism imbued with progressive certainty. Schultz's and Agassiz's writings have been very popular and have been reprinted many times. Both contributed to demonstrating the barbaric inferiority of those born from interracial relationships. Nowadays, however, we are increasingly aware that the Creoles are part of a simultaneous and historic continuity with their parents' countries of origin. The child of the American soil, the Creole invents a New World from within complex relationships with others. Marthe Robert points out that the child, unlike Oedipus, "does not kill his father, he simply removes him from the family circle, while granting himself the ideal father from which he hopes to claim the qualities"[59] of intelligence, wealth, and independence, which are some of the bases of dynamics leading to the *self-made man*.[60] In the contemporary world using social, educational, technological and economic mobility, the perfect father, the ideal model of the desired object (from René Girard's perspective [1978]), is represented by people working on global relationships and on access to knowledge. Bill Gates, Mark Zuckerberg, and Steve Jobs represent a rejection of the essentialized attribution process pinpointed by Sarmiento, who remarked that people in the United States do not say they are poor, but that they are currently poor, as in the expression "poor right now."[61] The model is not given and established in the long term. It is built according to the needs of the moment, which indicates a determination to have the father that is desired. This, in turn, becomes a very singular declaration of independence, according to which each individual belongs to himself more than to a group. This individual then ambitiously aims to effect changes allowing an increase in the scope of abilities and access to networks. As Amy Tan writes,

> My mother believed you could be anything you wanted to be in America… America was where all my mother's hopes lay. She had come here in 1949 after losing everything in China: her mother and father, her family, home, her first husband, and two daughters, twin baby girls. But she never looked back with regret. There were so many ways for things to get better.[62]

Amy Tan is not moving towards the *self-made man* approach but to that of the *self-making man* and *self-making woman*. It is also evident in Kim Thúy's texts or in the portrayal of Dany Laferrière's character in *Cette grenade dans la main du jeune Nègre, est-elle une arme ou un fruit?*[63] The character asserts that he wants America, and he will have it. This desire to invent oneself thanks to an uncommon display of energy and intelligence can also be seen in Alain Savary's novel entitled *Le grand détour pour traverser la rue*.[64] The main character was born in a very poor neighborhood in Ottawa. However, he is able to "cross the street" and buy a house in a very rich neighborhood nearby after studying at the university of Ottawa and in Oxford, and making a fortune in Singapore. Geo-symbolic displacements lead to important identity change. It is interesting to note that many writers born outside the Americas present their characters as having dreams similar to those presented by Laferrière, Thúy or Savary. On the other hand, recently, a number of writers born in the United States, for example, tend to evoke the nightmare more than the dream. Long after *Le cauchemar climatisé* by Henry Miller[65] and *The Electric Kool-Aid Acid Test* by Tom Wolfe[66]—where the effects of the decomposition of revolution-driven hippie culture are seen—authors like Hunter S. Thompson plunged the reader into the destructive drug world of Las Vegas in *Fear and Loathing in Las Vegas: A Savage Journey to the Heart of the American Dream.*[67] In it, all the horrors of the Americas occur in a context of total irresponsibility. The attribute of "savage" in a post-hippie society in the hands of corrupt politicians and greedy financiers reappears here, but without the complementary opposing pole (civilized), which may be the reason behind the author's suicide.

From Generation to Creation: From Ties With the Past to the *Self-Making Man*

What allows for the maintenance of a lineage, or a continuously linked identity that justifies territorial occupation and determines a system of common values? In the United States, since 1776, there has been a tendency to break from Europe and form a new democratic society. In this case the break was successful, bearing in mind that it is the current and future achievements that count. But for the rest of the Americas, the new Nation-States were often defined through continuity. These societies therefore favoured approaches that did not allow for everyone to prosper according to their inclinations. In Sergio Kokis' Brazil, ambition—that is, aiming for success through the exploitation of the modern world—collides with traditions[68] and with the fear of being devoured by others in a type of cannibalism in which Brazil is seen as the victim of foreigners. This anxiety of being devoured is illustrated by a character in Kokis' *Pavillon des miroirs* (as seen in section: Escaping Dualism and the Legitimization), and in media articles such as "Amor e ódio no comércio internacional."[69] In the article, the journalist emphasizes that one of the stereotypes based on the interior/exterior paradigm (linked to protection/aggression) assumes that Brazil opts for external trade, thus causing a shortage of products on the domestic market, which privileges the rich at the expense of the hungry poor.[70] Thus, the interior/exterior dualism (close to that of civilization/barbarism) is marked by the fear of being devoured by others. This dualistic belief in turn gives way to the prevalence of the commonly perceived notion of life as a zero-sum game.[71] This presupposition is the organizational basis for social, cultural and economic representations in a vast intertext that flows through languages, discourse and media. It crosses national, linguistic and discursive boundaries, emerging as an argumentative foundation in the Americas, which are strongly engaged in identity, cultural and economic redefinitions. In Brazil, in the Americas and across the globe, the push away from the belief in the zero-sum game indicates a transition from a modern nationalistic territorial discourse targeting the distribution of identity capital, to a postmodern/postcolonial liberal discourse displacing limits and reconfiguring self-images. One could say that the zero-sum game relies on protection and that the non-zero-sum game is linked to proactivity, these being the two terms that recontextualize Bagehot's notions of generation and creation. An interior-survival/exterior-cannibalism paradigm is put in place in Brazil. It reveals a victim mentality, whereby the government elites are supposed to provide protection against the devouring foreign predator. This situation focuses the country on itself and its suspicions of exports and of all that is foreign. As Ferron's short story "Retour au Kentucky" (published in *Contes anglais* [1.9]) demonstrates, in Quebec the victim status was dominant until the 1970s. This status maintains continuity which, in this case, is based on fear of the other, and on resentment. In fact, sometimes resentment turns the status of victim into a positive value, leading to a reversal of values and towards a pseudo-restorative ideology which does not permit the control of success-oriented affirmation. George Woodcock suggested this when comparing the interest in Louis Riel, victim, and Gabriel Dumont[72], hero. This active resentment acting as a tool towards change is also evident in *Nègres blancs d'Amérique* by Pierre Vallières, who outlines the history of the exploitation of the population of New France from the Conquest until 1969. It could be said that one of the goals of these texts is to keep the victimization narrative operative, ensuring historical continuity and maintaining a collective identity in the tradition of the victim seeking redress. If we refer to René Girard's theory emphasizing that appropriation mimesis is the dynamic established between a model showing the object of desire and a rival aiming to seize the object in order to become the model, we see that in the 1960s, this fight was renewed by left-wing discourse which took the object of desire (that of being a victim) from the hands of the traditional clergy. It was this object that established continuity, merging identity across generations and giving a direction to the community. The "we" was differentiated from "the others" because the community was a victim seeking redress. Within this resentment—exposed in a Marxist speech criticized by Éric Dupont in *La logeuse*—a willingness to assert oneself was manifested by those who were exploited in the 1960s, who identified themselves with the great legitimizing narrative of the class struggle. The internationalist objective of this narrative was strategically influenced by Marxist politicians to assert national independence within the context of decolonization. There are good examples in Quebec publications, such as Françoise Marcel's text, *42 ans de service*: "Le poing fermé—tenant bien serré—le drapeau noir—toujours présents,—nous avançons—dans le temps—seuls ou regroupés, entre camarades,—pour continuer—la lutte à finir."[73] A similar line of thought is found in Latin America, from Cuba to Nicaragua and Venezuela, via Argentina, Uruguay and the Montoneros, and is evident in the violent political and dictatorial reactions to these speeches. But these statements are often oriented towards a past whose workings do not match the power relations of an imperfectly acknowledged present. These societies consume themselves in ideological, economic and sometimes very physical fights that result in thousands of deaths. This chain of events is clearly shown in the film *No*, which analyzes the strategies used to defeat Pinochet's government in Chile. The non-rejection of the extension of Pinochet's authority was won by only 54% of votes against Pinochet (with 46% of votes for him). The results make clear that a campaign based solely on resentment against Pinochet, rather than on the ability to consider the future optimistically, could not have attracted the crowds who were kept in passivity and fear by the government. Hence, an insistence on negativity would have the "yes" vote to win. As Camila Reimers (2006) explains, dictatorship wins if it stirs resentment and reactivity in people rather than proactivity, which implies an ethic of forgiveness able to free people from the weight of the past, allowing engagement in relevant struggles with new issues linked to the rest of the world.

The Rejection of Homogenizing Nationalism

> I launched into my recitation of "La cigale et la fourmi." From the first words, a black wave of hatred hit me; I feel it still… It was hatred of an alien sound…How can one not want to know what other people think and feel, stated on their terms.[74]

Nowadays, the thematic based on biological continuity (belonging to a family tree), or on historical continuity (belonging to the same country), is displaced in texts presenting transitions which value change outside of these biological, militant political and nationalist identifiers. These texts share a perspective also found in contemporary novels by Michael Ondaatje and Yann Martel; novels which reject national identifiers. The questioning of traditional nationalism, though scarcely considered by literary critics, can be found in many works predating Ondaatje and Martel. Consider, for example, the criticism of nationalism and the sharp distinction between "us" and "them" in Gabrielle Roy's short story "Wilhelm" in *Rue Deschambault*, where a character wants an immigrant to receive the recognition he deserves, but only amongst his own, in his own country, away from Manitoba (Canada). Additionally, consider the many forgotten comments by writers who cast doubt on all nationalism, including the nationalism of identity affirmation in Quebec and postcolonial affirmation in English Canada. These writers have often made unambiguous remarks through narrators or characters either by fostering a strong cosmopolitanism or by rejecting nationalism. An example in the interwar period is found in the short story "Hélène du XXVe siècle" in Jean-Charles Harvey's *L'homme qui va*. The story criticizes the principle of nationality which was used to rebuild Europe after the Great War, advocating the hope that the League of Nations will succeed in establishing world peace: "Avant d'être Français, Anglais, Allemands, Russes, Japonais, Chinois, Américains ou Brésiliens, nous sommes des hommes."[75] In English Canada, the democratic and internationalist liberalism was also evident in W.A. Deacon's description of a world parliament: "Under the present conditions, the force theory must be retained… With the League of Nations serving as a world parliament for the service and welfare of humanity, with national federal bodies to deal with such matters as railroads and national utilities, with states or provinces having legislation, with greater local autonomy, with considerably more power in the hands of the municipalities over matters of vital and immediate moment to the people—then, and not till then, can the moral motive theory be safely adopted."[76] These ideas were resurrected in a post-World-War II context by known dissidents like Claude Gauvreau: "Accepter comme naturelle et bienfaisante la multiplicité des différences; les racistes et nationalistes sont des semeurs de haine."[77] Borduas' words are also relevant in this context: "Non pas question de nationalisme. Je les ai tous en horreur."[78] This is also evident in many remarks by characters in Réjean Ducharme's novels who reject roots: "Un vrai Autochtone, si j'ai bien compris, est un être qui naît dans sa tombe; il bouge un peu, pas plus qu'une racine, et se tord dans un sens, se tord dans l'autre sens, puis ne se tord plus du tout"[79]; "se battre pour une patrie, c'est se battre pour un berceau et un cercueil, c'est ridicule et faux, ça sent l'excuse pourrie. Le seul combat logique est un combat contre tous"[80]; "pourquoi m'enfermerais-je avec eux dans un de ces réduits pleins à craquer de fumée de cigarette appelés pays ?"[81]; "c'est cela le droit qu'ils ont pris de diviser comme une tourte, la terre en parties supposées égales et de te barricader dans celle qu'ils ont convenu de considérer comme tienne."[82] Notwithstanding Ducharme's dualistic us/them perspective with respect to the fight against all and his use of voracious self-cannibalism in *L'avalée des avalés*, his discourse transcends notions of the nation common to many literary works of the 20th century. However, in *L'avalée des avalés*, his reaction ignores relationships, including interracial ones. Subsequently, Mavis Gallant criticizes the anxieties of Frye and Atwood about the emptiness of identity in *Home Truths*, questioning the fact that Canadians do not know who or where they are. Believing this to be untrue, Gallant rejects nationalism as a dangerous avenue for self-assertion: "What I am calling, most clumsily, the national sense of self is quite separate from nationalism, which I distrust and reject absolutely, and even patriotism, so often used as a stick to beat people with."[83]

Ondaatje's novel *The English Patient*[84] is part of this current, taking World War II as a background to assert detachment with respect to national allegiance, allowing a dynamic encounter in which everyone is transformed and gains knowledge. However, if with Gauvreau or Ducharme one senses an activist tone close to total refusal, Ondaatje shows an openness to the movement of people, writings, ideas and things as encounters leading to a transformation in permanent transition. The fight of "all against all" fades away, permitting life to exist beyond dualistic paradigms; leading to the recognition of alterity: the other is in us, as we are in the other. In other words, there is a move away from the paradigms used in the 1960s and before. It touches upon the desire for self-invention (with others), in a future-oriented present. In *Imagining Canada*, Pico Iyer's reading of Ondaatje's *The English Patient* is revealing. Iyer says the novel is "charting the outlines of a new world, in which strangers could interact and love and talk in a new kind of way, 'unconscious of ancestry.'"[85] In the development of the new world order in which Canada and the Americas are finding their place, the nation's allegiances and definitions (bloody prerogative of World War II used in *The English Patient*) have a tendency to abate: "At the very moment when the world was being convulsed by nationalistic divisions, and people were killed on the basis of passports they carried, or their religions, these four semi-posthumous beings told us we could define ourselves in new ways and step into a different kind of community."[86] This reading echoes the words of a character in *The English Patient*: "Gradually we became nationless. I came to hate nations."[87] This is in accordance with Antonio d'Alfonso's claim in *In Italics*:

> Perhaps one day people will no longer be classified according to the land they come from; nor will they be identified by predetermined genetic qualities. And they will

> not be identified by the language they speak. Then, I believe, identity will be set by consciousness alone. More than all the flags of the world, more than all the religions and languages of the world, it will be the kind of society you choose to participate in that will determine who you are. Let no one tell you otherwise.[88]

From the action aiming at rebuilding a nation, as seen in the writings of Ferron and Margaret Atwood, a movement towards disengagement emerged. It proceeds from the understanding that any agreement on a victimization process constantly results in more exclusion. What emerges in Michael Ondaatje and Pico Iyer's works (in the world of globalized liberalism) is an opening to a future in motion that tends to elude the synthesis of various cultures into a whole dominated by people of European origin. This dynamic is portrayed in Jose Vasconcelos' writings. However, today, we can find numerous examples of a blending which does not lead to a dominance in the fields of literature, the arts, economics and science. For instance, painter Peter Doig, born in Scotland, educated in Montreal and living in Barbados is one of them. Nathalie Petrowski says that Doig "s'est senti à la fois nulle part et pourtant chez lui"[89]; hence the title (*Nulle terre étrangère*) of his first major exhibition in North America at the Musée des Beaux-Arts in Montreal, in the spring of 2014.

Pico Iyer envisages syncretism rather than synthesis. He relies on the encounter of existing cultures with long, continuous pasts (indigenous and European), or a discontinuous one, as highlighted by Glissant regarding Blacks. Creoleness is defined by Glissant as hybridity plus surprise.[90] Creoleness is thereby an unquantifiable addition, which is always in the process of further additions.[91]

Moreover, compared to the status of the victim who transfers the past into present resentments in an essentializing, constantly dominated identity, a new dynamic has recently revealed itself in the postmodern/postcolonial context: the dynamic of choice. This is what Pico Iyer emphasizes regarding his grandparents and himself:

> I often think, in all these contexts, of my grandparents, all four of whom were born in India. For all of them, I think, there came at birth a very strong, perhaps oppressively strong, sense of where they belonged, what they believed, who their friends and enemies were and where they would likely pass all their days. Now for more and more of us, the very facts that were a given for our grandparents are, you could say, a chosen; we have the chance—which is also a challenge—to invent from scratch our sense of tradition, of neighbourhood, of home and even of self. The oldest and simplest question in the world—"Where do you come from?"—suddenly brings new and more open-ended answers, or no answers at all for those strong enough to live in the spaces between categories.[92]

In the context of globalization, the paragraph clearly and effectively demonstrates the significant changes experienced by the Americas, and the ability to choose rather than being forced to bear the burden of ancestors' resentments and national canonical stories that require that the enemy, as well as the victim and the scapegoat, be defined. It is thereby possible to go beyond Anne Michaels' claim in *Fugitive Pieces* that "even if an act could be forgiven, no one could bear the responsibility of forgiveness on behalf of the dead. No act of violence is ever resolved. When the one who can forgive can no longer speak, there is only silence."[93] When we understand that these very harsh words are linked to a parable told by a rabbi who does not see how to pardon a definitive exclusionary process, the path that certain writers ask the reader to follow is clear (writers such as Laura Esquivel, Isabel Allende, Yann Martel and Éric Dupont, as seen earlier). They ask for the recognition of the other as an attempt to escape the transfer of resentment. It is a far cry from the hard line expressed in the rabbi's last words, whose forgiveness is sought by the bourgeois: "All this time you have been asking the wrong man. You must ask the man on the train to forgive you."[94] Indeed, the rabbi appears temporarily in the guise of a farmer in order to avoid conditioned automatic respect, so to experience the life of the excluded.

Reincarnation

> Il existe un schéma transculturel de la violence collective… C'est-à-dire que la crise et sa résolution victimaire se déroulent toujours et partout selon un processus identique.[95]

The incarnation of characters subjected to exclusion has been the topic of numerous factual and journalistic publications throughout the last thirty years, with White reporters masquerading as Black Americans in the United States[96] in order to denounce rampant, ambient discrimination. Exclusion also manifests itself in fiction. However, it is important to go beyond the denunciation of the discrimination faced by a particular group, conveying a sense of the historical and anthropological workings that causes people and populations to disassociate themselves from their actions (especially that of excluding others), an attitude criticized by Milan Kundera in *L'Art du roman*.[97] That is why, in contemporary literature, recognition and intimate knowledge of violence and exclusion are going through major transformations within the aesthetics of realism; excellent examples of which are found in the reincarnation[98] themes and the techniques used in *The Law of Love* by Laura Esquivel, *Self* by Yann Martel and *Myra Breckinridge; Myron* by Gore Vidal.[99] The dynamics of reincarnation allow an exploration of scenarios related to human violence in various contexts. In *Self*, the protagonist is a man, then a woman who has been raped, and then a man again. In *Myra Breckinridge; Myron*, Myra (who was gay and was called Myron) becomes a woman. She questions machismo as well as feminism, to finally become the man who happily breaks down the taboos. In Laura Esquivel's novel, the indigenous woman raped by the conquistador (as it is always presented in the official historical stereotype in Mexico) is reincarnated several decades later, returning to life as a man. She dominates the conquistador, who has become a woman, in a constant exchange of positions of power lasting until the 20th century. This exploration of violence is also thematized in Clarice Lispector's *Selected Crônicas* where the female character is suddenly seized with terror after being invited by a man "for a little stroll." She then suggests that during the Stone Age, she was probably abused by a man who loved her. Transsexual and transhistorical reincarnations transform power struggles, as they explore the violence suffered by victims in a dynamic of change through role-reversals. This leads to a change in the official historical narrative controlled by the nation-state's policy. In other words, the internal becomes external, eliminating the barbarism/civilization dualism and the synonymy between these paradigms. This promotes a process of reflexivity on the legitimization of the discourse, as it is constructed through narrativity. As we will see (section: Causality and Narrative), narrativity and its causal consequence structure tends to lead readers to look for a bad character to be excluded. A narrativity based on reincarnation deters the reader from seeing the text as truth incarnate (who is good?/who is the villain?), in order to focus on the storytelling process[100] and the invention of the character who is simultaneously one and the other. This is what Camila Reimers shows in *Tres lotos en un mar de fuego*.[101] She insists that to be reintegrated into the future, immigrants who have been tortured and/or raped in Chile, Cambodia and Algeria must forgive and overcome the scars and the physical allocation by suffering. The inhospitable space—the nation of birth and torture—must be left behind, requiring a departure from temporality and from the past.

Reincarnation proposes the idea of a long continuity, but in a completely different way than through the operation of the victimhood process legalized by the lynchers, who tell the official history that spans centuries. Reincarnation is intended to question the legitimacy of these essentialized relations and to denounce the state and national history, controlled by victimizing winners, while maintaining a new type of continuity: the continuity of the discontinuous, through reincarnation based on encounters. Reincarnation's playfulness opens the door to the possibility of recognizing the other in oneself, as demonstrated by Lévinas[102], through the intermediary of unacknowledged and/or forgotten sufferings by the nation-state's grand legitimization/homogenization narrative which, like much human suffering, transcends politico-ideological options.

As Girard remarks, Jesus' position is pertinent here; exactly at that defining moment when he was silenced by the lynch mob and did not react violently. Girard says about Jesus: "Il faut que cette victime réussisse à nous atteindre au moment où la violence lui ferme la bouche."[103] Everyone feels the horror of this moment of physical, intellectual and spiritual violence when the group gangs up against the scapegoat. What matters in these narratives of reincarnation, where the encounter and the exchange of power positions recontextualize the continuity and challenge historical continuity and truth, is the moment of violence that strikes. This moment transcends the dichotomies of self/others, civilization/barbarism, interior/exterior. It also transcends the long term/short term opposition. Indeed, this moment is simultaneously ephemeral in its immediate violence and very long with respect to the process of torture; it is in fact very long with respect to its impact on memory. It is also found in *La nuit* by Jacques Ferron. In the novel the main character is brutally attacked by the police, and although there is no reincarnation (because the aesthetics of the time did not allow for it), there is duplication and an exploration of encounters with otherness, resulting in an identity transformation. Thus, this moment escapes entrenched dualities in order to gain a value that crosses time and place. Also, like Camila Reimers' statements[104] about torture and rape, all widely used by terrorists and repressive regimes, this moment of violence permits the consideration of the encounter through the recognition of differences.

From a literary point of view, reincarnation subverts the coherence of the fictional character, who, from a traditional critical perspective, is often described as being sure-footed and whose action concords with stable causal/temporal functional structures, and is made plausible by a culture controlled by active historical narratives through intertextual simultaneity.[105] The character is no longer constructed according to the verisimilitude of a predictable identity based on a sequence of actions related to causality and descriptive paradigms that set restrictive limits on his means of mobility and psychosocial transformations. The character becomes a network of dominant discourses and forgotten or diminished ones, which he/she comes upon and can influence, provoking encounters with others in geographical spaces, which serve as unedited rhetoric for them. The character becomes the focus of encounters for diverse cultures. His self-image may proliferate in partially unpredictable ways and lead to new, networked identities. He is a transhistorical chameleon who is built on the knowledge of political systems and interpersonal violence.

Dualism and Victim Status

References to lineage, roots and family trees, themselves entwined in long narratives managed by nation-states, impart a sense of stability and simplicity to identity by basing it on a binary dualism. For example: barbarism/civilization, reframed to reflect political and discursive perspectives between operator/operated, colonizer/colonized, the others/self. However, this dualism does not take into account the multiplicity of power relations in the Americas: take the example of French Canadians and Quebeckers who are both minorities when compared to Anglophones in Canada or the United States, and majorities when compared to Blacks and immigrants. This power dynamic is pointed out by the Italian-Quebec writers of the 1970s.[106] It is also apparent when comparing Pierre Vallières and Lorena Gale, as seen earlier (section: Rethinking Relations). Quebeckers have a double status, like all children born on the soil of the Americas; with respect to at least two other groups, including one considered to be dominant (European or American), and the other, less important (Black, Indigenous or recent immigrant). This situation is the same in many regions of the Americas. Take English Canadians, for example, as presented in *Survival* by Margaret Atwood: "Let us suppose, for the sake of argument, that Canada as a whole is a victim, or an 'oppressed minority,'or 'exploited.' Let us suppose in short that Canada is a colony."[107] In the 1960s, English Canadians feel threatened by the United States after having been dominated by England and its colonial power. At the same time, they are in a position of superiority over French Canadians. Indeed, Margaret Atwood points out that Francophones, too, are engaged in a process of survival but she sometimes forgets to specify against whom! One has the impression that, according to her, Anglophones cannot be both victims and victimizers; therefore, they cannot be in relationship with at least two 'others'. Indeed, she is looking for ways to avoid saying that English Canadians share the responsibility in the uncomfortable situation of French Canadians' survival. She refers to the character of Philibert in Roch Carrier's novel *La guerre, Yes Sir*[108] and asks who is responsible for this situation. Roch Carrier points to the system, to English Canadians who are exploiting French Canadians, as well as to the capitalists who are exploiting the workers: "But the fact remains that it is not the System that wrecks Philibert's car: it is himself. His role as a victim is certainly imposed on him by the System, but it has also been imposed on him by his family and his culture, and he has internalized it very early."[109] When *Survival* was published, Margaret Atwood was well aware that French Canadian culture was still partly a victim culture, as seen previously in a passage by Claude-Henri Grignon:

> Nos pères… nous ont jetés dans le commerce, les industries, les professions dites libérales où nous essuyons une défaite éternelle parce que nous manquons de capital. Nous possédions le plus riche capital qui existe: le sol. Vous le constaterez après la guerre. Nous l'avons perdu. Et nous sommes perdus aujourd'hui dans les masses étrangères.[110]

As for English Canadians, theirs is also a culture of victimhood and dependence, but Margaret Atwood mostly blames the individual and not the relationship of domination established between English Canadians and French Canadians. Yet this relationship is clearly denounced by Roch Carrier in *La guerre, Yes Sir* (both in the novel and in the play). Atwood rejects the double role for English Canadians—that of both colonizer and colonized. Writings asserting national identity in the 1960s are inevitably based on a dualism consistent with barbarism/civilization; those whose identities are uncertain cannot or do not want to acknowledge the even more marginalized groups, many of whom are almost invisible, as in the case of Franco-Ontarians, Franco-Manitobans and Franco-Albertans. All of these even smaller minority groups are threatened by continuity, by the conception of the long term and by dualistic paradigms that define them negatively in their quest for recognition, expansion and the possibility of redeeming the promises offered by the Americas. Promises which meet with basic universal democratic aspirations of having a place in the sun and of belonging to oneself and defining oneself within a constant evolution.

Contemporary Concerns Regarding Hybridity

Despite the general openness towards encounters, uncertainties regarding hybridity persist to this day. These uncertainties appear more in social discourse relayed by the media than in artistic or literary works which, since the

1980s, have been mostly oriented towards the exploration of contextual and hybrid relationships. The title of an interview from the Montreal newspaper *La Presse* in 2000 illustrates the perspective in which these social discourses emerge in a sentence illustrating a photo: "Les traits métissés, l'accent québécois." The article then starts with the following comments: "Valérie, Annie et Marie-France Lemaine, nées à Montréal d'une mère québécoise et d'un père haïtien, se sentent parfois étrangères dans le regard des autres."[111] For some, if it were possible to be "old-stock" by virtue of one's culture, accent, school references and proxemics, while appearing foreign through the presence of an "obvious" feature (more or less swarthy skin), then it would no longer be possible to differentiate between people according to ethnic-historical criteria. This situation was perceived as dangerous between the two world wars. Gratien Gélinas warned French Canadians to be wary of foreigners who, one day, would speak French like them and would be difficult to exclude, being no longer recognizable: "Nous répandons le français? Sans doute, au point que, dans quelques années, les juifs, par exemple, qui seront habiles, auront appris eux-mêmes notre langue et remercieront les nôtres de leurs services. Et le public ne remarquera pas la différence; il sera même fier qu'un juif lui parle la langue de Dollard des Ormeaux."[112] Today, however, Mark Kingwell says:

> Citizenship can be defended, then, but it can no longer be conceived the way it was a thousand, hundred, or even fifty years ago. The oldest models of civic belonging are forms of virtual racism, tribal fear given a political formulation… None of these three historical models—the models based on blood, belief, or law—has been complete in its attempted domination of the political realm…What we need is a new model of citizenship based on the act of participation itself, not on some quality or thought or right enjoyed by its possessor. This participatory citizenship doesn't simply demand action from existing citizens; it makes action at once the condition and the task of citizenship.[113]

The word "action"—meaning acting together in the context of encounters with others—is linked to building a present and a future made up of personalities in the process of transformation. Action in this sense is supported by José Antonio Giménez Micó.[114] With respect to immigrants, he refers to active blending rather than to integration or assimilation. In the new culture legitimizing transformation (in the context of the knowledge-based society), action and access are keywords in new social relations escaping the static social relationships criticized by Kingwell.

This active blending complicates the multiple relations envisaged among different facets of identity (citizen, retired, student, mother), which form the foundation of an active participation by an individual in economic, cultural and social activities. This participation is measured increasingly within social and media discourse. For example, Dr. Yves Lamontagne, President of the College of Physicians of Quebec from 1998 to 2010, said he was pleased that "foreign doctors, after five years in office under a restrictive permit, obtain a regular licence."[115] Note, however, that foreign doctors can obtain Canadian citizenship within three years of residence. In other words, because they did not grow up and were not trained in the host country—and even if they are legally no longer foreigners (as they have become Canadian citizens with Canadian passports)—the accreditation process stipulated by the medical doctors' union accords them the professional status of foreigners. We should take into account the shift from noun to qualifying adjective. Indeed, Dr. Lamontagne would not have said, for example, that Alvaro Ramirez is a foreigner, but that Ramirez is a foreign doctor. In other words, these days, one could be a Canadian citizen and a foreign doctor, depending on how those in power define those waiting to have a little more power in order to participate actively in scientific, economic and social life. This proves the veracity of Mark Kingwell's reasoning when he insists on the recognition of participatory action as a key category of citizenship. However, the situation can sometimes lead to very qualified taxi drivers with degrees in engineering, etc., as seen in Denys Arcand's film *Les Invasions Barbares* (2003), where a Somali taxi driver helps deliver a baby born from a lady herself born in Québec while affirming that he is a family member, in an underfunded Montreal hospital with overworked staff.

Nowadays, there is an increasing divergence from accreditation processes based on nationalism, precipitated by the need to increase social capital to complement knowledge capital in professional and economic networks within given territories in competition within a global market. The participatory action of all is a crucial issue on the interdependent economic, cultural and civic fronts. The identity question is therefore of some importance, but it is no longer based on fixed structures, like the professional accreditation process and its essentialized link (by means of the verb *to be*) to any noun leading to cultural and economic exclusion. As we have seen, a noun and its link to ancestors help define the basis of a community which recognizes itself through naming. Nowadays, however, individuals are increasingly becoming more like network centers, instantly interconnected and in permanent transition according to fields of interest and constantly recycled issues. Action and proactivity are key to encounters.

Where Is Here? Concerns From the Sixties to the Present

The contemporary dynamic outlined above shifts the question posed by Northrop Frye in the sixties about ties between identity and territory. Indeed, identity has become a constant production of multiple self-images within a territory that is at once local, global and virtual. This conception of identity was not the same in the sixties: "But in Canada, as Frye suggested, the answer to the question 'Who am I?' is at least partly the same as the answer to another question: 'Where is here?'"[116] Where is here, how do we define here, what can I do here, and how can I act here? These were the questions English Canada tried to answer in the sixties and seventies; the question formed part of the identity quest of uncertain Canadians facing English colonial domination, the U. S. economy's progress and culture, and new technology. An appreciation for the depth of the question was important, highlighting the need to focus on *what* and *how* to live within a seemingly unfamiliar space. Nonetheless, *Where is here?* was part of the context of Northrop Frye's thinking. He insisted on the importance of the past and on history:

> Trying to sharpen one's sense of the future is useless, as the future has no existence; trying to see the present as an interim in which anything may go at any time merely adds to the mood of destruction… What kind of people we are is perhaps determined, and certainly conditioned, by what we realize of our past, and sharpening our sense of the past is the only way of meeting the future.[117]

That much is clear. Ensuring a basis for a heritage was certainly necessary; however, it was not necessary to reject the future and technology, as did Frye: "The only possible economic alternative to capitalism, we feel, is socialism, but if capitalism is a destroyer, socialism is even more one, because more committed to technology."[118] But what about Marshall McLuhan and Pico Iyer, leading us to a world where complexity bears more nuances than this simple dualism! Iyer compares Canada and the United States, underlining the fact that Canada is neither obsessed by the future (like the United States), nor a prisoner of the past (like the United Kingdom). It represents a clear balance according to the evolution of the planet marked by new knowledge, access to networks and globalization.

These days, the question "Who am I?" and its complement "How do we define here?" is often asked, not by the Canadians born in Canada, but by a certain number of immigrants who have confronted hostile environments in their countries of origin as well as in host countries like Canada. This is apparent in Rawi Hage's work. Hage is a Montreal writer of Middle-Eastern descent whose main character, wandering in downtown Montreal, feels like a cockroach: "Where am I? And what am I doing here? How did I end up trapped in a constantly shivering carcass, walking in a frozen city with wet cotton falling on me all the time?"[119] Similar reactions are also found in Brazilian writer and artist Henfil's text entitled *Diário de um cucaracha*[120]. Henfil's text tells the story of a Brazilian immigrant in the United States. He doesn't fit in and feels as if he is turning into a cockroach in other people's eyes, like in Kafka's *The Metamorphosis.*[121] He goes back to Brazil full of resentment. Montreal in Hage's writing is quite different from Dany Laferrière's ironic perspective in *Comment faire l'amour avec un Nègre sans se fatiguer*, where he makes ample provision for encounters in spite of the continuous interference of stereotypes. Hage's writing also differs from the more rationally controlled comments in Antonio d'Alfonso's works. In the novel by Hage, resentment expresses an inner pain that constantly intensifies the psychological imbalance of the character, who becomes more and more dangerous to those he joyfully threatens or whom he robs. Now let us compare Torres-Garcia with Northrop Frye.

Where Is Up? Where Is Here?

In 1935, Torres-Garcia drew a famous map entitled *América invertida* in *La escuela del Sur*. The map put the South Pole at the top, meaning the North Pole was at the bottom. Though an interesting retaliatory measure, Torres-Garcia's map is not immune to the usual dualism: like barbarity/civilization, it merely changed the place of the poles. Even so, the map reflected the Southerners' rejection of any perceived dependence on the North. This reprisal could be identified as "*Where is up?*," forming a link with Northrop Frye's "*Where is here?*", rejecting dominance but also embodying the ideology of dependency theory. Barbarism/civilization was thereby recycled in dependent/dominant or South/North inter-American relations. The inverted America shown in the map whose legend "*Where is up?*" can be compared to the famous question "*Where is here?*" asked by Northrop Frye. He pointed out that place and identity in Canada were at best vague and uncertain, as opposed to what the inverted map suggests, namely that Latin America knows its place in a world where the South is dominated by the North. Hence, we can see that for Canada, the socioeconomic question seemed less critical than in Latin America. This is also highlighted by Seema Ahluwalia in an analysis of the Indigenous peoples' situation: "Les Canadiens sont ainsi confrontés à une contradiction inconfortable entre leurs valeurs libérales démocratiques, et le racisme et la colonisation qui font partie intégrante de notre société."[122] Of course, this comment, made in 2012 after Canada's extensive evolution and after the implementation and integration of multiculturalism into the Canadian way of life (contributing to a national renewal), has not been made at a time when the uncertainty expressed in "*Where is here?*" was being diffused. Nonetheless, sometimes Canadians were informed of very serious problems taking place in residential schools. In February 1967, the very popular *MacLeans Magazine* published the story of Chanie Wenjack (age 12) who fled the violence of the residential school in Kenora (Northern Ontario), and died alone a few days later.[123] The story was quickly forgotten! The more so because of the preparation of the Universal Expo 67 taking place in Montreal.

In the sixties and seventies, the identity uncertainty pointed out by Frye and Atwood was a symptom of a possible evolution towards questioning identity definitions. Hence, at that time those who felt colonized (African Americans, English Canadians, Quebeckers, etc.), wanted to be recognized and have their voices heard. It was important to self-identify, to define oneself, to think of ourselves as Canadians or as Quebeckers, to feel attached to HERE. A "here" that could be specified without feeling a sense of being invaded by the others (dominant Americans or French and English colonizers), and without forgetting all those who were dominated and displaced, like the Indigenous peoples.

As seen earlier, not all writers naturally work according to this logic. Réjean Ducharme questions nationalist allegiances (section: The Rejection of Homogenizing Nationalism) in l'*Avalée des avalés* and in l'*Hiver de force*. In these books Ducharme creates parodies of anti-establishment discourses looking to create a populist link and in which characters spout ultranationalist clichés. According to the ultranationalist, "C'est un tyran éclairé qu'il nous faut au Québec."[124] The pseudo-indigenous anti-establishment discourse is represented with: "C'est Louis Caron, l'être joual supérieur… il porte un bandeau à plumes, se fait appeler Raton Rêveur et répand la théorie que le joual est une langue sauvage, donc indienne."[125] Ducharme highlights that these anti-establishment discourses aim to lead a new elite that ignores known contradictions, in this case the synonymy between savage and "Indian." These discourses of stereotyped protest, aimed at a new consensus leading to new exclusions, opens with the remark "I WAS HERE!," which is subtly critiqued: "[…] ces mots terribles, les seuls que n'importe qui peut écrire n'importe où sans se tromper: I WAS HERE!"[126] Ducharme may be the only author from the 1970s to take on issues already questioning dominant anti-establishment discourses (like nationalist ones), and dramatizing what is essential in life: a change of perspective of the world and an obsession with chaos.

This perspective is linked to Rutherford's questions regarding matter at McGill University, then to Einstein's theory of relativity, in which he explains "that there is no such place as here."[127] Stephen Leacock humorously plays with the concept in his story about two fishermen: "We should have marked that place where we got all the fish," said one fisherman, to which the other replied, "I did: I marked it on the boat. Well, that's it. That's here."[128] The world chaos already contemplated by Leacock is explored by Ducharme and by his characters, lost in the consumption of objects, people, faiths and ideologies and shaken by exclusions but standing erect, like Bérénice Einberg in *L'Avalée des avalés*, in their assertive individuality. These ideas were not clearly shown in Frye's *Where Is Here?* Ducharme understands that discoveries are possible only in an undetermined place and time. His characters find themselves in an already chaotic context, in which few encounters make sense. In a way, Ducharme is a precursor of a thematic later explored in *La logeuse* by Éric Dupont[129] (section: The Variegated Land).

In different ways, the children of the soil's position between two opposing sides was problematic in the sixties and seventies. One of the sides, from which they had to free themselves, was regarded as threatening: Europe, English Canada, United States; the anxious Northern continent. An effort was made to ignore the opposing side, made up of Indigenous peoples and different visible minorities. These minorities were ignored or only seen within established and exclusive paradigms. As Margaret Atwood says:

> *Where is here?* is a different kind of question. It is what a man asks when he finds himself in unknown territory, and it implies several other questions. Where is this place in relation to other places? How do I find my way around in it? […] Canada is an unknown territory for the people who live in it […] I'm talking about Canada as a state of mind, as the space you inhabit not just with your body but with your head […] Literature is not only a mirror; it is also a map, a geography of the mind […] we need to know about here [….].[130]

On the other hand, through *América invertida*, Latin America seemed to know where they were; having a place and being both politically independent and economically dependent and reacting dualistically depending on the dominant discourse of the class fight struggle against the traditionalism of the elites. On the contrary, for English Canadians who felt colonized, points of reference were limited because of partial political dependence and economic comfort. Therefore, self-assertion was less likely. In this case, many Canadians felt *not quite*, as Bhabha says—not quite English, not quite American, not quite European, but certainly not descendants of the Metis or Indigenous peoples: at a crossroads, without a compass. They were neither this nor that, which was also expressed in the eighties by Franco-Ontarian author Patrice Desbiens in *L'Homme invisible/The Invisible Man*[131] by focusing on the Francophone minority in Ontario. *The Invisible Man* by Black American writer Ralph Ellison[132] is referenced, showing the possibility that Francophone minorities in Ontario are, like Pierre Vallières' Quebeckers, the Black Whites of America.

In 1960s Canada, a reflection would take place—achieved through cultural and linguistic affirmation—requiring the study of Canadian and Quebec literatures rather than that of Racine and Shakespeare. Thereafter, for the small communities, which were forgotten or invisible at the time (such as the Franco-Ontarians), a dynamic transformation would also take place. It would require the study of Franco-Ontarian literature rather than a curriculum using works exclusively derived from Quebec and France. It was the same in 2012 for the Indigenous peoples and the Métis who claimed their economic and cultural presence in various academic and political institutions and who participated in the Truth and Reconciliation Commission, which, it is important to note, was limited: "Où se trouvent le leadership, les ressources et l'encouragement du gouvernement lorsque vient le temps de rassembler les témoignages des colons canadiens sur la domination, la violence, le racisme et l'indifférence envers la souffrance humaine? Quand les Canadiens reconnaîtront-ils leurs crimes contre l'humanité afin que nous puissions amorcer le processus de guérison par rapport au comportement oppressif qu'ils continuent à adopter à l'égard des peuples autochtones?"[133]

The uncertain identity articulated in the sixties also affected French Canada, but it was by eliminating the Anglophone ruler/colonizer who imposed his exclusive vision that other invisible groups could be recognized, so that Quebec (linked to the Americas more than to Europe) could be defined by all its diversity and through the coincidence of encounters. This is mentioned in *La Nuit* by Ferron: Frank/François, the French Canadian assimilated by the Anglophone world, finds his way by eliminating the authoritarian "coup de poing"[134] received in his youth by a repressive police force while at a demonstration for independence. François eases the shock of the punch and uses a "pot de coings" (bowl of quince)—which are poisonous and deadly to Frank—as a means to kill his dominating Anglo alter ego. François thereby rids himself of the integrated Anglo assimilator Frank, making a submission to the establishment within the context of nationalistic Anglophone domination. This allows him to regain his powers, to self-define by escaping the mimetism and the *not quite*. It is important to remember that this Anglo assimilator is related to colonial domination, which, in the eyes of Francophones, is part of an uninterrupted filiation defining the Anglo-Canadian. However, in Ferron's *La Nuit*, this liberation does not aim to establish a homogenous society assimilating others or throwing them away as a negligible quantity. Indeed, François' feeling of independence implies being in possession of his means and not being dominated by the others' codes. This dependency was also thoroughly explored in the 1930s by many writers in Latin America and particularly by José Vasconcelos ("If we simply imitate, we lose"[135]). The independent republics of the Latin Americas have known this for a while. This greater security assurance with regards to one's identity leads to a clearer view of others. In *La nuit*, François, thanks to his newly asserted identity, knows how to reach others by crossing the unstable waters on Montreal bridges thanks to the ferryman-taxi driver, Alfredo Carone. These crossings lead from the little bungalow steeped in diurnal boredom to downtown Montreal—a ship-island open to the discovery of a new continent, to the night, and to characters from other cultures like Barbara, a Black woman from the Caribbean. Through Ferron's writing François/Frank passes to another level of reality, escaping the realism of repression and the boredom of daily life, using a timid approach that nonetheless sets off the magic of realism and the metamorphoses of nocturnal life. He discovers that cultures and perspectives cross and do not always conform to a single vision, system of values or ethic. Interculturalism in Quebec and multiculturalism in English Canada are emerging in literature because one of the values shared by Canadians is the recognition of identities at a perpetual crossroads. These identities are multiple self-images in transition—in a coincidence of self-images—that do not depend uniquely on a filiation, but rather on unforeseen and interesting relationships. By accepting coincidence rather than continuity, certain literary texts from the mid-sixties have a connection to the dynamics of the Americas and can be linked to the novels of the 2000s. This journey then leads to Quebec and to interculturalism. It acts in the context of a double positioning: from the perspective of minority French-speaking communities in English Canada and the United States, and from the majority French-speaking community's perspective in Quebec. This implies the rejection of multiculturalism by the population of Quebec[136], who still sees in it the possibility of domination by English Canada, through immigrants, among others. Without Bill 101 and interculturalism, the population of Quebec, and immigrants in particular, could have sent their children to English schools instead of French schools, leading eventually to a reduced Francophone population, and the dilution of French language and culture in Quebec.

This positioning has recently shifted, however, in *L'Autre modernité* by Simon Nadeau. The historically marginalized Quebec Francophones now know how to turn their peripheral position in the context of the federal canadian state into a force in the context of globalization. They can both be provincial and global, reaching humanity in its entirety, particularly given the democratization of access to knowledge: "Cette souveraineté retrouvée, c'est celle du 'provincial émancipé' qui use de sa *différence* comme d'une arme à double tranchant: d'un côté, il coupe le lien communautaire qui enserre l'individu dans les rets d'un contrat social non remis en question et imposé (lequel se fait passer pour la nature même); de l'autre côté, il se sert de cet écart pour rester libre par rapports aux modèles universels d'émancipation qui ne sont souvent qu'une nouvelle façon d'embrigader les individus de sociétés les plus développées dans de nouveaux moules sociaux et de juguler, par le fait même, ce qu'il y a d'irréductible et d'inassimilable chez les individus, la part la plus sauvage et en même temps la plus substantielle de chacun, là où le soi est seul à être soi."[137]

This new fluid certainty about identity (*in-between ... at the same time ... neither one nor the other, one and the other*) knows how to attain the savage side turned positive. It represents the unassimilable through systems, whether they are national, local or pseudo-universal. Yvon Rivard affirms this in *Le siècle de Jeanne* and Jocelyne Saucier explores it in her novel *Il pleuvait des oiseaux*, from a less intellectual imaginary (see section: Escaping Dualism).

Development of the uncertain identity can also be measured by comparing the Group of Seven paintings, where the vast and splendid empty spaces ask, "*Where is here?*" and avoid using a dominant face to represent all the groups that make up English Canada, where everybody should also feel at home. This is different from the Quebecker Clarence Gagnon, who fills his scenarios with local people, because they must be present in order to assert the homogeneity of the group.[138] With respect to the aesthetics linked to the power relations of the two founding communities, we can measure the gap thanks to the recent paintings of new Canadian Jin Mee Yoon.[139] Asian men and women are shown in the paintings; whether tourists or immigrants, we don't know, especially as they are painted with their backs turned to us in stereotyped landscapes, like the Prince Edward Island of Lucy Maud Montgomery's *Anne of Green Gables* (1908) for example.

If they are tourists, the national stereotype of the idyllic place is reinforced, especially given the Japanese fascination with *Anne of Green Gables*.[140] However, if they are immigrants who bought a farm to work their land, the image of traditional Canada becomes global through the questioning of the mythic link between the body and the earth. The child of the soil and all the stereotypes connected to it are carried away by a new frontier: that of multiculturalism, which concerns not only the nucleus of large urban centers but also local territorial roots. Sarah Phillips Casteel points this out when asking the exclusion question in the context of *Where is here?*: "The deep sense of ambiguity surrounding place and its relationship to conquest indicates that to construct a sense of place is always to run the risk of displacing someone else."[141] Those who are moved, however, are mostly spectators who do not know how to interpret a painting, though realistically crafted; maybe even too realistic, as the official interpretative tradition is questioned in this case.

These spectators have been trained using well-defined interpretations, as explained by Jésus Martín Barbero[142] and Susana Vellegia.[143] Martín Barbero underlines that the national bourgeoisies share the same infatuation for the type of representation that grafts itself onto a form of patriotic progressivism. This provides an idea of finality related to a duty to progress that pragmatically replaces the religious idea of finality. Susana Vellegia specifies that the nature of shared representation constitutes a power group. It is related to the impossibility of understanding otherness, the unknown and the distinct, and to the desire for domination. Realistic representation is a code of communication, broadcasting evidence shared amongst all, that is, amongst all of those who count socially and economically. This representation introduces "una normatividad para la percepción del mundo real. Desde este punto de vista, el realismo es uno de los mayores logros de la burguesia, en tanto lógica universal de la representación capaz de apuntalar la reprodución de su poder simbólico."[144] The effect is to naturalize a unique vision, which is thereafter reinforced in popular films, resulting in a generalized bourgeois vision of the world, aiming through technology and science to offer the truth of detail as an expression of progress related to well-being. Realism thereby presents the rejection of its aesthetics as folkloric, delirious or mythical, which is well paired with the non-recognition of otherness and with the dominance of the barbarism/civilization paradigm. The latter focuses on the monism of hegemony as a positive term; the bourgeois realistic world of European origin claims to be based on facts and clarity. Yet, realism in the context of the 21st century is no longer that of the rise of the national bourgeoisie. It has transformed itself for example into hyperrealism like in Colville's paintings, where everything looks important and thus almost magic, because unwarranted.

Going back to Jin Mee Yoon, we understand that the national story linking territory and identity ("O Canada! Our home and native land!") becomes vague, because the context is no longer homogenous but colourful. What story is then told from these paintings of Jin Mee Yoon! Which story can we believe to be true or conclusive? This is the question that Yann Martel also asks in *Life of Pi*, using stories told by Piscine Patel to two Japanese representatives of an insurance company. They are not able to say which story is true: did Pi eat his mother on a raft, or did he survive with a tiger on a raft in the middle of the ocean after the shipwreck? This is also Dany Laferrière's approach in *Je suis un écrivain japonais* (2008). Laferrière says that when a Japanese reads his work, he becomes a Japanese writer. This shows that the meanings produced by his text are related to the hermeneutic abilities generated by Japanese culture—its myths, its evidence, its stereotypes and its historical and communal stories. Incidentally, this is affirmed by Edwidge Danticat: "Even without globalization, the writer bound to the reader, under diabolic, or even joyful circumstances inevitably becomes a loyal citizen of the country of his readers."[145]

Henceforth, otherness (particularly that of the readers) has its input in works, texts and discourses. As we have seen in the discussion dealing with interculturalism, this requires that accommodations take the communities into account: settled for a long time, they have things to say and values to be recognized, as Charles Taylor[146] recalls. The long-established communities like English Canadians and "old stock" Quebeckers likewise have to take newcomers, writers and others into account so that groups can communicate and actively take part in the creation of an ever-changing society. These various groups, however, tend to manage their relations with otherness in different and complex ways. We are far from the barbarism/civilization dualism, inscribed in a national story based on a homogenizing hegemony, imposing a unique reading dictated by a convention controlled by specialists centralizing the power of their knowledge. Henceforth, complexity is within us.

The Variegated Land: Where Is the Wind?

The relationship with the land as the basis of a cultural hermeneutic from textual and pictorial stereotypes is thereby questioned. This can lead to resentment, as evidenced in Rawi Hage's novel entitled *Cockroach* through the loss of the immigrant character's territorial connection. This resentment is however almost absent in Éric Dupont's novel *La logeuse*, even though the territorial legitimation contributing to the meaning of existence is strongly undermined, and even though the malaise relative to contemporary dynamics is definite. In Éric Dupont's novel, cultural and ideological struggles are shown through the portrayal of a domestic migrant, Rosa Ost, who moves from the oppressive militant Marxist nationalist modernity of her Gaspe village to the multiplicity of unexpected encounters in multi-ethnic Montreal in a chaotic post-liberal society.

Initially, the reader is informed that Karl Marx and Jeanne d'Arc are the two discursive models that dominate currents of thought governing the vision of identity embodied in MERDIQ (le Ministère pour l'épanouissement des régions désolées et isolées du Québec).[147] The goal of this organization is to achieve a socialist paradise in a Gaspe village, protecting local and national identities. The connection between Marxism and nationalism[148] is linked to an oppressive boredom and a repression based on a silent violence. However, reading about Rosa Ost's tribulations escaping the organization's reach is a lot of fun. MERDIQ, led by dogmatic politico-unionists, is thwarted by her quest for wind in Montreal. Her little Gaspe village, Notre-Dame-du-Cachalot, has a problem: the wind has suddenly stopped and it no longer shows the way to go (how and what to think), and the villagers are poisoned by deadly miasma. But in the city, Rosa quickly discovers that her new contemporary urban world "était un immense bordel dont elle était la tenancière."[149] From this point, the poles of local identity shorted-circuited by an unbridled liberalism are explored. First, in Notre-Dame-du-Cachalot, conventional and orthodox bureaucrats create a nationalist community and socialist paradise even while the socialist countries of the Soviet Union are being dismantled (the burlesque horrors of which are referenced by Montreal writer Elena Botchorichvili[150]). These bureaucrats organize a society wherein the individual and, in particular, the marginal who diverts from the norm, has no place: "Notre-Dame-du-Cachalot, malgré tous les mensonges qui circulent à son sujet, représente l'achèvement le plus méconnu du rêve politique socialiste d'inspiration marxiste."[151] It is to demonstrate the disinformation on which this dream is based (so to refute the lie), that pyramid-shaped tumuli, which are said to be tombs erected in the past by the natives, are found at the entrance of the village. Simultaneously, the narrator reveals a more primal ritual. Each time a villager expresses himself singularly, by means of a flowering Christmas mini-cactus placed to announce winter storms, for example, he is stoned by a delirious mob, which confounds causality and coincidence.[152] In doing so, a story of causality that establishes the victim's culpability (according to a known Girardian schema) is constructed. It is important to note here that the lynchers use excluded minorities such as Indigenous peoples as victims to serve their purposes.

In other words, the bureaucrats not only produce the archives but also their referents (the tumuli) as disinformation worthy of the most experienced dictatorships; the word "disappeared" hides criminal acts committed by the state, and the gulags are universally ignored. This socialist realism does not succeed in hiding its foundations, as can be seen on a sign at the entrance of the village: "Comprenez qu'en quittant le paradis dans lequel le MERDIQ vous avait généreusement donné la chance de naître, vous renoncez à la possibilité de rentrer chez vous sans goûter à l'opprobre et à la rancœur."[153] Later on in the novel, in Montreal, figures complementary to Marx appear in Quebec's evolution from the Quiet Revolution, alongside a quasi-diabolical Jeanne d'Arc embodying authoritarian catholic powers. These powers complement the facility with which the village submits to the Marxist community. Jeanne Joyal, the landlady who rents a room to Rosa Ost and to other immigrant women, is the reincarnation of Jeanne d'Arc. She reveals the imposture of the myth of Jeanne d'Arc to Rosa Ost, along with the imposture and repressive powers linked to catholic identities fostering a traditional nationalism. Moreover, she forces on Rosa and the other tenants a disastrous instruction about the history of Quebec's identity. Following the stereotyped narrative: "Le monde avait commencé avec et par Duplessis. S'ensuivit la liste des suspects habituels, le clergé étouffant, la bourgeoisie canadienne anglaise perfide et le milieu des affaires obnubilé par la recherche du profit."[154] Here, we are in search of the ideological and national purity embodied by Jeanne Joyal who refuses "d'inclure dans ses devoirs de mémoire, des souvenirs hors Québec."[155] This purity is based on the traditional Québécois view of the city as a place of perdition and the village as a civilized, protecting space, which is ironically evident in the Gaspe pronunciation of Rosa Ost. Indeed, in Rosa's mouth, the phoneme "k" is replaced by the phoneme "g." "Au village, on associait toute prononciation plus dure du 'k' à la ville de Montréal, donc à la perdition et à la trahison."[156] This local purity is helped by the historical convention anchored in Jeanne d'Arc's myth; driving out the English from the territory and recasting the consensus. We thereby see that for Jeanne Joyal, on the very subject of language, Rosa is a little barbaric, and to the Gaspe village, the city is a little barbaric. A dynamic of exclusion is in place which aims to reconfigure the values of the barbarism/civilization paradigm. In a more traditional framework, the city is barbaric, but in a more modern national Quebec, the city is where the Quiet Revolution happened bringing civilized urban modernity to Quebec. This barbarism/civilization confrontation, and the various perspectives that value one or the other pole of the paradigm differently within the regions of the Americas, foreshadow what Rosa will face in Montreal. Different cultures, especially those of newcomers, will once again reconfigure her life and allow her to divest herself of barbarism/civilization dualism.[157] In order to achieve this, she has to reject the stereotype of the Quiet Revolution valued by Jeanne Joyal. Rosa dares to retort to Jeanne that it has nothing in common with a revolution, and that it is more like a missed revolution. Rosa is able to express these thoughts because revolutionary theory and the hatred of profiteers have nourished her childhood in Notre-Dame-du-Cachalot. The consensus on the development of national identity as embodied by Jeanne Joyal (also known as Jeanne d'Arc) is questioned through the desire expressed by Rosa Ost to redefine the parameters of the Quebec Nation.[158] This redefinition is based on a contemporary point of view—to be open to others and to the world, as Gérard Bouchard called for in his book *Interculturalisme: un point de vue québecois* (2012). Indeed, by chance in Montreal, Rosa meets a colourful group of immigrant women from Eastern European countries formerly occupied by the Soviet Union. As they couldn't find rewarding employment, they decided to put on an erotic burlesque show called Lenin's Great-Granddaughters. They dance, shedding their clothing (red army uniforms) piece by piece, while crude males cheer wildly (and more). The revolution and its socioeconomic ideals having been swallowed by the gulags, the massacres and the fall of the Berlin Wall are recycled in a music-hall strip show creating a trance in dance. This total mockery touches every situation connected to patriotic and national allegiances: "Jasmine… entrait en scène déguisée en fille du Roy et, sur l'air du Ô Canada, dévoilait lentement la terre de ses aïeux… Au moment où elle enlevait l'ultime feuille d'érable qui couvrait son foyer et son droit, on entendait résonner les premières mesures de l'Internationale."[159]

Rosa gets on well with these young women whose creativity in extricating themselves from their precarious situations stems from their status as illegal immigrants. However, these immigrants try to help one another in a world subject to the delusions of corruption. Indeed, some of these dancers frequent the Butler Motor Hotel where Rosa works as an accountant regularly. She sees some of these dancers spending a few hours with clients, "des chanteurs, des hommes politiques, des juges, des journalists…"[160]

In other words, the much quoted "*Where is here?*" is questioned in a new and relevant way. The question to ask is rather "where do we stand?" This is highlighted by Cassandra, a graduate of HEC who "hustles"[161] because she has already worked as an accountant for a big Toronto company. She made good money for "faire passer pour des ventes de titres les montagnes d'argent qu'ils encaissaient à faire du trafic d'organes au tiers-monde."[162] She wanted to blow the whistle, she had to run away and ended up as a whore at the Butler Motor Hotel. She says, "les organes, vaut mieux les sucer que les vendre."[163] After this disturbingly humourous assertion, she adds: "Que les grosses légumes t'en donnent (de l'argent) pour cacher leurs crimes dans une firme de comptables à Toronto ou pour les faire jouir dans un hôtel minable de Montréal, c'est le même fric."[164]

It is impossible to live according to classified certitudes with respect to paradigms offering bases to stories legitimizing clear options, allowing one to define one's identity as a function of roots caracterized by effective and integrated values. In other words, it is impossible to be certain which side is civilized and which side is barbaric. Rosa and these young immigrant women are stuck in lives wavering between the gulag and the whorehouse. They are simultaneously familiar with nationalist Marxist linguistic/rhetorical disinformation, generator of massacres, and the mafia's criminal, numbered accounting disinformation. There is no such thing as a defined safe haven.

For Rosa, there is neither a place which could be a home, nor a narrative which could generate meaning. This is different from transnational allegoric novels in contemporary Mexico which tend to embody collective cultural practices beyond national identities. They recognize the local, the subaltern without taking refuge in the defense of the local or the national; Juan Villoro's *Arrecife*[165], for example, strongly criticizes neo-liberalism. These novels explore how the global destroys the local but with the goal to create new subaltern solidarities, such as in Álvaro Enrigue's *Vidas perpendiculars*.[166] This novel explores love as a transgressive force and focuses on a transnational affective perspective reaching the global and recognizing the multifaceted aspects of exclusion and domination. Hence, these novels engage in the recognition of other cultures inside and outside of Mexico. However, they also maintain the Latin American stereotype of failure (*fracaso*) as ground for reinvention and a counter-hegemonic dynamic aiming at reconfiguring power relationships. They propose hope and occasionally have a utopian flavour, something which is rejected by Laura Esquivel in *The Law of Love*.[167] As we will now see, for Rosa Ost an affective perspective is not considered because everybody is built by ideological narratives, which, in a situation of stress, tend to dominate ethic perspectives aiming at protecting those who are in a position of subalternity.

Finding a Niche in a Vacuum

What can provide anchorage, if not love of country or respect for values? Love for a loved one? Unfortunately, love is not in the cards. The story in this case is not one about rape, massacres, domination and a long learning curve leading to a better understanding of the other, but rather one about the exclusion in the form of expulsion, leading to death. Réjean, Rosa's attentive admirer, is a policeman who carries out a raid at the Butler Motor Hotel. He is looking for young women without a visa, aiming to deport them to their countries of origin. There, they will either work or die from despair. Shu-Misty, for example, who ends up working in a cannery in China, lets herself fall onto a conveyor belt and is cut to pieces by fish-processing blades. She returns to Canada in tin cans. Having witnessed Réjean's cold, wicked determination in his treatment of these women and coming to appreciate his belief in his own righteousness, Rosa is petrified with fear. She understands that Réjean acts according to a causal narrative that defines good and bad without worrying about the consequences. The belief in the values of law and order, and the way the policeman puts them into practice leads ultimately to death and terror: these values separate the self from the others, the interior from the exterior, and finally, civilization from barbarism. In performing what he considers to be his duties, Réjean thereby reveals his own profound cruelty. He is just a soulless bureaucrat following watchwords. Rosa leaves behind the moderate optimism that guided her. She realizes that under certain circumstances, anyone could send her to the gulag to face death and torture. Again, nothing holds together. What kind of world is this? she asks herself.

Yet, she has already suffered rejection: her friends had suddenly decided to gang up on Quebec and on Quebeckers' attitudes, onto which they projected numerous stereotypes: "Ils conduisent comme des fous! … Ils n'apprennent rien à l'école! Ils baragouinent une langue qu'ils veulent imposer à tout le monde !… Ils ne comprennent rien, à part le hockey et les frites!"[168] Rosa's friends thereby impulsively renew prejudices based on resentment. This concert of charges "adressées à tous par tous"[169] troubles Rosa, because although she knows nothing about hockey and she doesn't drive, she knows how to conduct herself. Collective resentment suddenly emerges in the rejection of otherness.[170] In this case, "the other" in Montreal is Rosa Ost, the Gaspe women who has already been rejected by contemporary urban stereotypes based on a cacophony of exclusive socioeconomic and cultural demands: "Partout on cherchait ce qu'elle n'était pas: bilingue, cinq ans d'expérience, minorité visible, etc."[171] But, in *La logeuse*, everyone in the city comes from somewhere else. They try to live, to adjust to a world that no longer relies on religious, ethic, linguistic and historic values or on any ideal: everything is reduced to illusions in an unrecognizable territoriality.

Refuge is only a temporary solution in this case. Even if the wind has returned to Notre-Dame-du-Cachalot, finally allowing the inhabitants to escape the noxious fumes of boredom, and even if the villagers no longer have to express themselves literally and die of boredom, it is nonetheless clear that finding the wind's direction is impossible. We go from a reading of the monosomic socioeconomic and cultural situation as performed by Jeanne Joyal—who is not able to extract any meaning from a tenant's story of a man turned into a toad[172]—to a world where all readings are possible, but are without a stable point of reference. The great stories of legitimization and the dualist paradigms that provide a foundation have proven to be dangerous disinformation. Everything then should be read in a cacophony of interpretations, as emphasized by the last sentence of the novel: "Un jour, il faut bien apprendre à compter."[173] This also means that it is important to be exclusively self-reliant: Rosa, in spite of a total collapse of values and failed social connections, has no taste for decadence.[174] She simply realizes that "tous les signes sont faux"[175] and that, in order to belong[176], she has to learn to find her voice, causing the least possible destruction in a knowledge-based society where encounters are in permanent transition, rather than looking for unique and hierarchically dominant meaning. Hence, Rawi Hage's main character affirms that "Nothing made any sense to me anymore. It was not that I was looking for a purpose and had been deceived, it was more that I had never *started* looking for one."[177]

The characters of Dupont and Hage are therefore forced to look for meanings exclusively in the short term. One important short-term objective is the preservation of their integrity, while trying to avoid Shu Misty's violent end. Territorial identity and the long term have become obsolete. What remains is to explore the benefits of the encounter and to become one with otherness, because what counts is the act of participation. Institutions are unsuccessful in providing the characters with a sense of security. They only provide the resources to create temporary solidarity. This is also evident in the work of

American Indian author, Sherman Alexie. His character meets with policemen at night: "'Well, where are you supposed to be?', he asked me, and I knew there were plenty of places I wanted to be, but none where I was supposed to be … I wanted to tell him I didn't really fit the profile of the country but I knew it would just get me into trouble."[178] Chicana-American writer Sandra Cisneros' character has a similar point of view: "I am going to tell you a story about a girl who didn't want to belong."[179]

In *La logeuse*, the trance-dance created by the strippers expresses the need for transcendence in a world where nothing holds together: people dissolve into the anonymity of systemic and bureaucratic demands in a generalized atmosphere of bureaucratic and economic corruption. This atmosphere works together with disinformation regarding murders committed under the influence of the Marxist ideologues of the small Gaspe village. Yes, all the indicators are false, a fact which Vaclav Havel illustrates in *Living in Truth*. From an ethical and sociocultural point of view, the essay analyzes the horrors experienced by people living under communist rule and taking part in its upkeep. *Living in Truth* is a critique of encounters between totalitarianism and economism. Vaclav Havel, following Aleksandr Solzhenitsyn in *The Gulag Archipelago*[180], comments on post-totalitarianism in Eastern European countries, examining the encounter between communist dictatorships and economism. He also undertakes a critique of the Western democratic world, where the irresponsible resign rather than face violent and anonymous authorities, and where people relish ordinary and comfortable consumption while turning a blind eye to genocidal regimes and to religious and state-supported terrorism. He calls for "a new experience of being, a renewed rootedness in the universe, and a newly grasped sense of 'higher responsibility' a new-found relationship to other people and to the human community."[181] This is all that Rosa aspires to, more or less confusedly, and is what is lacking in the people she encounters and the situations in which she finds herself. *La logeuse* is clearly the burlesque and critical expression of a hope for transcendence. We do not know where to find this transcendence (or even where to look), because the wind and a sense of eternity have been lost. Time passes inexorably without causal justification, as all causality relies on a dualism only aiming at determining who is good/who is bad, which leads to the worst moments of exclusion.

In this respect, Éric Dupont has joined a whole new literature of the Americas, alongside Laura Esquivel in Mexico and Camila Reimers in Ottawa. These writers explore permanent transitions: stories where the passage of time explored in new lives dominates any justificatory causality. In *Seulement attendre et regarder*, Elena Botchorichvili uses these temporalities to explore the relationships between newly arrived immigrants who have lost their sense of self and a purpose in life. Situated in Montreal, the short novel looks at the heart of relations between emigrants and people born in the province, asking: "Que savons-nous de l'amour des autres? Nous vivons tous comme si nous étions derrière le mur de Berlin."[182] Why? Perhaps because in soviet countries, the use of space and travel are strictly controlled; while in capitalist countries, time itself is controlled, as is proven by the numerous advertisements for luxury watches in fashionable magazines. As Jocelyne Saucier highlights in *Il pleuvait des oiseaux*, there is no access to that which is slow. In her novel, slowness is explored by old drop-outs. They are reborn to themselves in their cottages back in the woods. Slowness is also explored through reincarnation in *Self* by Yann Martel and in *The Law of Love* by Laura Esquivel, where reincarnation throws off the speed of the sequence from cause to stereotyped consequence. In *Seulement attendre et regarder*, slowness leads to the claim, "Nous c'est vous… vous c'est nous…"[183], like in *La Logeuse*, *Self* and *The Law of Love*. But this conclusion comes from individuals who have lived painful experiences. It is neither expressed by systems already in place nor by cultural and social environments which look rather noxious.

Notes

1. Francisco Bilbao, *El Evangelio Americano y paginas selectas* (Barcelona: Mauci, 1920 [1864]), 68. Our translation: "America lives in dualism. This dualism is made up of religious dogma and political ideals: Catholicism and the republic."
2. *Ibid*. Our translation: "The predominance of freedom like in the United States. There is no other solution. Let us seek one or the other but with faith we will be strong like Russia and like the United States."
3. Michel Maffesoli, *L'ombre de Dyonisos* (Paris: Méridien/Anthropos, 1982).
4. See the political influence of this bank in Canada. In the period of unrest that preceded the Revolt of the Patriots (1835–1837), the British lifted the veto on the creation of a second diocese in Quebec by the Holy See. Montreal became a diocesan seat in 1836, and starting in 1840, gave Bishop Bourget a platform to promote identity along more conservative lines. These compromises made by the English in Canada to strengthen their economic control doubled as a territorial compromise with the United States on a part of New Brunswick, north of Maine, where United States troops had entered in 1837. The British negotiator Alexander Baring (Lord Ashburton) was the president of the Baring Bank who handled the finances of the United States in England. Seven twelfths of the territory and four-fifths of the value of the disputed territory went to the United States, who chose not to exert military pressure to help the Patriots of 1838 (Stanley Bréhault

Ryerson, *Unequal Union* (New York: International Publisher, 1968), 224). It is important to remember too that in 1840, the Baring Bank imposed the Union of Canada, which the British Parliament voted for reluctantly. It was impossible to do otherwise, because Upper Canada could not repay its one-million-dollar debt to the Baring Bank without the help of Lower Canada.

5. Marcio Bahia, "Americanidad: towards the Mapping of a Concept," in *America's Worlds and the World's Americas/Les mondes des Amériques et les Amériques du monde*, collection des Amériques/The Americas Series/Colección de las Américas, eds. A. Chanady, G. Handley, and P. Imbert (Legas/University of Ottawa, vol. 5, 2006), 23–33.
6. Sergio Kokis, *Le pavillon des miroirs* (Montréal: XYZ, 1994), 78. Our translation: "All of the products he (the father) buys for his work have English names: Sylvania, General Electric, Westinghouse."
7. Marshall McLuhan, *Notes on the Media as Art Form* (Costa Madera, CA: Gingko Press, 2005), 13.
8. Tom Robbins, "How Do You Feel About America?", in *Wild Ducks Flying Backward* (New York: Bantam, 2005), 229.
9. Jerzy Kosinski, *Being There* (New York: Harcourt Brace Jovanovich, 1971).
10. Robbins, 228.
11. James Baldwin, "Notes for a Hypothetical Novel," *Nobody Knows My Name: More Notes of a Native Son* (New York: Dial Press, 1961).
12. Bill Schermbrucker, *Chameleon* (Vancouver: Talon Books, 1983), 53.
13. Esteban Echeverria, *El Matadero: La Cautiva* (Madrid: Catedra, 1986), 19. Our translation: "The evil afflicting the Republic of Argentina is its extension; the desert surrounds it from all sides and it creeps into its bowels: loneliness, lack of population and human habitation are usually unmistakable boundaries between provinces." This rhetoric is not completely lost, as evidenced by a hyperbolic subtitle in a recent article about Argentina: "Between the Buenos Aires area, urbanized and industrialized, and the rest of the country, desert and underdeveloped, there is nothing in common." *Géo*, avril 2002, p. 22. The Bertelsman multinational that publishes this magazine does not hesitate to use old stereotypes.
14. Jocelyne Saucier, *Il pleuvait des oiseaux* (Montréal: XYZ, 2011), 27. Our translation: "And with yet another great burst of laughter, accompanied by Charlie who had abandoned all restraint and laughed a hearty and loud laugh. The two old men took childish amusement in the idea of dealing a blow to the social workers of the world who want to lock up the old people in hospices."
15. Yvon Rivard, *Le siècle de Jeanne* (Montréal: Boréal, 2005), 287. Our translation: "And where, if not in Paris, can we conquer this wonderful land we inherited from the New World and that allows us to move freely among the others without wanting to compete with them, because a barbarian, must we be reminded, is not someone who flees others but someone trying to get closer to that part of himself that eludes him and which he sometimes finds in a tree or a face."
16. George Elliott Clarke, *Lush Dreams, Blue Exile, Fugitive Poems: 1978–1993* (Lawrencetown Beach, Nova Scotia: Pottersfield Press, 1994), 77.
17. Yvon Rivard, *Mort et naissance de Christophe Ulric* (Montréal: La Presse, 1976), 78. Our translation: "Where did the Indians come from before being savages?"

18. Robbins, 228.
19. Rivard, *Le siècle de Jeanne*, 94. Our translation: "because only beings, places and lost and found things are real."
20. Tomson Highway, *Comparing Mythologies* (Ottawa: University of Ottawa Press, 2003).
21. Rivard, Le *Siècle de Jeanne*, 291. Our translation: "The New World it is of course also made up of bodies, shop windows, goods, a world of new rich who no longer remember their poverty, a world of poor who dream only of being rich."
22. Daniel Mato, "Sobre la fetichización de la globalización y las dificultades que plantea para el estudio de las transformaciones sociales contemporaneas," *Revista venezolana de analísis de coyuntura* 5.1 (janvier-juin 1999): 139. Our translation: "Because if we abandon this, lots of things will be lost in the Indigenous zones, first botany, wild fauna, the biosphere, biodiversity, the environment [...]."
23. *American Consumer* (Trinity: Flat Back Publishing, 2005).
24. Harrod Blank, *Art Cars* (New York: Lark Books, 2002), 117.
25. Alejo Carpentier, *Le partage des eaux* (Paris: Gallimard, 1976).
26. See Margaret Atwood, *Survival: A Thematic Guide to Canadian Literature* (Toronto: Anansi, 1972), 46.
27. Rivard, *Le siècle de Jeanne*, 92. Our translation: "This wonderful territory we have inherited from the New World and that allows us to travel freely among the others without wanting to compete with them..."
28. Andrés Neuman, *El viajero del siglo* (Madrid: Alfaguara, 2009), 417. Our translation: "According to Kant, says Sophie, killing a bastard son is less serious than an infidelity... He says that the most logical approach would be to ignore the existence of this son because, legally, he shouldn't have existed."
29. Marthe Robert, *Roman des origines et origines du roman* (Paris: Gallimard, 1972).
30. Our translation: "In Québec, we are all descendants of women who are orphans".
31. Marcos Aguinis, *La gesta del Marrano* (Buenos Aires: Planeta, 1991), 18. Our translation: "What need is there to teach history, arithmetic, geography and grammar in this desert of Christianity?"
32. *Ibid.*, 80. Our translation: "Here we are not in Madrid or in Rome. We live on a miserable earth, full of infidels and sins. Nobody has a library; that would be an eccentricity."
33. Lelia Area, *Una biblioteca para leer la Nación* (Rosario, Argentina: Beatriz Viterbo editora, 2006).
34. In her book entitled *Entre inclusion et exclusion. La symbolisation de l'autre dans les Amériques* (Paris: Champion, 1999), Amaryll Chanady criticizes the fact that, in an article published in 1992 by Michel Tétu, the sterility linked to the mule is still used to qualify the concept of hybridity. See Michel Tétu, "L'opposition hybridité/métissage et patrie/nation dans le contexte pluriculturel du Canada," in *Métamorphoses d'une utopie*, eds. Jean-Michel Lacroix and Fulvio Caccia (Paris: Presses de la Sorbonne Nouvelle/Éditions Tryptique, 1992), 157.
35. Aguinis, *La gesta del Marrano*, 48. Our translation: "This is an intruder species because it did not appear on the fifth day of creation, as have the other animals. It appeared much later, when a donkey, instead of coupling with a female of its species, did it with a mare. Is it wrong? I think it's wrong."

36. Denis Bertrand and André Lavallé (eds.), *Le Rapport Durham* (Montréal: Les Éditions Sainte-Marie, 1969), 17. Our translation: "They are a people without history and without literature."
37. Théodore Pavie, *Souvenirs atlantiques* (Paris: Robert, 1838, vol. 1), 163. Our translation: "[…] (on the northwest side of Montreal) there are only wild forests, black and blue hills like the firmament, oceans of wood, deserts, plains like the steppes of Asia, the sands of Arabia; then it all sinks and disappears in the west, lost in the frozen pole."
38. Philippe Aubert de Gaspé, *L'influence d'un livre* (LaSalle: Hurtubise, 1984 [1837]), 74. Our translation: "[…] Near the Baie-Saint-Paul, the Cap au Corbeau. This cape has something majestic and mournful. At a distance it could be taken for one of those immense tombs thrown in the middle of the deserts of Egypt by the foolish vanity of some puny mortal."
39. For Jocelyne Saucier, in *Il pleuvait des oiseaux*, the forest is a haven for the contemporary nomads, the *dropouts* who reject imprisonment by bureaucracy, health regulations and the police. This evasion of the codes of modernity is also reflected in a playful contrast between indigenous discourses and the discourse of European origin in Nancy Huston and Jacqueline Salmon's *In Deo* (Montréal: Silence, 1997).
40. This rhetoric can even be found more recently. In the book by Pierre Nepveu entitled *Intérieurs du Nouveau Monde*, one can read the following sentence linked to a comparison between small cities and regions in Québec with Montréal: "ces lieux limitrophes…là où la québécitude s'effrite dans le Sahel du bilinguisme … ." ("these spaces at the limit… where Quebec identity crumbles in the Sahel of bilingualism…"). What is the reason for using the comparison with the desert of Africa (Sahel) except for the influence of a canonic and outdated rhetoric?
41. W. L. Morton, *The Canadian Identity* (Madison/Toronto: The University of Wisconsin Press/The University of Toronto Press, 1964), 239.
42. Laure Conan, *Angéline de Montbrun* (Québec: Léger Brousseau, 1884).
43. Jean Simard, *Mon fils pourtant heureux* (Ottawa: Cercle du livre de France, 1956), 46. Our translation: "But 'noblesse oblige.'"
44. Adrienne Choquette, *Laure Clouet* (Québec: Institut littéraire du Québec, 1961), 49. Our translation: "She did not fail to remember that 'noblesse oblige.'"
45. Jacques Godbout, *L'Aquarium* (Paris: Seuil, 1962), 49. Our translation: "We … live with such nobility in such grandeur, don't we?"
46. Itamar Even-Zohar, "The Role of Literature in the Making of the Nations of Europe: A Socio-Semiotic Examination," AS/SA 1 (1996): 1–20, http://www.epas.utoronto.ca :8080/french/as-sa/ASSA/-No1/IEZ1.html
47. See Lelia Area, *Una biblioteca para leer la Nación*.
48. Amartya Sen, *Identité et violence* (Paris: Odile Jacob, 2001).
49. Pico Iyer, *The Global Soul* (New York: Vintage, 2000), 17.
50. Schermbrucker, *Chameleon*.
51. Gérard Bouchard, *Making of the Nations and Cultures of the New World: an Essay in Comparative History*, translated into English by Michelle Weinroth and Paul Leduc (Montréal: McGill-Queen's University Press, 2008), 314.
52. Réjean Ducharme, *L'Avalée des avalés* (Paris: Gallimard, 1966).
53. Quoted by Bouchard, *Making of the Nations and Cultures of the New World*, 313.

54. Pico Iyer, *Imagining Canada: An Outsider's Hope for a Global Future* (Toronto: The Hart House Lecture, 2001), 56
55. See *Territorio de Zaguates* (Consulted on September 20th, 2013) http://www.upworthy.com
56. Alfred P. Schultz, *Race or Mongrel* (Boston: L. C. Page & company, 1908). Here is the content summary: "A brief history of the rise and fall of the ancient races of earth: a theory that the fall of nations is due to intermarriage with alien stocks: a demonstration that a nation's strength is due to racial purity: a prophecy that America will sink to early decay unless immigration is rigorously restricted."
57. Professor and Mrs. Louis Agassiz, *Journey in Brazil* (Boston: Ticknor and Fields, 1869).
58. For racism and scientific discourse, see: *Le discours scientifique comme porteur de préjugés?/ Scientific Discourse as Prejudice-Carrier?*, eds. Alain Goldschläger and Clive Thomson (London, Ontario: The University of Western, Mestengo Press, 1998).
59. Marthe Robert, *Roman des origines et origines du roman*, 53.
60. Amélie Maxwell, "Le mythe américain du self-made man dans les littératures francophones du Canada: apprivoiser le changement en s'approvisionnant de déplacements," in *Américanité, cultures francophones canadiennes et société des savoirs: Le Canada et les Amériques*, ed. P. Imbert (Ottawa: Éditions Chaire de l'Université d'Ottawa: Canada: Enjeux sociaux et culturels dans une société du savoir, 2009), 111–42.
61. See in Michael Aaron Rockland, *Sarmiento's Travels in the United States in 1847* (Princeton: Princeton University Press, 1970).
62. Amy Tan, *The Joy Luck Club* (New York: G. P. Putnam, 1989), 56.
63. Dany Laferrière, *Cette grenade dans la main du jeune Nègre est-elle une arme ou un fruit* (Montréal: VLB, 1983).
64. Alain Savary, *Le grand détour pour traverser la rue* (Ottawa: L'Interligne, 2019).
65. Henry Miller, *Le cauchemar climatisé* (Paris: Livre de poche, 1986).
66. Tom Wolfe, *The Electric Kool-Aid Acid Test* (New York: Farrar, Straus and Giroux, 1968).
67. Hunter S. Thompson, *Fear and Loathing in Las Vegas: A Savage Journey to the Heart of the American Dream* (New York: Vintage, 1998).
68. For a different approach of the modern world, see the comparison between Sergio Kokis and P.K. Page in Adina Balint, "Identités transmigrantes: Sergio Kokis et P.K. Page," *Envisager les rencontres transculturelles Canada-Brésil*, eds. Zila Bernd and Patrick Imbert (Québec: Presses de l'Université Laval, 2015), 177–96.
69. *Gazeta Mercantil*, Thursday, November 11, 1999, p. A3. Our translation: "Love and hate in international trade."
70. A similar situation is found in Argentina; the media highlight the fact that children are dying from hunger while the country produces food for export.
71. John von Neumann and Oskar Morgenstern, *Theory of Games and Economic Behavior* (Princeton: Princeton University Press, 1944). According to von Neumann and Morgenstern, a game is zero-sum when the players' interests are completely opposed; like in chess, for example. On the other hand, games which lead to a win for all players (i.e.,: to the creation of wealth), are non-zero-sum games.
72. George Woodcock, "Gabriel Dumont, the Forgotten Hero," *Saturday Night*, 88 (July 1973): 7.

73. Françoise Marcel, *42 ans de service* (Montréal: éditions québécoises-éditions vert blanc rouge (no date)), 90. Our translation: "The fist—holding tight—the black flag—always flying—we move forward—in time—alone or among comrades—persevering—fighting to the end."
74. Mavis Gallant, *Home Truths: Selected Canadian Stories* (Toronto: Macmillan, 1981), XVIII.
75. Jean-Charles Harvey, *L'homme qui va* (Québec: Le Soleil, 1929), 184. Our translation: "Before being French, English, German, Russian, Japanese, Chinese, American or Brazillian, we are people."
76. William Arthur Deacon, *Pens and Pirates* (Toronto: Ryerson, 1923), 33.
77. Claude Gauvreau, "L'esthétique: question de propagande," *Le Haut-parleur*, January 14th (1951): 5. Our translation: "Let's accept the multiplicity of differences as being natural and beneficent; racists and nationalists are hatemongers."
78. Paul-Émile Borduas, "Lettres à Claude Gauvreau," in *Liberté* 4.22 (1962): 249. Our translation: "There's no question of nationalism. I loathe them all."
79. Ducharme, *L'Avalée des avalés*, 300. Our translation: "A true Indigenous person, if I understand correctly, is an individual who is born in a tomb; he moves a little, no more than a root, bending this way, bending that way, until he no longer bends at all."
80. *Ibid.*, 296. Our translation: "Fighting for a country means fighting for a cradle and a coffin; this is ridiculous and wrong, it smells like a rotten excuse. The only logical fight is a fight against all."
81. *Ibid.*, 91. Our translation: "Why should I shut myself in with them in one of those hovels full to bursting with cigarette smoke called countries?"
82. Réjean Ducharme, *L'Océantume* (Paris: Gallimard, 1968), 94. Our translation: "They assumed the right to divide the land like a pie into supposedly equal pieces and to lock you into the part they decided was yours."
83. Mavis Gallant, *Home Truths: Selected Canadian Stories*, XVI.
84. Michael Ondaatje, *The English Patient* (New York: Vintage Books, 1992).
85. Iyer, *Imagining Canada*, 12.
86. *Ibid.*
87. Ondaatje, *The English Patient*, 12.
88. Antonio d'Alfonso, *In Italics: In Defence of Ethnicity* (Toronto: Guernica, 1996), 143.
89. Nathalie Petrowski, "Peter Doig," La Presse+Arts, Saturday, January 11th, 2014. Application for iPad. Our translation: "he felt like he was nowhere and at home simultaneously."
90. Édouard Glissant, *Introduction à une poétique du divers* (Paris: Gallimard, 1996).
91. His perspectives are resumed and popularized in different ways by Vincent Cespedes, *Mélangeons-nous. Enquête sur l'alchimie humaine* (Paris: Maren Sell, 2006), 42. Our translation: "Thereby, a truly vibrant existence is a continuous mixing, a sequence of identification and misidentification, of transportation and transformation, of external contribution and internal reorganization: It is mixture."
92. Iyer, *Imagining Canada*, 34.
93. Anne Michaels, *Fugitive Pieces* (Toronto: McClelland and Stewart, 1996), 161.
94. *Ibid.*, 160.

95. René Girard, *Le bouc émissaire* (Paris: Grasset, 1982), 33. Our translation: "There is a cross cultural process of collective violence ... This means that crises and victim-based solutions always develop in the same manner."
96. Richard Wright, *Black Boy* (New York: Harper and Row, 1937).
97. Milan Kundera, *L'Art du roman: essai* (Paris: Gallimard, 1986).
98. See also that references to reincarnation or after-life, as in Bernard Werber's *Les Thanatonautes*, about the New World (Australia in this case): "You have been given a new continent to explore. You must embrace thus the state of mind of the 16th century pioneers. They ignored the existence of a territory East of Indonesia. Those who would have mentioned it would have been considered as harmless madmen in the same way you consider nonsense the statements of the President... You just have to baptize your country of dead 'The New Australia' and embrace then an explorer's mentality." (Paris: A. Michel, 1994), 63.
99. Gore Vidal, *Myra Breckinridge: Myron* (New York: Random House, 1986).
100. As we will see later on, there is an important difference between a narrative based on the temporal causal, producing a certain amount of suspense, determining who is bad and defining the truth, and a narrative exploring the effects of encounters.
101. Camila Reimers, *Tres lotos en un mar de fuego* (Ottawa: Mapalé Publishing, 2006), 91.
102. Emmanuel Lévinas, *Totalité et infinité: essai sur l'extériorité* (La Haye: Nijhoff, 1961). See also, on the subject of the self in the other and the other in the self: Carlos Fuentes, *Cristóbal monato* (Mexico: Fundo de Cultura Económica, 1987), 546. "El otro soy yo porque me completa." Our translation: "I am the other because he completes me."
103. René Girard, *Des choses cachées depuis la fondation du monde* (Paris: Livre de poche, 1978), 317. Our translation: "The victim has to reach us at the very moment he is silenced by violence."
104. Reimers, *Tres lotos en un mar de fuego*, 102.
105. For example, the plausible in *Le Cid* by Corneille is activated by every chivalric romance related to the aristocracy. With Balzac, the plausible is constructed from economic relationships in an urban banking and industrial setting, which is in a process of rapid development.
106. Antonio d'Alfonso, *In Italics: In Defence of Ethnicity*.
107. Atwood, *Survival*, 35.
108. Roch Carrier, *La guerre, Yes Sir* (Montréal: Éditions du Jour, 1968).
109. Atwood, *Survival*, 222.
110. Claude-Henri Grignon, "Qu'avez-vous à dire aux étudiants ?", in *Les pamphlets de Valdombre* (March-April 1942): 39. Our translation: "Our fathers...threw us into trade, into industry, into the so-called liberal professions, where we live in eternal defeat because we lack capital. We had the richest capital of all: the earth. You will realize after the war. We lost it. And today we are lost in the foreign masses."
111. Rima Elkouri, "Les traits métissés, l'accent québécois," *La Presse* (Saturday, April 1st, 2000), B1. Our translation: "Facial features of mixed descent and a Quebec accent" "Valérie, Annie and Marie-France Lemaine, born in Montreal from a Quebec mother and a Haitian father, feel like strangers sometimes in the eyes of others."
112. Gratien Gélinas, "Du patriotisme ça?", *L'Action nationale* 5 (1935): 292–93. Our translation: "Are we promoting the French language? No doubt, to the point where in a few

years, Jews, for example, who are adept, will have learnt our language and thanked us for our services. And the public will never know the difference; they will even be proud that Jews can speak the language of Dollard des Ormeaux."

113. Mark Kingwell, *The World We Want* (New York: Viking, 2000), 12.
114. José Antonio Giménez Micó, "Latin-Americanizing Canada," in *Canadian Cultural Exchange/Échanges culturels au Canada: Translation and Transculturation/traduction et transculturation*, ed. Norman Cheadle (Waterloo, Ontario: Wilfrid Laurier University Press, 2007), 1–15.
115. Louise Leduc, "Le Dr. Yves Lamontagne tire sa révérence," *La Presse* (Monday, October 4th, 2010) : A7.
116. Atwood, *Survival*, 46.
117. Northrop Frye, "Canada: New World without Revolution," in *Divisions on a Ground: Essays on Canadian Culture*, ed. J. Palk (Toronto: Anansi, 1982), 176.
118. *Ibid.*, 174.
119. Rawi Hage, *Cockroach* (New York: W. W. Norton and Company, 2010), 9.
120. Henfil, *Diário de um cucaracha* (São Paulo: Record, 1987).
121. Franz Kafka, *The Metamorphosis* (New York: Bantam, 1972).
122. Seema Ahluwalia, "Exploiter la générosité et entretenir l'ignorance: Ô Canada, terre de nos aïeux," in *Canadian Issues/Thèmes canadiens, Les relations autochtones immigrants aujourd'hui* (summer 2012): 48. Our translation: "Canadians are thus confronted with an uncomfortable contradiction between their democratic, liberal values and the racism and colonization that are part of our society."
123. Ian Adams, "The lonely death of Chanie Wenjack," *MacLeans magazine* (February 1st, 1967), 37–45.
124. Réjean Ducharme, *L'Hiver de force* (Paris: Gallimard, 1973), 162. Our translation: "An enlightened tyrant is what we need in Quebec."
125. Ibid, 192. Our translation: "It is Louis Caron, representing the superiority of the joual race ... he wears a plumed headband and is known as Dreaming Racoon, spreading the theory that joual is a savage language, and therefore Indian."
126. Ibid, 143. Our translation: "[...] these terrible words, the only ones that anybody can write anywhere without fault: I WAS HERE!"
127. Stephen Leacock, "Common Sense and the Universe," in *Last Leaves* (Toronto: McClelland and Stewart, 1945), 46.
128. *Ibid.*
129. Éric Dupont, *La logeuse* (Montréal: Marchand de feuilles, 2006).
130. Atwood, *Survival*, 17–18.
131. Patrice Desbiens, *L'homme invisible/The Invisible Man* (Sudbury, Ontario: Prise de parole, 1997).
132. Ralph Ellison, *The Invisible Man* (New York: Random House, 1952).
133. The Truth and Reconciliation Commission was founded in 2008. Seema Ahluwalia, "Exploiter la générosité et entretenir l'ignorance: Ô Canada, terre de nos aïeux," 50. Our translation: "Where is the government leadership, resources and encouragement when the time comes to hear the testimony of Canadian colonizers about domination, violence, racism and indifference towards human suffering? When will Canadians recognize their

crimes against humanity so that we can begin the healing process with respect to the oppressive behaviour they continue to adopt with regard to the Indigenous peoples?"

134. Our translation: "Punch."
135. José Vasconcelos, *The Cosmic Race* (Baltimore: John Hopkins, 1997), 17.
136. More on this subject in: Afef Benessaieh and Patrick Imbert, "De Bouchard-Taylor à l'Unesco: ambivalences interculturelles et clarifications transculturelles," in *Canadian Studies: The State of the Art/Études canadiennes: questions de recherche*, Canadiana 10, eds. Klaus-Dieter Ertler, Steward Gill, Susan Hodgett, and Patrick James (Frankfurt: Peter Lang, 2011), 393–413.
137. Simon Nadeau, *L'Autre modernité* (Montréal: Boréal, 2013), 197. "This recovered sovereignty is that of the 'emancipated provincial' who uses his difference as a double-edged weapon: on one side, he cuts the community link that holds the individual in the trap of an unquestioned and forced social contract (which pretends to impersonate the nature of society); on the other hand, this gap is used to stay free of universal models of emancipation which are often only a new way to trap individuals from more developed societies into new social molds, halting, in this way, what is irreducible and unassimilable in individuals, the most savage and, at the same time the most significant in each, the place where the self is left alone to be himself."
138. Clarence Gagnon was born November 8, 1881 and died January 5, 1942.
139. Sarah Phillips Casteel, *Second Arrivals: Landscape and Belonging in Contemporary Writing of the Americas* (Charlottesville: University of Virginia Press, 2007).
140. Lucy Maud Montgomery, *Anne of Green Gables* (Toronto: McGraw-Hill Ryerson, 1968).
141. Sarah Phillips Casteel, *Second Arrivals: Landscape and Belonging in Contemporary Writing of the Americas*, 102.
142. Jésus Martín Barbero, "Globalizacion comunicacional y descentramiento cultural," in *La dinámica global/local*, Rubens Bayardo y Monica Lacarrieu (comp.) (Buenos Aires: Ciccus, 1999), 44.
143. Susana Vellegia, "Imagenes e imaginarios en la tension local/global," in *La dinámica global/local*, Rubens Bayardo y Monica Lacarrieu (comp.) (Buenos Aires: Ciccus, 1999), 235.
144. Ibid, 235. Our translation: "[…] a standardization of the perception of the real world. From this point of view, realism is one of the greatest successes of the bourgeoisie, as a universal representational logic able to support the reproduction of its own symbolic power."
145. Edwige Danticat, *Create dangerously* (Princeton: Princeton University Press, 2010), 15.
146. Charles Taylor, *Multiculturalism: Examining the Politics of Recognition* (Princeton: Princeton University Press, 1994).
147. Our translation: QRAPI (Quebec Regional Advancement for the Poor and Isolated). The translation does not explain everything because in French MERDIQ—though spelled *merdique*—means shitty.
148. See on this subject: George Orwell, *Notes on Nationalism* (London: Polemic, May 1945). [On line] [www.george-orwell.org/Notes_on_Nationalism/0.html (22/12/2012)].
149. Éric Dupont, *La logeuse*, 262. Our translation: "was an immense whorehouse of which she was the proprietress."
150. Elena Botchorichvili, *Sovki* (Montréal: Boréal, 2008).
151. Dupont, *La logeuse*, 12. Our translation: "In spite of all the lies circulating about it, Notre-Dame-du-Cachalot represents the least known achievement of the socialist political dream of Marxist inspiration."

152. *Ibid.*, 15. The words of W. L. Morton, fascinated by the Northern influence, are pertinent. He highlights that English Canadians, like the French Canadians, share certain tastes and conventions because of their northern location, especially "the cultivation of the African violet and the dwarf cactus." See: W. L. Morton, "The North in Canadian Historiography," in *Contexts of Canada's Past: Selected Essays of W. L. Morton*, ed. A. B. McKillop (Toronto/Ottawa: Macmillan/Carleton University Press, 1980), 237.
153. Dupont, *La logeuse*, 48. Our translation: "Understand that by leaving the paradise in which MERDIQ generously gave you the chance to be born, you give up the possibility of going home without tasting disgrace and bitterness."
154. *Ibid.*, 118. Our translation: "The world began with and by Duplessis. The list of usual suspects follows: the stifling clergy, the perfidious English Canadian bourgeoisie and the business community obsessed by the quest for profit."
155. *Ibid.*, 209. Our translation: "to include in her duties of memory, recollections from outside Quebec."
156. *Ibid.*, 26. Our translation: "thus to perdition and to treason."
157. This is relative in spite everything, because immigrants often see the Canadian city as civilized compared to the place where they came from. This is apparent for an immigrant from Costa Rica in Montreal in Monique Proulx's novel *Les aurores montréales* (Montréal: Boréal, 1996), 9: "If you see those shops, Manu, they have shops that you would call villages, just more civil and better stocked…" It is not certain that Monique Proulx could still write this in 2014, because for several years, the commercial centres of Costa Rica, especially in the district of Escazu in San José, are at least the equal of Montreal's commercial centres.
158. This is what happens in Laura Esquivel's *The Law of Love*. She reorganizes the religious history of the Mexican State as a function of the present, masking its process of exclusion under a progressive image by enlisting Marxist artists like Diego Rivera. Laura Esquivel thereby unblocks a national vision of Mexico different from the one proposed by modern schools of thought. She is open to all, especially to those who have always been excluded by the nationalist Mexican state, the Indigenous peoples.
159. Dupont, *La logeuse*, 82. Our translation: "Jasmine… entered the scene disguised as a fille du Roy and, to the tune of O Canada, slowly unveiled the land of her ancestors… The moment she took off the last maple leaf that was covering her home and native land, the first measures of *L'Internationale* could be heard …"
160. *Ibid.*, 69. Our translation: "singers, politicians, judges, journalists."
161. *Ibid.*, 102.
162. See also Matthew Little, "Des députés fédéraux se penchent sur un commerce horrible: Un sous-comité fait le point sur les prélèvements d'organes en Chine," Époque Times, (February 18 to March 3, 2013): 4. Our translation: "pass off the money they made by organ trafficking in the third world as property sales."
163. Dupont, *La logeuse*, 103. Our translation: "it is better to suck organs than to sell them."
164. *Ibid.*, 103. Our translation: "Either whether the bigwigs give you (money) to hide their crimes in an accounting firm in Toronto or to make them come in a lousy hotel in Montreal, it is the same dough."
165. Juan Villoro, *Arrecife* (Barcelona: Anagrama, 2012). It is worth noting that a pyramid, as in Éric Dupont's *La logeuse*, becomes a narrative pole of attraction.

166. Álvaro Enrigue, *Vidas perpendiculares* (Barcelona: Anagrama, 2008).
167. Laura Esquivel, *The Law of Love* (New York: Crown, 1996).
168. Dupont, *La logeuse*, 202. Our translation: "They drive like maniacs! ... They don't learn anything at school! They garble a language they want to force on everybody! ... All they understand is hockey and poutine fries!"
169. *Ibid.*, 203. Our translation: "addressed to all by all."
170. A similar expression of the Costa Ricans' rejection of Nicaraguans appears in Petronio Marcenaro's *Al otro lado del San Juan* (San José: editorial Costa Rica, 2007), 83: "Ah, los nicas! Dicen que en Nicaragua el que no es poeta es hijo de pueta... la poesia les sale regular, porque para nada más sirven." Our translation: "Ah, the Nicaraguans! They say in Nicaragua that he who is not a poet is the son of a poet (son of a bitch; a reference to a play on words using 'son of a bitch' and 'son of a poet') ... poetry comes out all by itself from them, as they have no other use."
171. Dupont, *La logeuse*, 61. Our translation: "Everywhere she went, they were looking for what she was not: bilingual, five years of experience, visible minority, etc."
172. *Ibid.*, 164–67.
173. *Ibid.*, 298. Our translation: "One day, we must learn to count."
174. *Ibid.*, 233.
175. *Ibid.*, 218. Our translation: "all the signs are fake."
176. This is different from Kim Thúy's experience while still bound by Vietnamese tradition, before integrating her knowledge from Quebec and Canada: "One day I wrote to a man: 'I want to be owned by you.' I was born at the wrong time... In this place, I could kneel in front of men, vanish behind their shadow without shaming the females, because it was a game, only a game, a moment of rest before returning to the everyday, to our common fragility." Kim Thúy and Pascal Janovjak, *À toi* (Montréal: Libre expression, 2011), 67.
177. Rawi Hage, *Cockroach*, 32.
178. Sherman Alexie, *The Lone Ranger and Tonto Fistfight in Heaven* (New York: Atlantic Monthly Press, 1993), 24.
179. Sandra Cisneros, *The House on Mango Street* (New York: Vintage, 1991), 89.
180. Aleksandr Solzhenitsyn, *The Gulag Archipelago* (New York: Harper and Row, 1973).
181. Vaclav Havel, *Living in Truth* (London/Boston: Faber and Faber, 1989), 118.
182. Elena Botchorichvili, *Seulement attendre et regarder* (Montréal: Boréal, 2012), 98. Our translation: "What do we know about others' loving the other? We are all living as if we were behind the Berlin wall."
183. *Ibid.*, 89. Our translation: "We are you... you are us."

Bibliography

Adams, Ian. "The lonely death of Chanie Wenjack." *MacLeans Magazine* (February 1st, 1967), 37–45.

Agassiz, Prof. Louis and Mrs. Louis. *Journey in Brazil*. Boston: Ticknor and Fields, 1869.

Aguinis, Marcos. *La gesta del Marrano*. Buenos Aires: Planeta, 1991.

Ahluwalia, Seema. "Exploiter la générosité et entretenir l'ignorance: Ô Canada, terre de nos aïeux." In *Canadian Issues/Thèmes canadiens, Les relations autochtones immigrants aujourd'hui* (summer 2012): 46–52.

Alexie, Sherman. *The Lone Ranger and Tonto Fistfight in Heaven*. New York: Atlantic Monthly Press, 1993.

American Consumer. Trinity: Flat Back Publishing, 2005.

Area, Lelia. *Una biblioteca para leer la Nación*. Rosario, Argentina: Beatriz Viterbo editora, 2006.

Atwood, Margaret. *Survival: A Thematic Guide to Canadian Literature*. Toronto: Anansi, 1972.

Aubert de Gaspé, Philippe, (fils). *L'influence d'un livre*. Ville LaSalle: Hurtubise, 1984 [1837].

Bahia, Marcio, "Americanidad: towards the Mapping of a Concept", in *America's Worlds and the World's Americas/Les mondes des Amériques et les Amériques du monde*, collection des Amériques/The Americas Series/Colección de las Américas, eds. A. Chanady, G. Handley and P. Imbert. Legas/Université d'Ottawa, vol. 5, 2006. 23–33.

Baldwin, James. "Notes for a Hypothetical Novel." *Nobody Knows My Name: More Notes of a Native Son*. New York: Dial Press, 1961.

Balint, Adina. "Identités transmigrantes: Sergio Kokis et P. K. Page." In *Envisager les rencontres transculturelles Canada-Brésil*. Eds. Zila Bernd and Patrick Imbert. Québec: Presses de l'Université Laval (2015), 177–96.

Barbero, Jésus Martín. "Globalización comunicacional y descentramiento cultural." In *La dinámica global/local*, Rubens Bayardo y Monica Lacarrieu (comp.). Buenos Aires: Ciccus, 1999: 27–49.

Benessaieh, Afef, and Patrick Imbert. "De Bouchard-Taylor à l'Unesco: ambivalences interculturelles et clarifications transculturelles." In *Canadian Studies: The State of the Art/Études canadiennes: questions de recherche*, Canadiana 10. Eds. Klaus-Dieter Ertler, Stewart Gill, Susan Hodgett, and Patrick James. Frankfurt: Peter Lang, 2011. 393–413.

Bilbao, Francisco. *El Evangelio Americano y paginas selectas*. Barcelona: Mauci, 1920 [1864].

Blank, Harrod. *Art Cars*. New York: Lark Books, 2002.

Borduas, Paul-Émile. "Lettres à Claude Gauvreau." *Liberté*, vol. 4, no. 22 (1962): 230–51.

Botchorichvili, Elena. *Seulement attendre et regarder*. Montréal: Boréal, 2012.

———. *Sovki*. Montréal: Boréal, 2008.

Bouchard, Gérard. *Making of the Nations and Cultures of the New World: An Essay in Comparative History*. Translated into English by Michelle Weinroth and Paul Leduc. Montréal: McGill-Queen's University Press, 2008.

Bréhault-Ryerson, Stanley. *Unequal Union*. New York: International Publisher, 1968.

Carpentier, Alejo. *Le partage des eaux*. Paris: Gallimard, 1976.

Carrier, Roch. *La guerre, Yes Sir*. Montréal: Éditions du Jour, 1968.

Casteel, Sarah Phillips. *Second Arrivals: Landscape and Belonging in Contemporary Writing of the Americas*. Charlottesville: University of Virginia Press, 2007.

Cespedes, Vincent. *Mélangeons-nous. Enquête sur l'alchimie humaine*. Paris: Maren Sell, 2006.

Chanady, Amaryll. *Entre inclusion et exclusion : La symbolisation de l'autre dans les Amériques*. Paris: Champion, 1999.

Choquette, Adrienne. *Laure Clouet*. Québec: Institut littéraire du Québec, 1961.

Cisneros, Sandra. *The House on Mango Street*. New York: Vintage, 1991.

Clarke, George Elliott. *Lush Dreams, Blue Exile, Fugitive Poems: 1978–1993*. Lawrencetown Beach, Nova Scotia: Pottersfield Press, 1994.
Conan, Laure. *Angéline de Montbrun*. Québec: Léger Brousseau, 1884.
d'Alfonso, Antonio. *In Italics: In Defense of Ethnicity*. Toronto: Guernica, 1996.
Danticat, Edwidge. *Create Dangerously*. Princeton: Princeton University Press, 2010.
Deacon, William Arthur. *Pens and Pirates*. Toronto: Ryerson, 1923.
Desbiens, Patrice. *L'homme invisible/The Invisible Man*. Sudbury, Ontario: Prise de parole, 1997.
Ducharme, Réjean. *L'Avalée des avalés*. Paris: Gallimard, 1966.
———. *L'hiver de force*. Paris: Gallimard, 1973.
———. *L'Océantume*. Paris: Gallimard, 1968.
Dupont, Éric. *La logeuse*. Montréal: Marchand de feuilles, 2006.
Echeverria, Esteban. *El Matadero: La Cautiva*. Madrid: Catedra, 1986.
Elkouri, Rima. "Les traits métissés, l'accent québécois." *La Presse* (Saturday, April 1st, 2000), B1.
Ellison, Ralph. *The Invisible Man*. New York: Random House, 1952.
Enrigue, Álvaro. *Vidas perpendiculares*. Barcelona: Anagrama, 2008.
Esquivel, Laura. *The Law of Love*. New York: Crown, 1996.
Even-Zohar, Itamar. "The Role of Literature in the Making of the Nations of Europe: A Socio-Semiotic Examination." *AS/SA*, n°1 (1996): 1–20. http://www.epas.utoronto.ca:8080/french/as-sa/ASSA/-No1/IEZ1.html
Kafka, Franz. *The Metamorphosis*. New York: Bantam, 1972.
Frye, Northrop. "Canada: New World without Revolution." In *Divisions on a Ground: Essays on Canadian Culture*. Ed. James Polk. Toronto: Anansi, 1982. 167–80.
Fuentes, Carlos. *Cristóbal nonato*. Mexico: Fondo de Cultura Económica, 1987.
Gallant, Mavis. *Home Truths: Selected Canadian Stories*. Toronto: Macmillan, 1981.
Gauvreau, Claude. "L'esthétique: question de propagande." *Le Haut-parleur*, January 14th (1951): 5.
Gazeta Mercantil, Thursday, November 11, 1999, p. A3.
Gélinas, Gratien. "Du patriotisme ça ?" *L'Action nationale*, vol. 5 (1935): 292–93.
Giménez Micó, José Antonio. "Latin-Americanizing Canada." In *Canadian Cultural Exchange/Échanges culturels au Canada: Translation and Transculturation/traduction et transculturation*. Ed. Norman Cheadle. Waterloo, Ontario: Wilfrid Laurier University Press, 2007. 1–15.
Girard, René. *Des choses cachées depuis la fondation du monde*. Paris: Livre de poche, 1978.
———. *Le bouc émissaire*. Paris: Grasset, 1982.
Glissant, Édouard. *Introduction à une poétique du divers*. Paris: Gallimard, 1996.
Godbout, Jacques. *L'Aquarium*. Paris: Seuil, 1962.
Goldschläger, Alain, and Clive Thomson. (eds.). *Le discours scientifique comme porteur de préjugés?/Scientific Discourse as Prejudice-Carrier?* London, Ontario: The University of Western, Mestengo Press, 1998.
Grignon, Claude-Henri. "Qu'avez-vous à dire aux étudiants?" In *Les pamphlets de Valdombre*, (March-April 1942): 39.
Hage, Rawi. *Cockroach*. New York: W. W. Norton, 2010.
Harvey, Jean-Charles. *L'homme qui va*. Québec: Le Soleil, 1929.

Havel, Vaclav. *Living in Truth*. London/Boston: Faber and Faber, 1989.
Henfil. *Diário de um cucaracha*. São Paulo: Record, 1987.
Highway, Tomson. *Comparing Mythologies*. Ottawa: University of Ottawa Press, 2003.
Iyer, Pico. *Imagining Canada: An Outsider's Hope for a Global Future*. Toronto: The Hart House Lecture, 2001.
———. *The Global Soul*. New York: Vintage, 2000.
Kingwell, Mark. *The World We Want*. New York: Viking, 2000.
Kokis, Sergio. *Le pavillon des miroirs*. Montréal: XYZ, 1994.
Kosinski, Jerzy. *Being There*. New York: Harcourt Brace Jovanovich, 1971.
Kundera, Milan. *L'Art du roman: essai*. Paris: Gallimard, 1986.
Laferrière, Dany. *Cette grenade dans la main du jeune Nègre est-elle une arme ou un fruit*. Montréal: VLB, 1983.
Leacock, Stephen. "Common Sense and the Universe." In *Last Leaves*. Toronto: McClelland and Stewart, 1945. 35–51.
Leduc, Louise. "Le Dr. Yves Lamontagne tire sa révérence." *La Presse* (Monday, October 4th, 2010), A7.
Le Rapport Durham. (Eds. Denis Bertrand and André Lavallée). Montréal: Les éditions Sainte-Marie, 1969.
Lévinas, Emmanuel. *Totalité et infinité; essai sur l'extériorité*. La Haye: Nijhoff, 1961.
Little, Matthew. "Des députés fédéraux se penchent sur un commerce horrible: Un sous-comité fait le point sur les prélèvements d'organes en Chine." *Époque Times* (February 18-March 3, 2013): 4.
Maffesoli, Michel. *L'ombre de Dionysos*. Paris: Méridien/Anthropos, 1982.
Marcel, Françoise. *42 ans de service*. Montréal: éditions québécoises-éditions vert blanc rouge (no date).
Marcenaro, Petronio. *Al otro lado del San Juan*. San José: editorial Costa Rica, 2007.
Mato, Daniel. "Sobre la fetichización de la globalización y las dificultades que plantea para el estudio de las transformaciones sociales contemporaneas." *Revista venezolana de analísis de coyuntura*, vol. 5, no. 1 (janvier-juin 1999): 129–47.
Maxwell, Amélie. "Le mythe américain du self-made man dans les littératures francophones du Canada: apprivoiser le changement en s'approvisionnant de déplacements." In *Américanité, cultures francophones canadiennes et société des savoirs: Le Canada et les Amériques*. Ed. P. Imbert. Ottawa: Éditions Chaire de l'Université d'Ottawa: Canada: Enjeux sociaux et culturels dans une société du savoir, 2009: 111–42.
McKillop, A. B. (ed.). *Contexts of Canada's Past: Selected Essays of W. L. Morton*. Toronto/Ottawa: Macmillan/Carleton University Press, 1980.
McLuhan, Marshall. *Notes on the Media as Art Form*. Corte Madera, CA: Gingko Press, 2005.
Michaels, Anne. *Fugitive Pieces*. Toronto: McClelland and Stewart, 1996.
Miller, Henry. *Le cauchemar climatisé*. Paris: Livre de poche, 1986.
Montgomery, Lucy Maud. *Anne of Green Gables*. Toronto: McGraw-Hill Ryerson, 1968.
Morton, W. L. *The Canadian Identity*. Madison/Toronto: The University of Wisconsin Press/The University of Toronto Press, 1964.
Nadeau, Simon. *L'Autre modernité*. Montréal: Boréal, 2013.

Neuman, Andrés. *El viajero del siglo*. Madrid: Alfaguara, 2009.
Nepveu, Pierre. *Intérieurs du Nouveau Monde*. Montréal: Boréal, 1998.
Ondaatje, Michael. *The English Patient*. New York: Vintage Books, 1992.
Orwell, George. *Notes on Nationalism*. London: Polemic, May 1945. [Online] www.george-orwell.org/Notes_on_Nationalism/0.html (22/12/2012).
Pavie, Théodore. *Souvenirs atlantiques*. Paris: Robert, 1838.
Petrowski, Nathalie. "Peter Doig." La Presse+Arts, Saturday, January 11th (2014). [Application for iPad].
Proulx, Monique. *Les Aurores Montréales*. Montréal: Boréal, 1996.
Reimers, Camila. *Tres lotos en un mar de fuego*. Ottawa: Mapalé Publishing, 2006.
Rivard, Yvon. *Le siècle de Jeanne*. Montréal: Boréal, 2005.
———. *Mort et naissance de Christophe Ulric*. Montréal: La Presse, 1976.
Robbins, Tom. *Wild Ducks Flying Backward*. New York: Bantam, 2005.
Robert, Marthe. *Roman des origines et origines du roman*. Paris: Gallimard, 1972.
Rockland, Michael Aaron. *Sarmiento's Travels in the United States in 1847*. Princeton: Princeton University Press, 1970.
Saucier, Jocelyne. *Il pleuvait des oiseaux*. Montréal: XYZ, 2011.
Savary, Alain. *Le grand détour pour traverser la rue*. Ottawa: L'Interligne, 2019.
Schultz, Alfred P. *Race or Mongrel*. Boston: L.C. Page & company, 1908
Schermbrucker, Bill. *Chameleon*. Vancouver: Talon Books, 1983.
Sen, Amartya. *Identité et violence*. Paris: Odile Jacob, 2001.
Simard, Jean. *Mon fils pourtant heureux*. Ottawa: Cercle du livre de France, 1956.
Solzhenitsyn, Aleksandr. *The Gulag Archipelago*. New York: Harper and Row, 1973.
Tan, Amy. *The Joy Luck Club*. New York: G. P. Putnam, 1989.
Taylor, Charles. *Multiculturalism: Examining the Politics of Recognition*. Princeton: Princeton University Press, 1994.
Tétu, Michel. "L'opposition hybridité/métissage et patrie/nation dans le contexte pluriculturel du Canada." In *Métamorphoses d'une utopie*. Eds. Jean-Michel Lacroix and Fulvio Caccia. Paris: Presses de la Sorbonne Nouvelle/Éditions Tryptique, 1992.
Thúy, Kim, and Pascal Janovjak. *À toi*. Montréal: Libre expression, 2011.
Thompson, Hunter S. *Fear and Loathing in Las Vegas: A Savage Journey to the Heart of the American Dream*. New York: Vintage, 1998.
Vasconcelos, José. *The Cosmic Race*. Baltimore: John Hopkins, 1997.
Vellegia, Susana. "Imagenes e imaginarios en la tensión local/global." In *La dinámica global/local*, Rubens Bayardo y Monica Lacarrieu (comp.). Buenos Aires: Ciccus, 1999: 217–58.
Vidal, Gore. *Myra Breckinridge: Myron*. New York: Random House, 1986.
Villoro, Juan. *Arrecife*. Barcelona: Anagrama, 2012.
Von Neumann, John and Oskar Morgenstern. *Theory of Games and Economic Behavior*. Princeton: Princeton University Press, 1944.
Werber, Bernard. *Les Thanatonautes*. Paris: Albin Michel, 1994.
Wright, Richard. *Black Boy*. New York: Harper and Row, 1937.
Wolfe, Tom. *The Electric Kool-Aid Acid Test*. New York: Farrar, Straus and Giroux, 1968.
Woodcock, George. "Gabriel Dumont, the Forgotten Hero." *Saturday Night* 88 (July 1973): 7.

· 3 ·

THE CONTEMPORARY INTERCULTURAL, MULTICULTURAL, AND TRANSCULTURAL DYNAMICS

> Le véritable lieu de naissance est celui où l'on a porté, pour la première fois, un regard d'étranger sur soi-même: mes premières patries ont été des terres étrangères. J'ai aimé ces rapports étrangement élusifs, étrangement intimes qui existent entre un homme et des terres chaudes dont il est dépossédé pour miser ses efforts sur des terres promises, désormais objet de son désir.[1]

Transcultural Citizenship

Pico Iyer evokes the loss of benchmarks as the positive side of the invention of new perspectives by giving as an example his journey migrating from England to Canada, and highlighting that what attracts him is the multifold and hybrid side of Canada.[2] It is interesting to note that Pico Iyer controls, like many contemporary writers, the art of recycling as defined by Jencks in his study of the postmodern world.[3] For example, he claims that Toronto, according to the United-Nations' report, is the most multicultural city on the planet and, at the same time, statistically the safest in North America as well as one of the better organized ones. He adds: "And you could believe that a multi-culture could go beyond the states we knew and give a new meaning to that outdated term, the 'Commonwealth.'"[4]

One must not forget that one of the architects of the multicultural recognition in Canada in the context of the Commonwealth was Lord Tweedsmuir, the Governor general of Canada from 1935 to 1940. In 1936, he commended a group of Icelandic in Gimli, Manitoba:

> You have become in the fullest sense good Canadians and have shared in all the enterprises and struggles of this new nation and at the same time I rejoice to think that you have never forgotten the traditions of your homeland. That is the way in which a strong people is made—by accepting willingly the duties and loyalties of your adopted country, but also by bringing your own native traditions as a contribution to the making of Canada.[5]

In 1938, he underlines in a speech at Bishop's University in Quebec that these double identities are the strength of the monarchy, for unity is in diversity, which in fact defines the Commonwealth. But this vision of double identities is close to what we would nowadays call a kind of plural monoculturalism, because Lord Tweedsmuir seeks essentialized identities cut off from one another. This perspective related to the kind of multiculturalism conceived in the 1970s was strongly criticized by Neil Bissoondath in *Selling Illusions: The Cult of Multiculturalism in Canada*.[6] The Commonwealth was seen as a planetary relationship united around a center that was England, and divided into separate cultures. In *The English Patient*, Michael Ondaatje presented it as a microcosm of wounded World War II soldiers from various regions of the Commonwealth, Sri Lanka, India, Africa or Nepal. It was slowly transforming into an encounter of individuals who became citizens of newly independent states thanks to decolonization. A new era started.

The new citizenship evoked by Pico Iyer is contextualized in a new process, not that of the geographical *frontier*, but that of the cultural *frontier* where an immense collection of self-images is possible. Hence, people are able to develop themselves in numerous ways based on their capability for defining themselves in a permanent transition, for "one is many". One is no longer in a world dominated only by the dualistic Aristotelian logic of the excluded third that is based on the following axioms: the principle of identity: A is A, of non-contradiction: A is not non-A and of the excluded third: there exists no third term T, which is simultaneously A and non-A. In other words, citizenship has changed, despite the sports/leisure incentives to identify with the national as underscored by Iyer: "Yet the Olympics, famously, insists on national divisions at precisely the time when those are coming to seem most beside the point, and enshrines the cult of the flag when the logo is coming to seem more central."[7] Lynn Diamond pushes this thought even further: "À quoi tu crois, toi, Minnie?—À l'ecstasy."[8] Minnie asks the same question: Il a répondu: "'Je crois que la vie est courte.'"[9] Citizenship is consequently linked to much more than the national attribute as is also emphasized by Kingwell[10] (section: Contemporary concerns). These new attributes are based on elements leading to rewarding experiences in terms of movement, travel and meetings, without neglecting the sense of a coherent self in relation to different spaces—that of childhood, for example, as Nancy Huston underlines in *Nord Perdu*[11] or Margaret Laurence in *Heart of a Stranger*: "I am not very patriotic in the usual meaning of that word… But one thing is inalterable, for better or worse, for life. This [her small village in the Prairies] is where my world began."[12] However, in *Mort et naissance de Christophe Ulric* by Yvon Rivard[13], the space of childhood appears as a beautiful, protective landscape, a forest, rather than one defined by its national character. This space is about progression towards self-knowledge as a permanent transformation by love or access to another culture, which is also the case in *Le singe grammairien* by Octavio Paz.[14] One can therefore be moving, enjoy the movement, and be attached to spaces until people recognize themselves in glocalized spaces. In this sense, the humorous question advertised by the Four Seasons Hotels and Resorts is quite relevant: "Is it possible to become homesick for a hotel?"[15] (section: The Hotel as *Home*).

Multicultural citizenship is linked to the legitimation of displacements in the geographic, intellectual, cultural, and technological sense. What is more transportable than language? Nowadays, semantic contents are mixed and transform in contact with other semantic contents, writes Iyer: "I've thought about language as perhaps the only portable home a global mongrel has, though my own language, in my lifetime, has, like the cities around it, gone from the clear distinctions of Henry James's world to the polymorphous mish-mashes of Salman Rushdie's."[16] In exchanges, languages hybridize because they cover a larger space, a space made of relations with other cultures. Moreover, technology is transforming the planetary space into a restricted location where everything has become close, a kind of archipelago, to use a term dear to Édouard Glissant.[17] Furthermore, this language carries stories, which are no longer related to a single space with which one identifies. The narrated space now involves multiple spaces. These spaces are formed continuously from both recent and active memories. In other words, the spaces coinciding through the chance meetings of different people interacting with each other become a series of networks in constant transformation. Thus, in the structure of different narratives, the causality/consequence paradigm often leading to exclusion is amended by chance and coincidence. Similarly, the short temporality/long temporality binary is displaced by moments of violence or seduction and produce a discourse based on a shared memory of encounter which is very different from the legitimation of exclusion found in official histories.

Temporal Vector, Historic Canon, Causality, Multiculturalism

> Lili était intervenue avec un petit air ironique en disant que le défi du XXIe siècle serait de comprendre les liens de cause à effet.[18]

Temporality and causality. In *Comparing Mythologies*, Tomson Highway emphasizes the distance which separates the narratives of the Indigenous people of America from the Christian story of Genesis. Both cultures explain their origin. It is mother earth for the Natives and clay modelled into Adam by the father God, for Christians and Jews. Temporalities are also very different. Indigeneity is a vagina, a circle generating life cycles, whereas Christianity, as Teilhard de Chardin[19] points out, is a vector going from point alpha to omega. This vector, if it is freed from the religious end, is called modern progress and it is very different from the vagina envisaged by the Indigenous peoples of the Americas:

> North America, quite on the end, is the most spectacularly beautiful continent on Earth, as all who have seen it can attest. It is not a curse from an angry male. It is a gift from a benevolent female god… Christian mythology arrived here on the shores of North America in October of the year 1492. At which point God as man met God as a woman—for that's where she'd been kept hidden all this time, as it turns out—and thereby hangs a tale of what are probably the worst cases of rape, wife battery, and attempted wife murder in the history of the world as we know it. At that point in time, in other words, the circle of matriarchy was punctured by the straight line of patriarchy, the circle of the womb, was punctured, most brutally, by the straight line of the phallus. And the bleeding was profuse.[20]

The object of desire for the Indigenous peoples is the relationship with nature and the cosmic where there is a place for everything. For the people of European origins, the object of desire is the domination of nature by humans. This domination is carried out by work, either in the biblical perspective ("Tu travailleras à la sueur de ton front"), or in the practical rationalistic perspective imagined by Sarmiento and expressed by Étienne Parent ("le travail c'est la liberté"[21]). In the perspective of the Europeans, the problem in the Americas is that the Indigenous peoples do not engage in work. The solution criticized by Parent has been to import slaves from Africa. However, they were not given the choice to take the object of desire since the definition of slavery is to be forced to act according to the system of those who own it without having access to any of that system's components. In other words, these people are barbarians because they have no access—for lack of interest or prohibition[22]—to the object of desire of the Christian Europeans.

Thus, these narratives do not agree on the essential point: the object to be desired. In his actantial model for analyzing the basic elements of the plot structure, Greimas[23] rightly underlines that the subject/object relationship of desire is fundamental to the story, and that holds for all cultures. The importance of this situation is even more evident for the Indigenous peoples than for the Black slaves. Indeed, for Indigenous people the competition with Europeans is not about a common desired object (to dominate nature by industry), but on the nature of the relationship to the cosmos, which for Europeans is constructed as a nature to be exploited and for Indigenous people is linked to respect and balance. This cosmic approach to nature is developed for instance in Carlos Castaneda's best-selling novel *Journey to Ixtlan*.[24] The two systems of values are incommensurable. For the Blacks, however, the ones who are completely cut off from the cultures that formed them in Africa, the problem will be to allow them to fit into the great story of Christian legitimacy combined with the practical rationalism of nature domination. For them, the aim will be to share the same goals as Whites if given the opportunity by the abolition of slavery. As the struggles of Martin Luther King and Malcom X demonstrate, it is only in the sixties that they started to gain access to the competition for the object determined as desirable by the socio-economic game in the United States. For the Indigenous peoples, the goal imposed on them by Whites is to give them the desire of an object which, in their master narrative, has no important meaning.

We know that stories more than languages determine cultural orientation. It is the narrative, the cultural and social contexts defined by causality and temporality, that give meaning to a group. Therefore, from the European perspective, it will be necessary to erase Indigenous civilizations that thrived throughout the Americas. For instance, in Lima, Peru, the convent and the Church of the Dominicans, located next to The Plaza de Armas, were built on the recently revealed foundations of an immense pre-Colombian pyramid.[25] In view of this connection, nowadays, many institutions are considering ways to recognize the fact that most Indigenous peoples are bicultural and master at least two narratives, two systems of meanings. This is what one finds, for example, in the program of the Toronto District School Board: "Ses mesures comprennent la création d'un programme de cours axés sur les modes de vie traditionnels comme il est défini par les *First Nations Schools* de Toronto, ainsi que l'ajout de cours sur l'histoire et les perspectives autochtones au sein du programme d'étude."[26] If this occurs, it is because the teachers have found that there is a gap between what the children experience at home, what they are taught, and the goals that are assigned to them in schools based entirely on a rationalist perspective and practice of Western model. Nevertheless, it is significant that these programs on Indigenous cultures are only designed for Indigenous children, which means that non-Indigenous people, according to the scheme referred to by Homi Bhabha in *The Location of Culture*, can take the liberty of ignoring everything about these cultures. However, one notes that recently the University of Winnipeg in Manitoba imposed a first-year course dealing with Indigenous cultures to all students.

As we can see, the descendants of Europeans, from one end of the continent to the other—the soldiers in search of gold, the coureurs des bois seeking fur, the seringueros in search of rubber, the farmers, the urbanites, and the techno-trendy—are molded by the long-term Christian-Western vectored duration. It can be opposed to a cyclic aboriginal temporality and an Afro-Caribbean temporality, built in the discontinuous, as specified by Édouard Glissant in *Introduction à une poétique du divers*. If the European descendants are much more open to otherness in the 21st century, they still do not feel the need to understand the cultural bases of other groups, because these other groups are not important enough to have a cultural and economic stand.

Temporality and multiculturalism. The question of long term and of short term is defined according to those who want to use it particularly for specific identity purposes. For recent immigrants, short term can mean adapting to the host society established for a relatively long time, even if it is not as long as the national historical narratives of their origins try to establish, narratives of which immigrants are carriers. As Charles Taylor[27] points out, this new and democratic society has something to say to the newcomers. He rejects cultural relativism because, in the context of the nation-states, the culture of the host country, having been there for a long time, has something special to offer newcomers.[28] For Taylor, it is not enough that we accept the initial hypothesis that the values are equal, for it creates the risk of falling into absolute relativism. We must go further and promote a better understanding of different values, as well as their importance and the consequences linked to the recognition of these values. What is even more important than the recognition of these values is knowing how to perceive others and how to establish efficient relationships from a constitutional, institutional and practical point of view. All of this, of course, in the context of an established society that has its own values, but is open to accommodate some of the differences brought by the newcomers. This is also highlighted by Gérard Bouchard in his recent book *L'interculturalisme: un point de vue québecois.*[29] For Bouchard, there is a Francophone majority in Quebec with things to say to the newcomers, especially from the point of view of the language, history, and system of values. This is what is less emphasized in the Canadian multiculturalism, which tends to present cultural relationships as taking place between minorities in the absence of a majority. The vision of the Canadian multiculturalism is therefore pluralistic and seems much more relativist than what proposed Gérard Bouchard for whom interculturalism is dual. But it is good to further discuss the issue of social values from a multiculturalist perspective, as there are diverging views on the subject by different thinkers. For instance, Will Kymlicka[30], Daniel Bonilla Maldonado[31], and Tariq Modood[32], each offer a different view on the subject, the latter two being familiar with the theories of Kymlicka.

Take for example Tariq Modood's critique of multiculturalism, which proposes a greater institutional recognition of Islam in the context of the United Kingdom. This discussion is related to Canada because Modood cites the Canadian example and especially Will Kymlicka's theory. This theory argues that any liberal society (therefore the Canadian society) can neither accept the complete relativism of values nor accommodate illiberal and discriminatory perspectives, or practices which are dangerous to the integrity of the individual. In fact, for Kymlicka, it is clear that multiculturalism is an extension of the Human Rights.

Modood acknowledges that certain values, such as gender equality, embedded in the laws as well as in social norms, pose some limitations on the nature of the recognition that he hopes to achieve: "Norms and laws and constitutional principles concerning the appropriate place of religion in public life general and in specific policy areas (such as schools or rehabilitation of criminals) consist of such public values and are reasoned about, justified or criticized by reference to specific values about religion of politics…"[33] He then suggests that these social values and norms (including gender equality) are negotiable, that they may be justified or criticized, and that "they are constantly being reinterpreted, realigned, extended and reformed."[34]

This call for the negotiation of values and norms attempts to prepare the reader for the rejection of the claim that in the new society that is the United Kingdom, certain core values are of great importance for the immigrants. In this perspective, it is understood by Modood that national identity is weak in contemporary Great Britain. He points out that in Canada, Australia and Malaysia, multiculturalism, however, has coincided with the nation building project.[35] Therefore, for Modood, multiculturalism in Canada is part of a form of established power, an accepted social consensus and a definition of identity that would be difficult to challenge. According to him, it is just the opposite in the United Kingdom: "But if the goal of wanting to become British, to be accepted as British and to belong to Britain is not a worthwhile goal for Commonwealth migrants and their progeny, what then are they supposed to integrate into? And if there is nothing strong, purposive and inspiring to integrate to, why bother with integration?"[36] This apparent weakness is the opposite of the perception of a Great Britain as the historical center of a powerful empire and can be linked to what the Canadian writer Margaret Atwood wrote about Canada of the sixties and seventies in her book, *Survival.* In this book, the Canadian identity was perceived as weak as a result of the British colonization and the impact of the American cultural and economic influence. However, Robert Fulford reminds us that geography unites Canadians who are conscious, nevertheless, that they live in different worlds in which their ideas and even their rights are separate. It is true for Indigenous people as well as for Francophones from Québec who do not share the same legal system as other Provinces in Canada. Yet they are in a continuous and constant process of learning and understanding one another: "It is only in the age of mass communication that genuine pluralism can flourish, because it is only in this age that we have the means to learn about each other", emphasizes to Robert Fulford's in his foreword to Janis Kraulis' book entitled: *Canada: A Landscape Portrait.*[37] The size of the country—its physical diversity combined with democratic traditions and with new technologies, prove that encounters of differences occurred. Canada is no longer based on the valorization of an essentialized rootedness separating people. Rather, Canada is seen as a meeting place of different cultures, which are still linked to childhood memory, providing a stable basis to an identity in constant transformation, as Margaret Laurence said so clearly. Thus, the alleged identity weakness based on the ability to be subjected to numerous influences has been transformed into a strength. All this thanks to a multiculturalism that has formed a dynamic nation determined to help immigrants participate actively in a society that is brandishing the democratic values in an exemplary manner, as Pierre-Elliot Trudeau points out in 1965 in *Le fédéralisme et la société canadienne-française*.

Qualifying the British identity as weak allows Modood to argue in his book that there are no core values worthy of attention in the United Kingdom, and that they cannot be linked to significant definitions: "Brown[38] wants to derive a set of core values (liberty, fairness, enterprise and so on) from a historical narrative yet such values, even if they could singly or in combination be given a distinctive British take, are too complex and their interpretation and priority too contested to be amenable to be set into a series of meaningful definitions."[39] However, as pointed out by Michael Finkenthal[40], efficient management of cultural meetings is always complex. Even more astonishing, by an illustration of what could be termed as a colonialist perspective stemming from somebody who uses anti-colonial arguments, Modood uses the dualistic argument "either…or" to reject any legitimate base of sharing core values: "Definitions of core values will either be too bland or too divisive and the idea that there has to be a schedule of value statements to which every citizen is expected to sign up is not in the spirit of a multi logical citizenship (Brown: 2005)."[41] This contradicts the way in which Robert Fulford defines Canada: "We avoid deciding upon that definition (of the Crown) precisely because to do so would be divisive."[42] Not to decide can sometimes be a strength. Not to decide is, as shown by Yann Martel in *Life of Pi*, knowing how to navigate without losing one's directions, even though the drift forces are big. It is about living in the best possible conditions in a world always on the brink of conflict and often engulfed in dynamics led by appropriation mimesis and the production of scapegoats as underscored in René Girard's theory.[43]

Let's discuss again Modood's arguments about the Canadian situation. In Canada multiculturalism is linked to fundamental values which must be respected. Recently, a survey was conducted in an Islamic school in Toronto where the educational material from Iran was inappropriate, because it presented the Jews as enemies and encouraged the boys "to keep fit for jihad."[44] Multiculturalism is a Canadian value among other Canadian values and its basic principle is to treat all immigrants and non-immigrants with respect[45], in order to encourage them to participate in different aspects of the established society and access the power centers if they wish to do so. In addition, we should not encourage children to dream of exclusions or killings, or to consider the others as inferior or dangerous beings. This is in agreement with the fact that, as pointed out by Kymlicka, multiculturalism should not contribute to the recognition of practices and perspectives of groups that are related to the exclusion of others. Kymlicka insists that there are values such as freedom of expression (*The Satanic Verses* by Salman Rushdie are part of this freedom), gender equality, etc., which are not negotiable in a liberal democracy. According to Taylor and Kymlicka, all liberal societies share fundamental values that are not negotiable, such as the rejection of torture, the refusal of mutilations such as clitoridectomy, equality between men and women, non-discrimination against sexual orientation, etc. These must also include protection of the individual against the group (whether a majority or minority group)—a point strongly disputed by Moodod who dismisses the fact that a person can leave Islam and belong to himself with assertiveness and not in submission.

Contrary to what Modood wishes, multiculturalism may not recognize some of the values of certain non-liberal minorities who oppress certain subgroups or individuals within the minority group, or who demonstrate behaviours or values that are discriminatory against some members of the group. As Kymlicka points out in *Multicultural Odysseys*, some groups submit their members to the authority of traditional hierarchies, religious or not, where some of the practices such as honour crimes or a fatwa promoting murder in the name of religion or politics, are not acceptable in a liberal democracy based on the respect of Human Rights. Therefore, Kymlicka and Taylor understand multiculturalism as a dynamic process of active participation in an established, democratic and liberal society chosen by the newcomers because of its values, its economy and the opportunities it offers them. Both parties, those who are long-established and the newcomers, need to learn to share the cross-cultural differences in good faith and in a peaceful manner, in order to provide access to the fundamental principles that have drawn people to the new country.

It is essential to understand that democratic values are part of the long term in the United States and in Canada. In fact, the democratic values on which multiculturalism is based have been established for much longer than in many countries outside of North America. Some immigrants claim that they come from long established societies: Europe, Africa, China, and the Middle East. They tend to consider that the Americas live in the short term, thus under less established operations and more subject to redefinition. This sometimes leads to a contempt for the continent, particularly if they fail to get a job, as we see in Rawi Hage: "He either gave me long monologues about Persia and the greatness of its history, or he re-enacted the tears of his mother, whom he will never see again before she dies because, as he claims, he is an unfortunate exile."[46] However, it should be understood that these countries have almost all experienced long historical periods of domination by nobles, dictators or others, which is reflected by a monopoly of wealth leading to the construction of sumptuous palaces and various grandiose historical monuments, but of very short durations if compared to a democratic practice and life where people self-belong and can grow.

The Long-Term and the New

> Canada [...] was the land that looked ideal in theory because [...] it was not hemmed in by the weight of its past, as the Old World could be, not burdened by the promise of an unlimited future, as its neighbor in the New World often is.[47]

After this comment by Pico Iyer, the question of the long term should be rethought. In fact, the Americas rest upon a long term compared to the rest of the planet, in any case a part of the Americas, including Canada and the United States. This long term is that of the development of democratic, parliamentarians and/or republican values rather than official or monumental historical attachments. These values are those that most immigrants who seek to develop their individual potential within new collective communities are sharing. In this context of democracy, of interesting and tolerant encounters with the other, what is the meaning of the word new? One could say, from the perspective of René Girard, that the new as in the contextualization of the Old and the New Testament, is what brings that which is original in human relationships, and that this original is much more in line with the origin (for *The New Testament* it is the word of God) than the narratives that have been established for a long time such as the *Old Testament*.

Indeed, from René Girard's perspective, the whole vision is based on the fact that *The New Testament* calls into question the universe of the myths of exclusion producing scapegoats in order to found a homogeneous community that is built as such, because it shares the belief that the socially excluded are guilty of the sins with which they are charged. *The New Testament*, as we have seen, points a finger at the moment where the exclusion shuts the victim's mouth. Although Jesus is presented as guilty, he is innocent of what he is accused of—in particular, to divide the community. *The New Testament* is thus both original in its approach, as suggested by René Girard, and is linked to the origin, because it is closer to the word of God. Indeed, it connects us to the origin of the Word of God that says "Love one another", rather than "an eye for an eye", which could be connected to *The Old Testament*. Contrary to what was stated in the historical narratives associated with myths, *The New Testament* is, for Girard, closer to the origin while at the same time it engages the entire future of humanity. This is shown in the call of Jesus to migration, breaking allegiances based on an established past: "Leave everything and follow me." By this positioning, the new gathers in itself the moment that contains everything, seduction or violence, as well as the origin and the future as discussed by Yvon Rivard in *Le siècle de Jeanne*.

The new world can thus be understood in this way. It is original in its desire to promote democracy, as in its intention to put in place tolerant and efficient multicultural encounters. Therefore, it is closer to an origin, the non-localizable and non-temporal that demands to recognize the other as always present, because the whole self is in relation with the other. Hence, the rootedness, limited by national territories, becomes a planetary rhizome. In this way, the creation of Adam from clay, the link between body and territory would not be limited by cultural or territorial boundaries, but be open to the entire planet. This dynamic shapes a number of texts as seen in Christian Bök's work referring to fractals open to adventure and encounters in the imaginary, and distant from returns towards an elusive origin: "A fractal confining a finite/ space plots a dream perimeter,/ a route composed of Nothing/ but detours, an imaginary/ line that goes nowhere even/ as it returns to its origin."[48]

The Long-Term and the Instant

The long-term of liberal democracy integrates the momentary awareness of violence and its long-term impact that makes us reflect on the word of God: "Love one another". This democratic long term is long because democracy aims to invent a present and a future where people can live together, rather than foster resentment or exclude people because of their appearance, their sexual orientations or their opinions.[49] In that case, the instant can be lived not as a moment of violence but as a moment which encompasses a whole life from birth to old age, as pointed out by Yvon Rivard. He offers his conception of the mobile eternity of the instant, which contains all: "[…] je m'entêtais à croire que les erreurs, les ratés et les horreurs de l'Amérique ne procèdent pas tant de la perte de la mémoire, comme on le pense trop souvent, mais qui est au contraire la plus grande mémoire, la plus vivante, celle qui me rend à chaque instant contemporain du commencement et de la fin du monde."[50] For Yvon Rivard, this instant can be lived as a hub of the beauty of all that lives. Hence, Rivard values taking the risk to live fully and to expose oneself to the danger of being alive, in all its human and ethical sense, because: "Il faut maintenant tout recommencer, recommencer à voir, à sentir, à comprendre que ce monde et nous-mêmes n'avons pas d'âge puisque nous naissons ensemble à chaque instant et que chaque instant est une frontière mobile où se rencontrent tous les siècles passés et à venir."[51] How to better symbolically define the fascinations between individuals and groups of different cultures and backgrounds? The experience of beauty is one of the engines driving the individuals to be assertive, to take the risk of becoming themselves, that is to say self and the other in the revival of an affirmation of self-belonging, which is the freedom of always running the risk of being singular with the others.[52]

For Rivard, this mobile frontier of the moment, coupled with an awareness of the aesthetics of life gets closer to the *frontier*, but in a temporality born of the fusion of the here and now in order to prevent the world from growing old and dying. Willingness to live in the new and the renewal of the New World, the intensity, the feeling of the rediscovered vastness, attention to life, to the beauty in the exploration of slowness—this attitude is not lost on Tomson Highway, who speaks of the Americas in *Comparing Mythologies* or even on Jocelyne Saucier in *Il pleuvait des oiseaux*: "Nous étions installés dans la lenteur que j'aime et il m'a lancé, comme si nous avions discuté du sujet pendant des heures: —un endroit idéal pour ce que tu cherches."[53]

For Yvon Rivard, one of the keys of this full moment is located in the following: "Qu'est-ce qui nous permet d'être heureux, sinon cette chose en nous qui nous éloigne du bonheur et nous en donne le désir, qui voit dans tout ce qui est une image menacée par tout ce qui est?"[54] What is revealed here is the anxiety generated by coincidence in what is not expected, in what is new, and from the new threatened by the new, which in turn threatens that which is already here. Fragility. The beauty of the encounter and the fear of the disaster in the hope of the moment, of what is still virtual, is the basis of the New World for Yvon Rivard.

In the New World, generations, those of the immigrants, the Creoles, the African Americans or the Indigenous Peoples, are seized by dreams to achieve their goals, to escape both the continued dominance of the long term, and the discontinuous, economic and cultural violence, which has ruled encounters in the world. Remembering to escape both the vector of the master narrative and traces of the discontinuous, which marks the aging and potential death of civilizations, is one of the elements mentioned by Yvon Rivard. That is why *Le siècle de Jeanne* is the century of Jeanne, that is, the encounter between Alexander, the grandfather, and Jeanne, the grand-child who teaches him to be a child again, and whom Alex loves because it is Jeanne who brings out the child in him:

> Le Nouveau Monde n'était peut-être possible que si nous arrivons à percevoir à la fois et en même temps le début et la fin d'un monde, et pour cela quel meilleur exercice que d'entendre sur une plage déserte les pas de ceux qui sont passés et les pas de ceux qui viendront, comme de voir au milieu d'une foule ou dans les bras d'une femme cet espace vide que personne ne pourra jamais combler, le centre immobile de tout mouvement, le moyeu de la roue.[55]

As we can see, the New World, unlike what Vasconcelos believes, does not seek to resolve the contradictions through a narration that seeks unification, but rather to constantly engage in the coincidence (space) of the simultaneous (time) and dynamically manage encounters. It is in the moment of the coincidence that something can happen, because in the New World something is always expected to happen. But what occurs is not of the order of the narrative that closes on a negative consequence originating in the exclusive logic of causalities linked to any narrative structure. "Keep it moving"[56] said Alexander, as encounters in the unexpected are permanent. This permanence of displacements is also highlighted in the parabolic novel *Life of Pi* by Yann Martel. The New World (or at least a part of it) tries through its dream of the Garden of Eden, then by practices related to democracy and, more recently by implementing multiculturalism and interculturalism, to reject the old myths of exclusion. The goal is to manage the encounters of people who carry old stories and insert them into new dynamics, as shown by the recycled official Mexican story in *The Law of Love* by Laura Esquivel. The new countries, and those who inhabit them in successive waves, look to escape the homogenizing victim-based narratives linked to the place from which the majority of the immigrants come from: the Middle East and its massacres, Europe and the Holocaust, the Czarist, Soviet or Maoist persecutions, the Armenian genocide as we see it represented in the movie *Ararat* by Atom Egoyan, the Rwandan genocide[57], etc. The new countries of the Americas attempt to invent original narratives, such as those proposed by Moacyr Scliar in *Max and the Cat*, and even more by Yann Martel through Piscine Patel in *Life of Pi*. These stories can be connected to many texts produced by authors such as Jean-Charles Harvey who proposes a universal peace in *L'homme qui va*, or Gabrielle Roy who, in her humanistic humour, offers a deep recognition of the others in *Rue*

Deschambault or *Un jardin au bout du monde*. That is to say, the narratives of encounters, even if they are part of a relatively long term, that of the development of democracy in the Americas, are designed to incorporate the throbbing of the continuous and the discontinuous since the encounters are with groups who have left a place in order to reinvent themselves elsewhere, and also because these intertwining narratives produce multiple potential branching networks in permanent transitions.

Continuous and Discontinuous

Nowadays, we understand that the Americas develop their culture by playing within the relationship between the continuous and the discontinuous. This was already explored by Édouard Glissant who underlines that the mixing of people from Europe, Africa, and the pre-Columbian Americas is based on the fact that civilizations are not solely dependent on continuity but that their very existence can be definitively disrupted. They do not completely die in spite of the dreams of the politicians who aim to create homogenized states. These politicians are often backed by anthropologists who express their exclusions through construction of monuments to their own glory, as in Argentine: "La provincia de Jujuy y la Comisión de Homenaje a los arqueologos Juan B. Ambrosetti (1865–1917) y Salvador Debenedetti (1884–1930). De entre las cenizas milenarias de un pueblo muerto exhumaron las culturas aborigenes dando eco al silencio."[58]

We keep in mind that these words inscribed on a monument are meant to disseminate the work of anthropologists, and not the memory of Indigenous peoples in Pucara de Tilcara, a place in the north of Argentina where many Indigenous people disappeared, while the hundreds of thousands who are alive are being marginalized by the non-Indigenous Argentinians. The descendants are well alive, and the millenary ashes are very metaphorical. However, in spite of everything, the life of these Indigenous people is completely different from their life before the arrival of the Europeans.[59] In this case, there is a continuum in the discontinuous, as also highlighted, for Africans in the Americas. Édouard Glissant[60] reminds us of the situation of Black people in the Caribbean: "Ce n'est pas dans des œuvres construites que nous puisons notre continuité, mais paradoxalement dans l'impossibilité historique de la continuité."[61] This continuum of discontinuous is based, for example, on the orality that penetrates the resources of the writing in processes of repetition, doubling, reassessment, suspense, circularity.[62] This type of discourse is characteristic of many West Indian, Indigenous or Métis writers. It is also evident in poetic interjections, as seen in *Manifesto* Antropófago by Oswald de Andrade in Brazil, or in a text such as *Refus global* by Paul-Émile Borduas.[63] Let's not forget the novel *Seulement attendre et regarder* by Elena Botchorichvili where throughout the story the modified chorus "Prolétaires de tous les pays unissez-vous" becomes "Même s'ils n'avaient rien en commun, hormis leur passé, leur passé exécré. Mais l'exécration peut-elle unir? Prolétaires de tous les pays, unissez-vous?"[64] It is in parallel with "Eux? Nous? Nous, c'est nous, vous c'est vous? Vous c'est vous, nous c'est nous?"[65] This sentence is also transformed in the sense of a successful encounter "Nous c'est vous… vous c'est nous…"[66] This passage evokes the continuity-discontinuity with the Eastern countries left by the post-communist emigrants. It manifests at the same time the attempt to reinsert the identities in a certain continuity disrupted by the communist/post-communist passage, and then by the adaptation to Canadian capitalist liberalism. This continuum of the discontinuous is also explored in the novel *Nikolski* by Nicolas Dickner through the references to Garifunas[67], these peoples issued from the meeting of the Indigenous Caribbean people with the Blacks and a few Whites, and who have migrated to the coasts of Belize or Honduras. They have known, in spite of all these moves, to perpetuate their culture.

This continuum of the discontinuous recently has taken huge temporal proportions, especially through Hollywood, which mediatizes the prehistoric monuments of the Americas; sites which, from Drumheller in Alberta to Argentina, reveal the skeletons of the dinosaurs or brachiosaurs and which find themselves in the children's games made of plastic. The presence of these skeletons is obsessive. It can be seen in Lynn Diamond's *Leslie Muller ou le principe d'incertitude*: "Pour payer ses études, elle (Anna) avait pendant deux ans reconstitué pour le compte d'un musée d'histoire naturelle le squelette grandeur nature d'un Albertosaure."[68] The historical monuments are represented by skeletons in the Americas more than elsewhere, because in the Americas in particular, we can see that civilizations and groups are mortals, that disappearance took place, or that we are close to disappearing. This is in part masked in Europe by the fact that there are not many obvious trace of very ancient groups[69], and that the long-term historical monuments override the extremely long timespan of the events related to prehistory. It is also symbolized in an issue of the *National Geographic* magazine showing an alligator watching the departure of a rocket to other planets in Cape Canaveral. As we can see in this image, the long timespan, which had been lacking in the New

World in the 19th century, is becoming greater and greater. This continuity-discontinuity that plays in the very long-term and, therefore, in the threat of extinction—because we know, as Bagehot pointed out in 1873 (section: The Nation), that the nations are not indestructible—depend on coincidences and not on the Darwinian laws of cause and consequence. Lynn Diamond notes that the meteorite that struck the earth and caused the extinction of the dinosaurs could have passed twenty minutes earlier or twenty minutes later, and then there would have been no collision, and maybe no development of the smaller animals after the extinction of dinosaurs. The continuum of the discontinuous takes extreme dimensions at the same time, because twenty minutes compared to millions of years, is temporally small and at the same time huge in its consequences. This puts into perspective the butterfly effect vulgarized by the economists' speeches stating that a minimal action in one place can lead to a planetary upheaval. This dimension raising the anxieties of a metaphysics of chaos is always at the forefront of Robert Lepage's work. In *La face cachée de la lune*[70] both the play and the movie, the image of the umbilical cord travels along with the cosmonaut connected to the spacecraft by his cord, which, if broken, would leave him turning in orbit like a meteorite and lost in the infinite background of galaxies, an anguish that is also present in the movie *Gravity* directed by Alfonso Cuarón Orozco (2013). This fascinating chaos[71] awakens the anxieties of the cultural and metaphysical divides that have turned the world upside down with the discovery of the Americas coinciding with the Renaissance and the Reform, the latter breaking up the unity of the Christian world. The Baroque as the jubilation of imbalance, of movement, of the spiral and the transverse as Jean Rousset[72] specifies, reappeared recently in the cultural productions of the Americas after having inspired the artists who, in the 17th century, built the convents and the churches of Salvador de Bahia in Brazil, Cartagena in Colombia, Quito in Ecuador or Oaxaca in Mexico. These productions are dazzled both by the differences, similarities and the challenges that restart the desire to take physical, cultural, scientific and economic risks in order to effectively manage the new data where the Americas and their multiplicities meet those of the planet. This new baroque lacks however the heavenly clarity of the domes in the baroque churches, directing the gaze, beyond the terrestrial vicissitudes, to God, the unique saviour. Indeed, for Lepage, we remain within an infinite bottomless black ink that has not yet been conquered.[73]

This continuum of discontinuous is also explored through the theme of postmodern/postcolonial recycling. We often witness, in contemporary texts, an archaeology of waste.[74] This is the case of the main character in *Nikolski* who digs in the piles of computers whose memories are discarded in the trash:

> En règle générale, les archéologues ne s'intéressent pas tellement aux nomades. Plus une population voyage moins elle laisse des traces. On préfère étudier les civilisations qui s'installent, construisent des villes et produisent beaucoup de déchets…—Et le territoire traditionnel, dans tout ça ?—Les Inuits n'avaient aucune idée de ce qu'était un dépotoir avant l'arrivée de la Compagnie de la Baie d'Hudson.[75]

Thus, Joyce retrieves the computer pieces and memories to build one that works in a rampant piracy parodying the hacks of the States that have filled the museums of treasures by looting the interesting places on the planet. But these memories, like the diverse debris in dumps[76], are the non-official history of people, groups, and networks who invent their lives outside of institutions mapping the paths they are trying to impose. What is noted, in this discontinuity, is the unpredictability of the future these encounters lead to. It is this unpredictability that often causes the kind of fear that Jacques Ferron describes in *La Nuit* in which he reverses the cliché that binds fear with not knowing where one is heading politically, geographically or socially: "De sorte que, ne sachant trop où j'allais, je n'avais pas lieu de m'alarmer."[77] This uncertainty is also perceived positively by Édouard Glissant in terms of the valorization of Creolity, which he defines as hybridity plus unpredictability. This unpredictability is symbolized in Elena Botchorichvili's *Seulement attendre et regarder* by the character Andros, whose encounter with love has gone wrong. Then, in an unpredictable and burlesque way, he transforms himself into a human nightingale perched naked on a tree branch in order to call his beloved before suddenly collapsing on the ground.

Unpredictability/Master Narratives/Women's Status

This unpredictability is seen as positive because it breaks with the expected, the traditions, and official narratives which stabilize the power relations and the ways to read texts or situations. Louky Bersianik demonstrates this playfully in *Le Pique-Nique sur l'Acropole* in 1979. In this book, which combines the novel and the essay in its form as well as the pictorial and the textual, we find citations from Plato, who says that men, by the maieutic, give birth to poetry or concepts which are much more essential than the bodies produced by women, because the body is inferior to the spirit. From this substrate of evidence, Louky Bersianik shows that this narrative has been around for centuries, leading to gender, economic and political discrimination towards women through the ages including violence such as clitoridectomy. A master narrative, such as the one imposed by Plato, spreads its evidence on the long term through a dualism that is linked to essence, to an unchangeable being and identity. One of these evidences is that the relationship with the other man/woman is as dual and uneven as any dualistic relation, because one of the terms dominates the other. So, are the long-term and cause/consequence relations which justify these exclusive arguments desirable? We don't think so, because they always give advantage to a group that is trying to perpetuate its dominance. And if the break is more desirable, with what will it break? This is the question asked by Isabel Allende in *Hija de la fortuna* in 1999. In Chili, Eliza Sommers is submissive to the power of tradition and of the men who define the order of the nation-state and marginalize the women who must serve the order. During the gold rush of 1849, Eliza flees to California disguised as a man where she appreciates her new freedom. Her new life is very different form the one in Chile, as she can control her life, self-belong and take initiatives: "Aqui las mujeres pueden ser dueñas de su tierra, comprar y vender propriedades, divorciarse si les da real gana."[78] Thus, in California a new society invents itself that is more open but far from free of racism and exclusion as Tao Chi'en highlights: "No puedes imaginarte lo que le importa los que hago o lo que sé, para los americanos soy solo un asqueroso chino pagano y Eliza es una grasienta. En Chinatown soy un renegado sin coleta y vertido de yanqui. No pertenezco en ningun lado."[79] But all this situation shows is that women have more opportunity for self-realization. This will eventually give impetus to the feminist movement, which will spread from the United States to many other countries and transform the face of the nation-state in the hands of (often) aging male groups, as Jean-Charles Harvey points out in *L'homme qui va* in 1929. This de-essentialization of the asymmetrical male/female power relationship is a break that permanently transforms sociocultural identities. It generates a different master narrative based on the recognition of individual freedom, self-control and responsibility: "Las leyes americanas favorecian a los individuos: cada propriedad se reducia al espacio que un hombre solo podia explotar."[80] The break in the dominant power relationships is connected to a new link to the territory, which would no longer belong only to an owner or to a nation-state run by the quasi-feudal owners, as it was in Chile in the 19th century, but could now be transferred through property title linked to the ability of people to work. This is very different from what the Chileans experienced: "Las compañas chileñas burlaban la ley registrando los derechos a nombre de cada uno de los peones para abarcar mas terreno."[81] The question of self-belonging appears again in a number of texts and in different forms. It is explored in bestsellers such as *Once minutos* by Paolo Coelho and is often linked to the question of chance. Maria, the young daughter born in the Brazilian *Nordeste* becomes a prostitute in Switzerland. She understands that nothing belongs to her in Brazil and that nothing corresponds to her hopes of love and a better life. She understands that she does not self-belong, neither in Brazil, nor in Switzerland. However, after months in Switzerland, she meets an interesting and rich artist painter who discovers a particularly intense brightness in her. She then claims that encounters are successful when we can die and be reborn emotionally and intellectually. In this novel, too, it is important to self-belong, to be reborn as another person, following the encounter: "Los encuentros nos esperan pero la mayoría de las veces evitamos que sucedan."[82] The possibility of failure produced by an integrated collective narrative imposing a negative vision of self, sometimes because of a repetitive acting out of a fear to succeed, is corrected by chance and by trial and error. Thus, it may be possible to create an effective partnership away from experienced rejections and the dualism of soul and body, because the body will learn to speak the language of the soul as Maria said in Paulo Coelho's novel.[83]

We can see that by taking charge of historic situations, male and female writers have in the recent years explored negative situations in order to draw a form of continuity, that of the recognition of difference in equality, in what lends itself to the disruption of an essentialist narrative cataloguing people in separate groups, classes, races, ethnicities, nations. This discontinuous continuity linked to a desire to invent oneself differently generates something new out of the confrontation of discourses that displaces the homogenizing and discriminating long-term dream to a space of coincidences in competition that creates new partnerships, if one accepts that every encounter generates change.

There Is No Guarantee

It is curious to see what one of James Baldwin's characters said after regretting his trip in Europe destroyed his optimism by the presence of monuments commemorating wars and genocides: " 'Americans should never come to Europe', she said, and tried to laugh and began to cry, 'it means they never can be happy again. What's the good of an American who isn't happy? Happiness was all we had.'"[84] History and tragedy also enter the character's life, this time not by understanding the experiences of the Indigenous peoples, but by learning about European horrors. The positive dream open to infinite possibilities is thus corrected by an encounter which reminds us that "There are no guarantees and, furthermore, our best dreams will flounder on the shoals of historical resistance."[85] Therefore, it is necessary to escape the historical determinisms by understanding them, that is to say, understanding that there is no guarantee! That is the key to the Americas that are meeting the tragedy, that is to say the fallibility of history. Nowadays one understands that the long term does not guarantee anything. It is in part because of a reflection linked to the situation of Europe during and after the Second World War, which shows that the long term is a disaster, that the Americas are going to discover gradually the others (Blacks, gays, lesbians, women, Indigenous peoples, Métis, etc.) and their stories of suffering. This discovery of violence through access to Europe is present in *Le ciel de Bay City* by Mavrikakis. In this novel, a paragraph written in the style of magical realism shows Amy, who lives in a small house in Michigan, encountering her grand-parents who were killed in Auschwitz-Birkenau. The history of Europe is a reminder of a catastrophic world, which does not circle around the frontier but rather around the suburban landscape mimicking the dream of vast spaces, sadly realized through its kilometers of bungalows and shopping centers.

This access to violence also reveals the ignorance of those nearest, for instance Indigenous peoples or Haitians in the Dominican Republic. This is explored in a hallucinated style by René Philoctète in *Massacre River*. He evokes the massacre of 20,000 Haitian semi-slave workers by the machetes of the henchmen of the dictator Trujillo in 1937: "No one has any guarantees against lost hope."[86] Surrounding this horror, a rhetoric develops where the solar images disappear in the darkness of the tombs: "The sunbeam is seeping deeper and deeper into the clayey soil."[87] In the name of the Dominican national pride, of the reason of the State, of purity of the nation, its authenticity, its specificity and its originality oriented towards whiteness, the machetes mutilated and killed men, women and children. It is what proudly proclaims the Dominican radio ending the account of severed heads by advertising Gillette or giving an excerpt from *La joie de vivre*. People joined in the violence of the moment of genocide because it was built on the desire of a national homogeneity. This moment still remains, in its horror, in a memory revived by literary discourse although the national historians remain discrete, if not silent.

Henceforth, it will be necessary, in the coincidence of the spaces to share, to manage this continuum of discontinuous in the simultaneous. It can be done by the prophetic pragmatism which Cornel West speaks of when he speaks of hope and memory, mostly a subversive memory defined as follows: "Subversive memory is memory of danger, a memory of past suffering, of past defeat, but also of past triumph and success."[88] Texts such as the one by René Philoctète or others by Gérard Étienne such as *Le Nègre crucifié*[89] or *La pacotille*[90] relate well to Cornel West, because they aim towards transformative encounters. But there are different attitudes towards violent moments and memory. In Yann Martel, Piscine negotiates with the tiger on his raft, while the Indigenous people and the Creole explore power relations they exchange through reincarnations in *The Law of Love* by Laura Esquivel, but without losing their personalities. In *À toi*, Kym Thúy highlights many difficulties encountered, but they are not definitive. By the energy and the dream stemming from the Americas, Thúy considers that many people can be successful: "Les professeurs m'ont accordé mon diplôme au bout de trois ans, en même temps que les autres étudiants. Mais, contrairement à celles des autres, mes notes étaient attribuables non pas à mon mérite mais à mon acharnement. Vingt ans plus tard, je me suis retrouvée devant eux, inconditionnelle des mots, amoureuse de la langue, messagers de l'imaginaire, pour partager un moment de littérature. Tout est donc possible?"[91]

It is in this awareness and ability to revisit the contradictions without resolving them, but by being engaged in a future open to difference, that the encounters of the Americas are played. They refuse the narratives that continue to exist with their quasi eternal resentments: like in Europe (in particular central Europe) or in the ancient civilizations such as Iran, India or China, where historical resentments are intertwined with more recent ones based on the history of the political and/or economic colonization, or on the violence due to the changes in dictatorship. Yet, it is in the ability to generate new worlds and new ways of doing from what was seen as contradictory, that the cultures of the Americas can be considered new and challenging, as Frank/François recalls for Jacques Ferron, Piscine for Yann Martel, and as underlined by one of the first brochures for the Apple computers: "Simplicity is the ultimate sophistication."[92] Steve Jobs specifies: "It takes a lot of hard work [...] to make something simple, to truly understand the underlying challenges and come up with elegant solutions."[93]

Knowledge of the self and knowledge of the other are superimposed in communicational and informative messages dealing with the relationship between the subject and its environment; this imbrication is also identified by the Palo Alto school and in particular by Gregory Bateson, and noted by McLuhan: "The new media have transformed the entire environment into an educational affair."[94] The knowledge-based society is everywhere, its center is nowhere, and certainly not solely in the structure of a linear narrative leading to supposedly transparent meanings and pathways where the individual is caught up in narratives nourished by prohibitions that make him comply with pre-normed actions: "This is how you set a table for tea; this is how you set a table for dinner… this is how you behave in the presence of men who don't know you very well."[95] And Jamaica Kincaid goes on for several pages in this style by extending the compliance of causality, which makes the majority of people self-impose narrow limits. Their identity comes back to reveal the path of their repetitive narratives imposed by social norms. In the face of this determinism, a world can manifest itself. It is open to the possibility of exploring new *frontiers* as emphasized by W. P. Kinsella in *Shoeless Joe Jackson comes to Iowa*[96] with his story depicting baseball as a game open onto the infinite. The knowledge-based society, in relation to these prohibitions that limit and obscure options, brings back the baroque movement open to the infinite. But this infinity is more cosmic than rooted in traditional orthodoxies. It can be translated in very significant concrete and technological cases as emphasized by Steve Jobs before his death: "But on the other hand, perhaps it's like an on-off switch", he (Steve Jobs) said. 'Click! And you are gone' Then he paused again and smiled slightly. 'Maybe that's why I've never liked to put on-off switches on Apple devices.'"[97] Incidentally, this infinite is more like the non-finite in its philosophical-artistic achievements as we see in the work of Escher or in the poems of Christian Bök entitled *Crystallography*. This work represents fractal dynamics playing on the non-finite: "Fractals reveal the same / degree of intricate detail / at every magnification:/ imagine a mirage receding / further into the distance, / the closer you get to it."[98] This fascination between words and repetitive systemic technological productivity that begins in the fractals continues in a differential systemic in snowflakes: "Snowflakes embody an absolute principle of difference."[99] The contemporary texts linked to the *frontier* of knowledge embodied by the global technology constantly oscillate between the repetition of the non-finite fractal and the infinite difference; another way to open up to the infinite logic of the moment of which Yvon Rivard talks in *Le siècle de Jeanne*, this moment that contains everything, the beginning and the end in an endless coincidence.

Causality and Narrative in the Americas

Canadians put their faith in luck and improvisation.[100]

What is said by Yvon Rivard is already perceived in *La ciudad sin nombre* by Torres-García.[101] He mixes images and handwriting to reject linear, causal and temporal connections, to rejoin the moments where the prehistoric, the pre-Columbian and the modernity of the constructivist art join in the exploration of encounters between civilizations including encounters which have not really taken place—particularly between European and pre-Columbian cultures, because in Uruguay there are no pre-Columbian traces. Nowadays, some of the narratives of the Americas tend to escape the dualism on/off, self/others synonymous with interior/exterior. They propose models of the positive encounters and productive outcomes of coincidences, surprises and simultaneity, mentioned also in novels like *On the Road* by Jack Kerouac, *Zen and the Art of Motorcycle Maintenance* by Pirsig or *Le singe grammairien* by Octavio Paz. These narratives of the contemporary Americas aim in part to escape the novels of strong causality linked to a certain conception of temporality. These narratives join the essayistic and theoretical reflections on subjects such as multiculturalism disseminated by Randolph Bourne already in 1916, and more recently Will Kymlicka and Charles Taylor. These thinkers much like writers such as Édouard Glissant, Isabel Allende, Pico Iyer, Yvon Rivard, Eric Dupont, or Carlos Castaneda, seek to produce a *new* narrative for the Americas. This narrative is related to the dissemination of a democracy based on the legitimacy of displacement and of travel. It would be a guide to thinking positively about the encounters of different cultural worlds, taking into account myths, as myths always hide, according to René Girard, the real killings and genocides. In this sense, as we have seen, the new worlds aim at establishing an original mode of being within the combination of difference and equality. One understands that any individual, from birth is shaped by various influences and discourses. This is the same for any society, which always invents itself in relations with other communities. The New Worlds (the Americas, Australia, New-Zealand) are based on their much longer democratic terms than the traditions brought over by newcomers, many of whom have never lived a life in a liberal democracy. The long term of democracies offers a reference that has no pure origin, because it invents itself in the present, in the moment of encounters and the conjunction of the different. The New Worlds offer, through the new, a reflection on the myth of the origin, which meaning is controlled by the mobs who exclude those who are different. The

New Worlds, contrary to what we have seen in the nationalist Marxist society accumulating fake Indigenous burial mounds in *La logeuse* by Éric Dupont so as to hide the fact that they murdered those who did not want to conform, redefine the very notion of origin based on the strategic needs of a present calling for the recognition of difference.

Thus, we see that the question of causality, as Lili pointed out in Lynn Diamond's work (section: Temporality and Causality), is important in the Americas, because it raises the question of the evaluation of the encounter between the Europeans and the others. Indeed, Columbus was not sent to discover a continent, but to open a route to India passing through the West because the Eastern route was blocked by Muslims. The purpose seemed clear, but the unintended consequences were huge. Tao Chi'en, a character in Isabel Allende's *Hija de la fortuna*, talks about what he and Eliza were looking for in California: "Parece que todos vinimos buscando algo y encontramos otra cosa."[102] Eliza, who wanted to see her fiancé again, has found the possibility for a personal development and a love for Tao Chi'en. As for all those who came for the gold, they found death, developed businesses, planted vines, etc. These unintended effects are read by some as the effect of the Providence that brought them in a new Garden of Eden where they were able to reestablish a better life much like various religious groups, Protestants, Doukhobors, Amish, Mennonites or others… even if, for the Doukhobors in Gabrielle Roy[103], the garden is in fact, as the agent of colonization said, a desert filled with dinosaur skeletons. For others, such as George Gilder in *Wealth and Poverty*[104], the unintended effects are perceived as the effect of what Adam Smith calls the invisible hand because if a commercial enterprise is a failure, it often leads to something else that is a success. In other words, in the unintended effects, the Anglo-Saxon Protestants often read a plan from God that reveals itself gradually in a life ordered by work, energy and spirituality. Hence, a form of Manifest Destiny is often at work and it was already present in the colonists who settled in Jamestown. For them, a superior causality guides what may sometimes appear as fortuitous, negative, and surprising.

These days, however, in the postcolonial/postmodern world, chance is an important motor of democracy and its culture. It is not necessarily constructed as the expression of a plan but as a form of chaos in the world that we must learn to manage in mobility and in versatility. How can chance be defined? It can be seen as the encounter of independent causes, a mixture of paths from causes to consequences. It is this meeting of independent causes that reorganizes the providential points of view and their myths, but according to different perspectives, because the providential narratives reflect on the future and the mythical narratives direct towards the past. In fact, the myths are always intended to give the origin, the first cause of a situation. As stated by Tomson Highway, they are therefore, like any mythology, located at "the exact halfway point between truth and fiction, mythology, the exact halfway point between science and religion, that most elaborate of all fictions."[105] This encounter of diverse narrativities, which establishes identity and culture explain the place of people, either in the desire to deny a right to this place, or in exploiting its potential. For the first case, we consider the paradigm of barbarism/civilization and the master narrative of progress, or even the rewriting of an encounter in a biblical dominant narrative as with the Mormons, who see the Indigenous people as one of the tribes of Israel who refused the message of Jesus. For the second case, we analyze the way an essayistic meta-reflection like the one Tomson Highway presents, or a symbolic/parabolic exploration such as *Life of Pi* by Yann Martel allows to go beyond established narratives of exclusion.

Chance, Causality, and Crime

However, there are different degrees in this differentiation placing chance and coincidence on one hand, and legitimation by the causal and the temporal on the other. The causal-temporal leaves place for misinforming tactics in the minds of the people, and therefore it results in a reading of history that serves a particular ideology. This is evident in Elena Botchorichvili's *Seulement attendre et regarder* and Éric Dupont's *La logeuse*. In this novel, situated at Notre-Dame-du-Cachalot, at the time of the post-Quiet Revolution, the bureaucrats of the nationalist Marxist thought attempt to create a paradise within a socialist national community protected by a culture of misinformation. It reveals to us a primary ritual. Every time a villager manifests his/her individuality, for example by way of growing a Christmas cactus, flourishing and announcing the winter storms, he/she is stoned to death in an expeditious manner by the delirious crowd, confusing causality and coincidence.[106] Indeed, the owner of the cactus is considered to be the one who made winter come. Hence, we can see that this Marxism is deeply linked to a world of religious traditions in which saying the name of Satan made him appear. The owner will then disappear under a mound presented as an indigenous tomb.

> Le 1er novembre 1987: camarade Madeleine Barachois, 55 ans, Balance, fut à son tour poursuivie et sauvagement assassinée en hurlant "non! non! non!". Fière pro-

> priétaire d'un cactus Noël qui, comme par magie, fleurissait toujours un jour avant les tempêtes de neige en décembre, elle avait pris l'habitude de prophétiser les pires blizzards. En ce matin du 1er novembre, Madeleine s'était vantée que son cactus allait fleurir tôt cette année-là. Les habitants, excédés par l'idée d'un blizzard hâtif, finirent par conclure que la pauvre femme désirait et provoquait ces tempêtes et, confondant causalité et coïncidence, donnèrent naissance à la deuxième sœur sous une pluie de pierre.[107]

Thus, the orthodox ideology always imposes a world of causality, eliminating those who are seen as a threat to the order of the community. The cactus that blooms is interpreted as a desire to harm the community on the part of the cactus' owner, who would see his powers rejected by the bureaucrats of the socialist paradise. This causality is understood as evil and leads to death by stoning. The individual does not self-belong, he should incorporate himself in the causality regime of an orthodox community and, as he deviates, he is labeled a traitor and becomes a scapegoat for everything that goes wrong. A master narrative is in place and it is controlled by the lynch mob who will rebuild the community in the face of adversity (here the blizzard). Faced with this orthodoxy of causalities and their relation to a temporality invented in the form of a reconstructed past, which helps deny the very existence of scapegoats as we see in *La logeuse*, Rosa Ost simply notes that "tous les signes sont faux."[108] This sentence reminds the reader of another sentence written by Werner Heisenberg in *Le manuscrit de 1942*: "Nous devons nous rappeler avant tout que la puissance politique s'est fondée encore et toujours sur le crime."[109]

The Semiotics of the Transcultural

> Zebras never wonder if they're white with black stripes. Or black with white stripes. They work together so they won't be lunch for a lion.[110]

Nowadays, a complex relationship to the production of meanings is manifested in the goal of transforming a dualistic antagonistic relationship into an efficient multiple cooperation. In following *Life of Pi* and the relationship between the tiger and Piscine on the raft, we would say that the meanings must be produced according to the context allowed by the encounter. The signs are not clues to be deciphered, as in a suspenseful plot where there are secrets to find, because a narrator who has authority controls the causality and aims to prove that there is always a culprit to eliminate. The signs are to occur in the shared spaces of the encounters born from coincidences. Yann Martel explains that a novel that has Portugal in the year 1939 as a background, may have little to do with Portugal in 1939.[111] This brings to mind Stephen Leacock's parodies of the English romantic-realistic codes. We remember "Gertrude the Governess or, Simple Seventeen". One can see that the scenic state of the soul and its transition to the realistic space is a technique that can be reversed, particularly in the Americas where the places are invented and change according to those who, as Jin Mee Yoon suggests, take charge of them through their actions and their culture. Here is Leacock's description which coincides with Martel's statement: "It was a wild and stormy night on the West coast of Scotland. This, however, is immaterial to the present story as the scene is not laid in the West of Scotland."[112] These spaces born of coincidences could lead to effective surprises or collaborations (though often temporary), if the partners found their place of survival, expansion, or dream. This is well illustrated by the relationship between Piscine and the tiger in *Life of Pi* by Yann Martel, two migrants on their way to a new world.

Life of Pi by Yann Martel is the story of Piscine Patel, a young man whose parents own a zoo in India and who want to immigrate to Canada. While Piscine dreams of being at the same time Buddhist, Christian and Muslim, he observes the territorial instincts of animals who are confined in their small territories, which distinguish them from humans. For humans are separated by national borders symbolized by spaces of different colors marked out by black lines in any atlas. Piscine Patel's family immigrates to Canada and takes some of the animals on a boat which sinks in the middle of the ocean. On the raft we find Piscine Patel and the tiger, also a hyena, a monkey and a zebra soon to be devoured. Piscine doesn't fear quasi-radical otherness, nor differences. He is the master of the ocean's vastness and movements waiting to be incorporated in the Americas.

What should Piscine do if he wants to survive the tiger and the ocean? He needs to activate his transdisciplinary knowledge, combining different levels of reality that are related to ethology, anthropology and history. The levels of reality which he faces are the following: on the side of the tiger, there are tendencies of dominance as studied by Henri Laborit[113] whereby the dominant eats first and has claim to the females while the others are satisfied by the rest. It will devour other species, as it did the zebra temporarily settled on the raft. The entire question for Piscine is to be regarded as more dominant by the tiger and, therefore, to operate effectively according to the level of reality of the tiger who manages its territoriality. But Piscine also knows another level of reality: it is René Girard's notion of mimesis of appropriation. It states that hominization, the affirmation of oneself as an individual subject, leads from the hierarchical violence established through dominance to the ability to compete, all against all, in order to obtain the object of desire shown by the one who is in a model position. He shows the others what they should desire: money or spirituality, and especially the power of having the ability to indicate what is desirable, therefore, what to do and what not to do, in other words a social order. This other level of reality non-A, rests on a democratized battle, on a dynamic to control a territory, a finite wealth as is the wealth in level A, that of dominance. However, Piscine is set on another level of reality, T, where the violence of dominance as that of the mimesis of appropriation—based on the territoriality where the self/others is synonymous with interior/exterior and civilized/barbaric, and based on the exclusions, the production of scapegoats, of wars and genocides—has been domesticated by a logic that is not dualistic but ternary. Cultural and scientific knowledge allows for creation of non-finite wealth as opposed to finite territorial logics. This logic of knowledge operates simultaneously with the other levels A and non-A on the raft, the cramped space of an encounter based on coincidence since Piscine and the tiger are on the raft because of a shipwreck (that is, by chance since nobody will know what caused the boat to sink). These levels of reality are based on Reality, that is to say, on that which resists our experiences and representations, as stated by Nicolescu.[114] These experiences, as highlighted by René Girard, are linked to the sacred, the sacrificial and a violence based on the perception that the other would represent a radical difference. This perception of the other as a 'radical other' can lead to his death. However, this death like any death represents an undeniable element, which is situated beyond any discourse. It is resistant to any representation, and therefore resists the disinformation and lies of the authoritarian institutions and the medias at their service, which connect negative meanings to the victims.

Piscine's talent will be, on the one hand, to convince the tiger that he is dominant, because he does not immediately have the means to kill it. On the other hand, he will have to combine reality A marked by the dominance with reality non-A, which would be that of the appropriative mimetic violence based on the dualism self/others; this should lead Piscine to kill the tiger at the first opportunity or to abandon it on the floating island. But Piscine goes to a different level T, because observing the zoo during his childhood and the reactions of the orthodox religious people living according to the appropriative mimesis of exclusion, and in relation to which he claimed to want to be (at the same time) Muslim, Christian and Buddhist, taught him to follow both the logic of knowledge and the territorial logic. He modifies the logic of dominance by feeding the tiger, an action which does not belong to a dominant who only leaves residues. He divides the limited space on the raft in two spaces because the tiger keeps its logic and is living thus according to A. He isn't looking to kill the tiger or leave it on the floating island, so he modifies the appropriative mimetic logic non-A that asks to get rid of the rival model. One of the invoked reasons is that, to survive for hundreds of days on the ocean, without losing his wits and his sense of orientation, it was necessary to have an interlocutor. It matters little that this radical other could destroy him, either as a dominant (in the ethological reading of the text), or as a symbol of appropriative nationalist murderers illustrated by the zoo and its division into homogeneous territories (in the Girardian anthropologic-historical reading of the text[115]). He combines A and non-A to reach the level of reality T that is based on the rejection of the static A, of the opposing dualism, A and non-A, to live a hyper-dynamism of the open space symbolized by the ocean: a new *frontier* that recycles in the liquid the *frontier* of the Americas. Piscine is then engaged in the transdisciplinary ethological/anthropological/semiotic-pragmatic level of reality of the knowledge society and not in the dualistic logic of finite wealth based on the territorial logic and the fascination of a rational and intellectual culture that is linked to Europe looking for clear definitions and distinct solutions to maintain homogeneity. Piscine, before even arriving to Canada is a Canadian, as Robert Fulford says: "Canada, because of its size and diversity, is not a country of *either/or* but a country of *maybe* and *I hope perhaps*."[116] It is this attitude that allows to effectively insert oneself in globalized encounters, where consensuses are formed and broken up in the temporariness of chances, and also in creative improvisations.

Levels of Reality and Social Capital

We retain that, upon arrival in Mexico, the tiger disappears without even looking back to take a last look at Piscine, who has fed him with fish the whole time. The social capital generated by the change of the level of reality (temporarily created on the raft), defined as "help people to advance their interests by co-operating with others,"[117] is based on a type of relationship that is, for Piscine, on the side of *bridging*. This means that the relationship is established with people of different backgrounds, but it is the *linking*, therefore a relation of hierarchy for the tiger, where the links of causes to consequences differ from one and the other.

Although the coincidence of being together on the raft remained incomprehensible for the tiger, for Piscine, it became significant in his transdisciplinary approach—the bearer of relationships from cause to particular coincidences. His experience then means living a transcultural practice on a daily basis with the radical otherness of the tiger. This allows him, upon arriving in Toronto, to live a life of dynamic transactions in various networks generating social capital "for a purpose maintained by supportive and productive interactions."[118]

The Choice in the Production of Meanings

"…it's foolhardy to think that a story ends.
There are as many possible endings as beginnings."[119]

Piscine has reached a principle of relativity that is consistent with what Nicolescu has said: "No level of Reality constitutes a privileged place from which one is able to understand all the other levels of Reality."[120] This is what we find when the Japanese insurers are going to the hospital in Mexico to investigate the shipwreck. He tells his story with the tiger, but it cannot be understood by the representatives of the insurance company accustomed to the discourse of factual, and plausible, bureaucracy. He tells a different story with human actors, more conform to the expectations of the employees. He thinks he knows how to adapt to the level of perception of the Japanese culture and that of a bureaucratic civilization that demands a true narrative; that is to say, a story consistent with prevailing stereotypes generated by nation-states based on the exclusion akin to what René Girard demonstrates in his analysis. Piscine asks: "You want words that reflect reality? […] Words that do not contradict reality? […] That will confirm that you already know."[121] He then tells his story and that of his mother and the cook on the raft and how they killed each other, based on the plausible logic of the mimesis of appropriation and a victimizing reading of the situation. Piscine speaks of the object of desire taken out of the hands of the model and with which Piscine kills him: "The knife was all along in plain view on the bench."[122] However, after the Japanese employees have admitted to not being able to discern between the true and the fictional story, the animal fiction and the more official story, they say that they prefer the one with the animals: "The story with the animals is the better story." To which Piscine replies: "Thank you. And so it goes with God."[123] Unfortunately, the Japanese bureaucrats do not have the necessary reflexive capacity to free themselves from the dualism and to reach a level T containing both A and non-A. They are "non-T" as opposed to Piscine, aware of the sacred and the strength of the new that displaces the predictable causalities linked to justifying slaughter. Therefore, they leave and write a bureaucratic report consistent with the expected professional discourse, stressing that the cause of the shipwreck remains a mystery. Chance and coincidence displace the argumentative bureaucratic order.

Coincidence and the Americas

Life of Pi is a parable that links globalization, the legitimacy of displacements and the call of the Americas as a multicultural context. It is clear when one considers that the different levels (A, non-A and T) are upsetting the relationships between fiction and reality, because the reality of some may be the fiction of others, as suggested by the episode with the Japanese insurers, and as shown already by a work representative of magical realism, Gabriel García Marquez's novel *One Hundred Years of Solitude*. The latter underlines the absurd realities of dictatorships leading to murders, torture and genocides for mad reasons such as not submitting to the complete dominance of the dictator. Reality is what resists our representations, which are in part constructed by the group that educates us. However, in the case of the writers of a new kind of magical realism like Yann Martel, what stands is the undeniable fact that there were people alive and that now they are dead. The causes of the shipwreck remain unclear and even more so the causes of the encounter between Piscine, the zebra, the monkey, the hyena, and the tiger on the raft. This is evidence of the crossing of independent causes, that is to say, chance. Moreover, it is the crossing of independent causes whereby people, in the Americas, are found to occupy spaces in contiguity, and are not bonded by a history as long as that of Europe's. Since there is no clear relationship between cause and consequence—the very basis of the narrative structure for specialists of narrativity such as Greimas[124]—it is necessary to invent a narrative that would give a meaning to this encounter. This is why Piscine offers two stories, the story of an encounter of two levels of successful realities and the story of a founding murder. On the one hand, there is the level of reality non-A of the mimesis of appropriation, since the employees of the Japanese insurance company find in the first story more of a delirious form than an acceptable story which, for them, would be that of the exclusionary and mimetic appropriative violence corresponding to all of the historical standards of the nation-states of the planet and of their educational dissemination in history books. On the other hand, there is the level of reality T of the successful encounter between Pi and the tiger, which is in accordance with the multi and transcultural perspectives.

Thus, through the Japanese insurers, Yann Martel agrees in a certain way with what Dany Laferrière proposes in his novel entitled *Je suis un écrivain japonais*. Laferrière believes that when a Japanese reader is reading his book, Laferrière is a Japanese writer. So, if it is read by someone who only refers to the positivist and dualistic modernity, this is how the novel will be read. But if it is read by someone who had access to several modes of cultural and narrative functioning, it will be understood as an animal parable symbolizing the successful management of a cross-cultural encounter despite the risks. This idea intrigues several other writers, such as Edwige Danticat, who says: "In the book, the fictional author, a stand-in for Dany Laferrière, explains his decision to call himself a Japanese writer, concurring with the French literary critic Roland Barthes that 'a text's unity lies not in its origin but in its destination.'"[125] The outcome, adds Danticat, is that there is probably "no such thing as an immigrant artist in this globalized age"[126], since all cultures intersect in coincidences produced by the use of technological networks that consistently lead to encounters where the cultures and aesthetics mingle. This view, in contrast to the traditional literary exegesis based on the life of the author attached to a territory, or on the intentions of the author, suggests that the productivity connected to the process of reading counts significantly. However, Laferrière suggests that this productivity is based on cultural differences that are blocked in the homogeneous national cultures. To understand his position, it is necessary to compare two books written by him: *Je suis un écrivain japonais* and *Comment faire l'amour avec un Nègre sans se fatiguer*. In the latter text, Vieux has several Anglo-Québécoises lovers whom he perceives as racist and naïve, this allowing him to fight against the remnants of the British Empire and its colonizing influences. The protagonist evokes *Le code noir*, which renders Blacks pieces of furniture. However, despite the fact that this code was produced by the French colonialists and applied in the Caribbean, especially Haiti, Vieux fights against the British Empire. In this sense, he manifests an attitude similar with that of the minority French-speaking Quebeckers and tries to not antagonize them. This is why there is no racist francophone student in the novel. By adapting, he is capable of controlling the stereotypes of the Franco-Quebecois readers who, through a reading consistent with their own interests and rejections, turn him into a Quebecois writer.[127] In other words, even if the reader is of great importance in producing meanings consistent with his experiences and perspectives on relationships with otherness, his or her reading may be controlled by the author who could lead him or her to approval rather than rejection. Thus, the author (here, Dany Laferrière) can buy himself the chance to become a bestseller author, because he may be able to comply with the identity structures that do not depend on relationships with the soil or the climate as stated by the positivist Buckle in the 19th century.

This functioning specific to a literature known as migrant, is not the same as that of *Life of Pi*. In the case of the migrant literature, as for René Girard, transnational and transcultural narratives direct the readings and the hermeneutical capacities of people to think in terms of causalities/consequences that always lead to looking for a culprit, thus to legitimize the dynamics of exclusion founding antagonistic communities. These narratives are included in national or regional cultures, according to particular modalities and themes, as we can see in the second story produced by Piscine for the Japanese insurers who cannot believe the multicultural story of survival with a tiger.[128] They clench to what they know, that is to narratives leading to finding a scapegoat. But these narratives relate to dynamics rooted in stereotypes such as those that govern the conduct of dominance, the mimesis of appropriation, and the fight of all against all, the production of a scapegoat ensuring the cohesion of the group and the territorial logic coupled with the belief that there is a finite sum of wealth. In contradistinction to these narratives, *Life of Pi* or *The Law of Love* by Laura Esquivel for instance are connected to the logic of the knowledge-based society, which offers an endless wealth of meanings leading to the recognition of difference. These narratives are themselves glocalized; they are related to themes that may be qualified not as migrant, but as globalized. These narratives allow to manage coincidence and simultaneity, in particular by the logic of the included third, which—while recognizing the limitations of those who adhere to a single level (A or non-A)—manage to recontextualize these levels in level T which produces win/win situations for all. According to a win/win logic, life is not a zero-sum game.[129]

It should be noted that this coincidence in contiguity—the symbol of the invention of the Americas whose regions are settled by people who arrived from the most diverse places on the planet—joined the dynamics of glocalization and its permanent and fast transformations. Indeed, the contemporary context is no longer that of the invention of the nations in the Americas where the dualism barbarism/civilization was the main reference. It is that of the progressive invention of a global brain. Hence, in this new context, the historicism, the basis of the perspective of the nation-state and its traditional representations on research, is partly unable to produce significations that would enlighten the contemporary dynamics, because it is linked to restricted places that it invents as homogeneous.[130] In other words, the transdisciplinary/transculturality produced in *Life of Pi* connects through a parabolic fiction the invention of the Americas to its planetary influence. The Japanese consul in *The Global Soul* by Pico Iyer points out: "America's great and lasting significance is its existence in the mind."[131] The Americas are a dream of well-being for the planet, especially regarding North America but of a well-being that, according to Yann Martel, cannot do without the belief in God even if this belief is escaping from the religious orthodoxies that are often being transformed in a kind of spiritualist polyculture.

In South America, the Americas are the utopia to achieve, as we are reminded by writers of magical realism such as Gabriel García Marquez, Isabel Allende, or even Laura Esquivel who questions utopian dreams, and proposes a recontextualization of historical discourses by demanding an egalitarian recognition of otherness. This utopian dream of the South Americas (controlled and parodied by Laura Esquivel), continues in a polycultural form the dream of the Jesuit missionaries. Indeed, the latter, in contrast to the proponents of practical rationalism, were not directly aiming at transplanting the European lifestyles in the Americas, but rather at re-creating the human being that would lead to equality in piety. This was the mission of the Jesuits as well as the Franciscans, who wanted to organize the lives of the Indigenous peoples according to the principles of Thomas Moore's *Utopia*, itself inspired by the Americas and the Indigenous lifestyles. In relation to these dimensions, in the coincidence of Piscine and the tiger, Piscine tries to reorganize the world and oneself in a scientific, fictional, spiritual, and emotional productivity related to level T including A and non-A, which leads to an effective transculturality based on the recognition of alterity in every sense of the term. Indeed, this level allows the production of new meanings from meanings—themselves a product of other meanings in a non-finite dynamic of interpretance, in the Peircian sense of the expression[132]—which facilitates living with the other temporarily and effectively in inclusion and creativity.

Girard and Greimas: Encounters and Narratives

Now what about the narrative and its ways of legitimizing exclusion by accepting the mechanism of causality managed by those who seek to build homogeneity? Let us reiterate that the narrative is understood by theorists (e.g. Greimas[133]) as a sequence of actions, to which are linked agents of action who make the transformation of an initial content into a different and final content possible. This transformation of semantic contents is produced by mechanisms, which combine actions and agents of actions in a narrative structure that rests on causality and temporality, generating interest for the reader. This syntagmatic connectivity is rooted in paradigms which are based on binary oppositions; the semantic squares of Greimas whose poles are connected by relations of contrariety and contradiction. In his analyses, in particular of a tale by Maupassant[134], Greimas reaches the fundamental opposition of life/death that can only coalesce in a unit expressed by the lexeme God. This lexeme is the place of the total indetermination from which all attributes can be generated: God is good, God is everything, God is everywhere, God is infinite, God is in heaven, etc. It is from this lexeme, too full or too empty, depending on the point of view of the reader, that narratives, which explore different perspectives of the world, will be generated. For instance, we can think that God is exterior as in the Christian world or interior to us as in the Buddhist world. In other words, the fundamental opposition is perhaps not life/death, but interior/exterior, which is also suggested in Yann Martel's *Life of Pi*. We can also say that this interior/exterior opposition governs all human semantics. Take, for example, the experience of someone who drinks water from a glass, spits it back into the glass and proceeds to drink it again. A lot of people will find this disgusting. However, there is nothing disgusting from a hygienic point of view since the same person is drinking his water and his saliva in his glass. But it has crossed the interior and exterior boundary, and this can be regarded as quite transgressive. Similarly, sexual penetration marks the crossing of the interior/exterior semantic limit, just as the territorial boundaries with their share of wars and genocides, not to mention the stories of spirits and the crossing of the Styx, all lead, in view of René Girard's theory[135], to consider this paradigm as fundamental.

Poor but Clean

If we take this hypothesis of the importance of the interior/exterior paradigm as our point of departure, we can see that it has important consequences on the conception that we may have of a narrative seen as a transformational structure linked to the dynamics of the encounter. Indeed, in this case, all narratives are a syntagmatization of the possibility, or not, of being inside the group. This is connected to different perspectives on how to be in contact with the exterior of the group as well as with others inside the group. This situation is also explored in poetry; that is, in texts based on weak narrativity as seen in *Outside, Inside* by Michael Penny.[136] The obsessive syntagmatization of this opportunity to be on the inside or the anguish of being rejected is true if one considers that a narrative is always a narrative of transformation. Nonetheless, this transformation is not always solely marked by the staging of actions and agents of actions, but sometimes also by the manifestation of conjunctions of coordination that modify binary stereotyped paradigms[137] and their implications. Let's take, for example, the phrase "poor but clean", an embodiment, as we will see, of a play on the interior/exterior. There are hundreds of instances of this phrase in the literatures of the 18th, 19th and 20th centuries, from Russia to North America, not to mention the copious resort to this stereotype in the media. Here are just a few examples: "La maison d'un prolétaire est modeste, simple, pauvre même mais propre comme le visage d'une honnête femme"[138]; "Entraron a una habitacíon pequeña, sin ventilacíon, pero limpa y ordenada"[139]; "La chambre qu'il occupait était pauvre mais proprette"[140] and "It was neat and clean but very dreary-looking and scantily furnished!"[141] Let's not forget the close or more distant synonymous structures from the basic concept: "La propreté est l'ornement du pauvre; qui s'en revêt se pare de beaux habits"[142] and "L'immeuble était vétuste mais bien entretenu."[143] What is the function of *mais* (but) in this oppositional paradigm? It displaces the binary paradigms poor/rich, dirty/clean, which in turn signal the more general opposition of exterior/interior. It especially transforms the stereotyped implications at the core of the media and literary visions of many societies. Indeed, rich implies clean (materially and morally) and poor implies dirty. This implication corresponds to an aristocratic society, not an industrialized one. From the moment industry is developed in the cities, poor but clean workers are needed, also people who have a certain degree of hygiene and are not a threat to the wealthy, and all the poor who are morally clean.[144] Thus, they will produce goods according to the imposed conditions, without getting involved in revolts and, most likely, without attempting to steal. We find a beautiful example of this situation in a recent issue of *The Economist*, on the subject of Kibera (Nairobi, Kenya), the largest slum in the world[145]: "The room is immaculate as are those of many neighbours. Kibera only looks like a slum from the outside." This quote illustrates the use of the paradigm interior/exterior in connection with "immaculate", thus very clean. It underlines a certain inner wealth from the point of view of shareable values. This demonstrates that poor but clean is often akin to poor, but honest[146]: "Un jeune pâtissier bordelais pauvre mais honnête comme on dit dans les histoires de l'oncle Paul."[147] Nowadays, we can put more emphasis on the fact of wanting to get out of this situation, to get comfortable, to strive for a better economic situation: "Ils sont pauvres, c'est vrai, mais ils sont fiers."[148]

The function of *mais* (but) is to break down the implication between poor and dirty, which has placed the poor at the exterior of the civilized world. *Mais* (but) leads us, therefore, to potentially tell the story of a surprise. This surprise leads to a release of shared evidence based on the stereotype of the binary paradigms and their received implications that, in particular, interior/exterior of which the modalities vary according to time and place. Surprisingly, both the poor and the rich can receive the qualifier clean. It is certain that the attribution process is also strongly related to the structure of the narrative, which plays on different moments in the definition of an identity, as Balzac illustrates in a caricatural way, in *Grandeur et décadence de César Birotteau*. In other words, *mais* (but) is the key element in the sequence of actions related to agents of action who are transformed by this adverb. The *mais* (but) not only modifies the implication, but it mostly transforms the interior/exterior paradigm. Suddenly, and this is the point of interest of fiction, we discover that the poor are part of the interior, thus of the socio-economic and cultural space profoundly modified. The reflexes of exclusion are no longer played the same way. This is highlighted by Sarmiento a few years after the publication of *Facundo*, in his stories of travel in the United States and in Canada.[149] He affirms that the process of attribution is not based on an unchangeable being. He states, as we mentioned before, that in the United States the people are not poor, but poor for now. The temporal adverb destroys the essence of the process of attribution and puts into perspective the hierarchy of social classes and, therefore, the narratives of exclusions based on the opposition interior/exterior. It opens to a narrative based on a future to build, and therefore, on a temporality that may be guided by Providence and thwart the established causal relationships. It will be the same when, in the sixties in the United States the speeches of Malcolm X or Martin Luther King state that *Black is beautiful*. This attribute brings into question the association of Blackness with non-aesthetic and dirty, which situates Blackness at the exterior and qualifies it as unsightly. Moreover, we retain in this context the analysis of the situation of Nicaraguan immigrants in Costa Rica, a democracy that thinks of itself as having a unique origin. However, Anyelick Campos Zamora and Larissa Tristan Jimenez demonstrate the construction of the self and the relations of exclusion legitimized by such a narrative. These researchers quote R. Soto defining Costa Rica's wish: "[…] una corriente de immigracíon sana, tanto en lo moral como en lo físico, inmigracíon exclusive de labradores, o mejor aun, de families de labradores, cuya sangre sea como la sangre magnífica de nuestro pueblo; y sus costumbres como las nuestras: campesinos españoles, italianos, franceses, irlandes…"[150] This vision leads to the exclusion of Black Anglo-protestants of the Caribbean coast settled there since the end of the 19th century, but who received Costa Rican citizenship only in 1948. Soto's phrase dates back to the beginning of the 20th century. However, in 2002, Carlos Sandoval García points out that similar discourses joining the words sane and moral[151] target the Nicaraguan immigrants. This point is also underlined by the two researchers, Zamora and Jimenez, analyzing the representations of Nicaraguans in the contemporary Costa Rican media. Here is what Carlos Sandoval García, quoting the two researchers, highlights: "En este contexto hay ciertas oposiciones que se repiten: legalidad versus ilegalidad es el contexto narrativo que predomina en el caso de los 'inmigrantes'; limpieza versus contagio es predominante cuando enfermedades es el principal topico…"[152] Thus, the others—the immigrants or the groups already there before the Europeans—are perceived as dirty and poor, they are "de piel oscura y pobres, mientras que el opuesto seria la propria blancura y una nación igualitaria de clade media."[153] At the very least, then, their moral and physical cleanliness must be verified if they cannot be sent elsewhere.

Returning to the *mais* (but) of the poor but clean, we see that everything happens as if we were no longer reading in order to seek the truth, the right decoding, the right meaning, as in Christian or Muslim traditions, or in their national, state and secular policy extensions. Everything rather happens as if the desire or the need to transform the basic interior/exterior paradigm, which governs all human semantics, was the issue of the narratives of modernity. The narratives of the 19th and 20th centuries appear to primarily rest on the action of conjunctions such as *mais* (but), changing the essentialist paradigms, or on adverbs such as *maintenant* (now) used by Sarmiento. They question the essentialized identity linked to dualism, rather than strengthen the causality's own constraints analyzed by Vladimir Propp.[154] Indeed, the use of *mais* (but) or *maintenant* (now) is always about exploring encounters and spaces of potential transformations, and thus to consider the possibility of changes in the complex sociocultural and economic relations.

Of course, these encounters are manifested by actions. We can even say that there are novels that are based on and fascinated by the causal temporal sequences of actions. This is the case of novels in the realistic aesthetic literary movement and its exacerbated variants: the mystery, espionage and horror genres. In this case, it leads to a strengthening of the interior/exterior paradigm akin to the good/wicked determination, and therefore the belief in a truth that resolves an enigma. This truth is always controlled by those who hold power. Engaging in the development of cause and consequence in a well-crafted, suspenseful story, is accepting the search of a criminal/bad character, which in turn leads to the renewal of dichotomies such as good/evil, interior/exterior. This process is parodied by Don Delillo in "Videotape": "The chance quality of the encounter. The victim, the killer, and the child with a camera. Random energies that approach a common point. There's something here that speaks to you directly, saying terrible things about forces beyond your control, lines of intersection that cut through history and logic and every reasonable layer of human expectation."[155] The insistence on this causal structure is called into question by a number of authors living in the context of the mortifying absurdity of dictatorships. Writers like Gabriel García Marquez,[156] Jacques Stephen Alexis,[157] René Philoctète or Augusto Roa Bastos,[158] realize that magical realism is a genre that leads to a new freedom; that of the stunning production of new meanings targeting "essentialized truths." It is also seen in *Mûr à crever* by Franketienne where "il y a bien un tracé narratif, mais il est dépossédé du statut habituel du fil conducteur."[159]

Other stories, not directly related to magical realism, emerge from the grip of a controlled causal destiny to exclude the deviants. These are mostly based on the exploration at the forefront of the encounter that targets the interaction, the crossing of boundaries in an adventure combining rationality and feelings as in Jack Kerouac's *On the Road*, Yvon Rivard's *Le siècle de Jeanne*, Octavio Paz's *Le singe grammairien* or Yann Martel's *Life of Pi*. Whether the novel is based on a linear plot or on a loose thread, there are always encounters. However, these encounters are not treated in the same way in the two types of narration those based on exclusion and those rejecting it. Encounters can lead to exclusion but they can also be for the purpose of loving the other or learning from him and helping him have multiple identities, because he will also be in us, which is one of the important elements of a multicultural or transcultural thought. Evidently, exploring the modalities of the passages from interior to exterior is important in these novels open to alterity. It often leads to stereotypes of the type "they are like us," which ensure the dominance of those who say this sentence unlike one such as "we are like them." If they are in fact like us, this means that we remain superior and they remain similar to us, this is what Homi Bhabha[160] means by *not quite*. In the short story by Gabrielle Roy entitled "Les deux Nègres" in *Rue Deschambault*, Catherine's mother, who is open to Black people to the point of renting them a room in her family home, has not yet reached the complementary pole, "we are like them". This expression could represent the basis of transculturalism, the invention of the new not from marginality but from liminality designed as an open space, as an in-between oriented towards a knowledge that can be transformed into a new symbolic and cultural *frontier*.

Non-Contradiction: Science and Literature

> Our purpose is to consciously, deliberately evolve toward a wiser, more liberated and luminous state of being; to return to Eden, make friends with the snake, and set up our computers among the wild apple trees.[161]

> We believe that it's technology married with the humanities that yields us the result that makes our heart sing. Nowhere is that more true than in these post-PC devices.[162]

> Reality, accordingly, is not something to which persons must assimilate, or run the risk of censure or marginalization. They are liberated because of the uncertainty found in the universe; the decisions made by persons, which are not predetermined, specify the parameters of reality. Reality is not a burden but an extension of ambitions.[163]

Escaping the causal/temporal structure of the narrative in order to enhance the encounter and the ternary of T that combines A and non-A, is to escape the dualism that establishes evidence and fashions the verisimilitude. This leads to the understanding that the elements perceived as contradictory in a dualistic frame of reference can be seen as complementary in the new non-dualistic framework. For Tom Robbins, the multiple Americas escape from dualism and open to the non-contradiction between ecology and technology, or between economy and knowledge; this is also the case for Kim Thúy who suggests: "Ce rêve américain a donné de l'assurance à ma voix, de la détermination à mes gestes, de la précision à mes désirs, de la vitesse à ma démarche et de la force à mon regard."[164] Living what is perceived as contradictory within the dual paradigm, but as complementary in the included third, is explored among many authors who have integrated more or less consciously the scientific, philosophical, and social contemporary scientific upheavals in their works in the Americas and in the world for some time already. These upheavals enhancing the change, the coincidence, the simultaneous and the encounter are manifested in the displacement of philosophical ideas rooted in Greek philosophy. Dewey explains this in his 1929 essay entitled "Escape from Peril". He exposes the reasons for which the Greek philosophers have valued:

> The idea of a higher realm of fixed reality of which alone true science is possible and of an inferior world of changing things with which experience and practical matters are concerned. They glorified the invariant at the expense of change, it being evident that all practical activity falls within the realm of change. They bequeathed the notion, which has ruled philosophy ever since the time of the Greeks, that the office of knowledge is to uncover the antecedently real, rather than, as is the case with our practical judgments, to gain the kind of understanding which is necessary to deal with problems as they arise.[165]

Through his pragmatism, the 19th century American semiotician Peirce had already developed a criticism of immovability and its rejection of change. Unfortunately, Peirce was not properly studied, disseminated and exploited until the end of the Second World War when scholars decided to publish his complete works: "Consider what effects, that might conceivably have practical bearings, we conceive the object of our conception to have. Then our conception of these effects is the whole of our conception of the object."[166] Here we retain two points. The practical impact of the theoretical, on the one hand, which manifests the idea of complementarity, and the productivity of meanings by the bias of effects, on the other hand, which according to the contexts are almost unlimited. Peirce's triadic logic is transitional and open on a *frontier* of meanings, because, for him, the meaning of a statement or a situation is specified by its effects, which are always numerous and often unpredictable.

This cultural and philosophical knowledge cannot be separated from the transformations of modern physics, relativity, quantum theory and the principle of uncertainty, which is based on the fact that the world is created in part by the observer. This is what Heisenberg underlines. He thought observing the phenomena changed them. This is also what John Gribbin confirms: "The strangest thing about the standard Copenhagen interpretation of the quantum world is that it is the act of observing a system that forces it to select one of its options, which then becomes real."[167] The option discussed here is the fact that electrons behave as waves in some experimental contexts, and as particles in others, which tends to give the phenomenon a probabilistic rather than causal description. These new perspectives validate movement and indeterminacy and fascinate thinkers, particularly José Vasconcelos in Mexico, the man who tried to rethink the relationships between ethnic groups and proposed the invention of a new race by mixing. In *Ética, la revulsión de la energia o Tratado de Metafisica*, he devotes himself to the will to found in a single expression "la física cuántica y la teoria de la relatividad con las humanidades y la religion."[168] Moreover, in his *Tratado de Metafisica*, Vasconcelos compares the physical waves to the waves of thought and of poetry,[169] which brings us close to the Nicaraguan poet Ernesto Cardenal and his collection *Cántico cósmico*[170] where he speaks of the dance of the stars and refers to Heisenberg. Let us also consider Vasconcelos' notion that everything is movement, and everything is relational rather than fixed: "El *número es apenas el signo de los instantes en que alterna el ritmo del movimiento…*"[171]

The recognition of otherness passes through a questioning of binary paradigms. José Vasconcelos isn't the only one thinking in those terms. But he is one of the first in Latin America to bring together scientific-theoretical changes, cultural changes and actions in the practice. The goal is to reorganize the chaos of the world by an activity of thought for which it is necessary to be aware that the possible syntheses are diverse: "Aparecen, sin embargo, desde el comienzo maneras diversas de entender el carácter de la síntesis."[172]

In this context of redefinition of the points of view on the world,[173] the observer, the reader of novels that play increasingly on the semantics focused more on the unexpected and the surprise, become participants that produce multiple meanings. The indetermination and the absence of linear causality are very present in the science issued by Heisenberg, Bohr, Planck and Einstein. They also appear in Borges, Cortazar, Fuentes[174] or even Stephen Leacock. These writers tend to evoke probabilities issued from operative knowledge always linked, for the reader, to a number of stereotypes creating expectations, which are themselves modified by various contexts. Leacock, with the use of mathematical formulas, draws parallels between the probability of encounters between him and a friend and the probability of the encounter between science, philosophy and theology. He compares this to daily life, which corresponds to the probability that three people rent apartments in the same building.[175] But if these stereotypes encounter a narrativity that rejects causality to explore an aesthetics questioning the realism and likelihood of the construction of the character (e.g., novels of magical realism, especially through the technique of reincarnation presented in Isabel Allende's *The House of the Spirits*[176]), then the reading process summons the learning of a new ternary logic. This logic has been particularly exploited by Yann Martel and Laura Esquivel. The singularity of readings transforms the reading and invents new possibilities to produce various meanings, one of the pathways leading to a multicultural or a transcultural society.

The Included Third

Many contemporary novels also explore the possibility that opposites come together. This is different from the religious or political discourses trapped in a conflictual dualism with which people think they can produce meanings based on a stable epistemological and linguistic foundation. We see this dualism in Tariq Modood's book on multiculturalism in which he defends a conflicting vision of the relationships between communities and where he wants to insert a powerful and orthodox vision of Islam in the context of the United Kingdom: "Moreover, citizens can learn several languages, but one cannot be a member of several religions at the same time, so while a multilingual state is an option, a multi-religious state is not."[177] Modood's reasoning does not hold, neither theoretically nor practically, because India and Germany, for instance, are states where several religions are recognized. Piscine Patel in *Life of Pi* wants to become a Christian, a Buddhist and a Muslim, and promotes syncretism in agreement with recent scientific texts such as William H. Harrison's *In Praise of Mixed Religion*.[178] Let us also consider Abla Farhoud's *Le bonheur à la queue glissante*. The character of Dounia manifests a large detachment from orthodoxies, because their representatives are blurry in her memories: "Un jour il eut l'idée d'aller voir le rabbin ou le prêtre ou l'imam, pour lui demander de l'aider."[179] The dream of syncretism, so powerful in the Americas and in particular on the Caribbean coast of Latin America, now captivates the contemporary writers and thinkers of the whole continent. They explore the multiple experiences of symbolic and discursive migration, and are open to taking symbolic and cultural risks. This is noted in *The Gum Thief*, where Douglas Coupland's character says the following in a constructive (not deconstructive) irony[180]:

> Speaking of biology, I think cloning is great. I don't understand why churchy people get so upset about it. God made the originals, and cloning is only making photocop-

ies. Big woo. And how can people get upset about evolution? Someone had to start the ball rolling; it's only natural to try to figure out the mechanicals of *how* it got rolling. Relax! One theory doesn't exclude the other.[181]

The character, Bethany, asserts that life is not a zero-sum game, that the excluded third is no longer valid. This is what Ronald Wright also underlines in *A Short History of Progress* where he shows the blind spots and dead-ends of positivism and dualistic antagonism that do not take into account the environment or the context by means of absurd arguments: "Someone fond of logical absurdities once defined specialists as 'people who know more and more about less and less, until they know all about nothing.'"[182] Thus, the binary paradigms are no longer effective and the creation of the world by God is no longer contradictory with Darwinism. The creation of species by God does not exclude their evolution, the adaptations to contexts, because everything is in motion and the motion is positive. The two interpretations are valid. To consider once again fixity, it would be sufficient to thematize cloning seeing as, in Coupland's perspective, Platonism mastered by science gives a new access to fixity. In other words, stasis and dynamism are now in the hands of writers and thinkers who, through cultural and techno-scientific knowledge, can play them according to their interests and the strategies they wish to elaborate in order to open perspectives on the sociocultural relations in gestation. Édouard Glissant is one of these thinkers who elaborates on the complementarity of Christ, Darwin and Buddhism: "La généralisation inspirée du Christ fut à ce moment relayée par celle que proposait Darwin, l'une et l'autre s'opposant d'abord. Il s'agissait dans les deux cas de transcender l'ancienne filiation mythique, liée au devenir d'une communauté, pour la dépasser dans une conception généralisante, qui eût gardé pourtant la force du principe de linéarité et qui eût 'compris' et motivé l'Histoire."[183] These views for Coupland, Glissant and others, join the syncretism of Piscine in *Life of Pi*, and lead to an affirmation of belonging to oneself and not to the group or the land. This syncretism demonstrates a distrust towards the exclusive and homogenizing community myths based on the dissemination of the belief that the victim was guilty of provoking division and destruction. This mechanism, which generates scapegoats is demonstrated by Glissant: "Il y a donc dans le Mythe une violence cachée, qui se prend aux mailles de la filiation et qui récuse en absolu l'existence de l'Autre, comme élément de relation."[184]

The Generalized Chameleonage

> Mon véritable pays est là où je deviens ce que je veux être.[185]
>
> ...(Antonio)...dijo que realmente no importaba dónde estuviera uno: una persona se podia adaptar a cualquier país.[186]

Chameleoning: From Negative to Positive. The included third leads us to a social and economic context where alterity is always present due to the fact that people meet through travel, databanks, the democratization of access to universities, competition, education (in particular for women) and migration. It also leads us to the metaphor of chameleon, which tends to sidestep the traditional metaphor based on roots and origins. While chameleon is now considered very positive, this has not always been the case, notably in the context of traditional modernity of nation-states. The negative view of chameleon is present in the derogatory words of Jean-Philippe Rossignol about Paul Claudel: "Ça donne sous sa plume de caméléon..."[187] Sergio Kokis, the Canadian writer of Brazilian origins, expresses thoughts which are not very favourable to the image of the chameleon. However, this is understandable for a character who finds him/herself in the situation of a minority and the experience of exile has been the discovery that he had "toujours été étranger partout"[188]: "Je me contente maintenant de passer inaperçu, de fuir les sollicitations, de faire le caméléon, de ne pas trop prendre au sérieux les ardeurs de mes semblables. La solitude, derrière une apparence de marionnette, constitue la seule position confortable dans mon cas."[189]

Yet, innovative authors who came before him, such as Ionesco, offer a more positive meaning of chameleon: "Si vous voulez, je suis tout de même le berger, le théâtre étant le caméléon puisque j'ai embrassé la carrière théâtrale, et le théâtre change, bien sûr, car le théâtre c'est la vie. Il est changeant comme la vie... Le caméléon aussi c'est la vie."[190] As we get closer to the end of the 20th century, we begin to think about human nature, comparing it to the chameleon, as Nando Michaud does when referring to Dali in *Les montres sont molles mais les temps sont durs*. The characters are asking themselves about the true colour of the chameleon. To find out they need to keep it from taking the ambient colour by putting it in a cage lined with mirrors![191] The chameleon is obsessed with the mirrors but, as we will now see, in many contemporary texts he is seen in a rather favourable perspective.

There are diverse ways of being a chameleon. In fact, it all depends on the context in which one acts as a chameleon. The concept of chameleoning is captured by the Canadian author Bill Schermbrucker who immigrated to Canada from a Kenya preparing for independence. He tells his situation of being a chameleon in a collection of short stories entitled *Chameleon*. We first measure how most Whites treat Black people: "I tell you, it would take these people *three hundred years*..."[192] The ellipses imply "to be civilized". They are thus, by definition, more than *not quite*, inadequate, in the sense described by Homo Bhabha. They are really incompetent. As for the narrator, he is in disagreement with this attitude: "The truth was I didn't quite fit."[193] It is he, the son of white owners, who is *not quite*, according to a new perspective. His inadequacy is based on not sharing the dominant trait of demeaning the others in a definitive way. In this he agrees with a writer like Doris Lessing, who says: "Colour prejudice is not our original fault but only one aspect of the atrophy of the imagination that prevents us from seeing ourselves in every creature that breathes under the sun."[194] In *Chameleon*, the narrator was qualified as the chameleon by one of his Black classmates in college: "One never knows exactly what is your own point of view. There is something strange about the way you look at people. One eye is looking on the left side, and one eye is to the right. So, when something is directly in front of you, you don't even see it. You called me *nyangau*, and I call you chameleon. Consider it a term of endearment."[195] At page 113, the narrator describes the eyes of the chameleon and their complex motor skills. He compares himself to them because of his alternating strabismus that makes him see beyond the stereotypes and understand what he wants to hide.[196] He then insists on the fact that he became a perfect Canadian, that he integrated himself and changed his vocabulary, but that the memories of Kenya and the times of war and terror remain alive. Thus, he was positively chameleon in Kenya and continues to be even more so in Canada, which tends to value the multiple. This is what allowed him to see the drawbacks of colonialism and qualities of Canada, while preserving in both cases a system of values based on the conscience of the suffering of the dominated otherness. Contrary to the "constant lie from the officials"[197] and their control over history, memory is the driving element of chameleonage. Memory allows to make contact with others beyond their suppression by the stereotypes in a zero-sum game imposing reductive and dualist choices. The narrator remembers what his Black friends told him before he left Kenya: "it was *either* equality, *or* development, take your pick"[198] or "It was never people like you we were against. It was the land barons, the settlers."[199] To be chameleon in this book implies a certain dosage of somewhat worrisome ambiguity but this ambiguity is seen nowadays as something positive and creative. This is especially the case today because of the legitimacy of displacements linked to democratic liberalism and glocalization.

Chameleoning in the Democratic Liberal Context. As emphasized by Gloria Anzaldúa in *Borderland/La frontera*, "The future will belong to the mestiza. Because the future depends on the breaking down of paradigms, it depends on the straddling of two or more cultures" (1999: 80).[200] This perspective is linked to the fact that the US-Mexican borderlands are neither the complete result of the Protestant-based ethic nor the copy of a development influenced in part by Europe and the USA like in Mexico. From California to Texas, a process of mixing has taken place for a long time.[201] It has always been a mixing of cultures and discourses blending aspirations for a well-being aiming at transforming the neither-nor (neither latino nor US) into a plus-plus (latino and US), the basic dynamic for becoming a chameleon. Being a chameleon, as we have seen for Bill Schermbrucker, to a certain point and within certain contexts, means taking risks, because it implies not belonging to any group. And to not belong is often to self-belong. The epigraph by Gloria Anzaldúa can be completed by many characters. For instance, by the house cleaner in Truman Capote's "A Day's Work" who inserts herself into the lives of other people and prays at the end so that they can change while she considers herself to be saved. Her friend says: "Mary, I want you to live forever."[202] We see that chameleoning is often combined with the consciousness of a temporality in tune with a non-finite future, a temporal *frontier*. Nowadays, acting as a chameleon in Canada leads to project wisely effective behaviours, as evidenced by the character of the novel *Self* by Yann Martel (a man who becomes a woman before reverting back to a man again after having been raped). In part, it is to be able to adapt to the context: "I could identify with up to three of those groups, which made me not so much a hybrid as a chameleon", says the main character in Yann Martel's *Self*.[203] In the same way, George Rodrigue, a Cajun artist from Louisiana, speaks of a pathway in charge of complexity:

> The wonderful thing about Blue Dog is that she's never hung up on playing a specific role; she will happily inhabit any world I put her in. Within Blue Dog is the history of the Cajun people and the history of myself, my joys and fears and visions, both of the world around me and the world yet to come… Through Blue Dog I can process the world around me, with all its complexity. Color, noise, and absurdity. The paintings in this book reflect this new path.[204]

Moreover, the authors are subtly working these identities, which shift in the process of attribution. We see this in *Anagrams* by Lorrie Moore.[205] Each chapter is a slightly reworded version of the first chapter, leading to what changes the characters are organizing with their lives while remaining in the routine of everyday life. Thus, Benna is a singer, an aerobics instructor and a professor of art history. In each chapter, the relations with the other vary until each person finds an acceptable accommodation with the environment, itself modified by these variations. Nowadays, a labile but more satisfactory identity is invented, a way of trying to self-belong in the world of cultural, economic, emotional and social constraints.

Nevertheless, it is necessary to differentiate between the attitudes, the projects and the context. A chameleon does not seek to adapt to the context to fit there permanently, but to enjoy the transition and to grow. This is understandable if we observe the attitude of those who want to live in a perpetual adaptation, to blend in with the background. This is referred to in Kim Thúy and Pascal Janovjak's book, *À toi*. Kim Thúy talks about Vietnamese immigrant parents who give their children names which will not stand out as different: "Pendant des semaines j'ai cru que Pi-r était un nom vietnamien des régions montagneuses qui signifiait peut-être 'renouveau' ou 'source,' ou encore 'sifflement du vent.' Mais ce n'était que Pierre, prononcé par une Vietnamienne clouée à sa machine à coudre jour et nuit, espérant que son fils porterait un visage aussi commun et banal que ce nom."[206] For many immigrants, there is often a desire of undifferentiating and this is because many immigrants wanted at some point in their lives to be part of the society where they came from but were not able to, because of the religious or political conflicts that prevented them. They found themselves in danger of becoming scapegoats because of the groups who controlled the social functioning. This is clear in *Man* by Kim Thúy where the mother of the narrator trapped in communist North Vietnam taught her daughter "à éviter les conflits, à respirer sans exister, à me fondre dans le décor… J'ai appris très vite à être à la fois invisible et utile afin d'être oubliée, afin que personne ne puisse me faire de reproches, afin que personne ne m'atteigne."[207] It was really to avoid problems while being productive and efficient. Despite the differences between the two texts, in both cases there is a desire to become like those who are already there: to have the right to reach out to the desired object, to work, to actively participate in the invention of one's own life by being actively participating in the new society where one now live.

Fear and Valorization of the Same. In other words, this is what is happening from the perspective of Girard's theory of exclusion. According to Girard, everybody in a group or in a society projects their hand towards the object marked by the model in order to obtain it. This is about, for example, getting a job, which means getting money leading to socio-personal growth. This struggle of all against all at the basis of the mimesis of appropriation is hidden by the sharing of a common language and culture, such as it is defined by Will Kymlicka: "I am using 'a culture' as synonymous with 'a nation' or 'a people' that is, as an intergenerational community, more or less institutionally complete, occupying a given territory or homeland, sharing a distinct language and history."[208] This definition has the disadvantage of being static (complete, native country, language, history), it conceives of its members as a homogenous entity with a distinct origin, not born of multiple relations founded on mixings. This definition leads to a rather dualistic reading of the cultural relations whereas Kymlicka's theory really isn't. He is therefore able to produce new ideas and engage in creativity by putting into practice these new ideas in a given context, itself changing, and this in spite of a definition that does not lead to the production of dynamic discourses about the contemporary world. Indeed, Kymlicka constantly insists on the ternary (majority group, minority group to protect against the majority group, individual to protect against the group) and on the fact that the relations are not based on a zero-sum game, but on the fact that it is possible to live multiplicity.

However, if we return to René Girard's definition of culture, the others who are at the exterior (outside the homogenous culture) are seen as not being able to hide their appropriative gesture with respect to the object of desire. They are excluded as job thieves, for example, not because they are different, but because they do the same as the dominant group—they project a mimetic appropriative gesture towards the desired object. This appropriative gesture remains hidden in the eyes of those who are members of the homogenous culture when they are among themselves. This foundation of the national where all cooperate, from the poorest to the elite, invents a market of social and economic relations claiming to be protective and fair. This type of functioning has been well analyzed by Seema Ahluwalia who is interested in the self-vision of the Indigenous people in a society that excludes them based on binary categories like "modern/primitive, civilized/barbaric, educated/illiterate, and evolved/atavistic."[209] There is visibly a competition between Indigenous people and immigrants. This study joins Lucia Madariaga-Vignudo's who studies the relations between the poor Indigenous people and the poor refugees in downtown Winnipeg in order to show the strong antagonisms regarding the access to social housing and work: "Quelques participants ont souligné que l'accès à l'emploi est l'un des secteurs où les Autochtones ont l'impression d'être en concurrence étroite avec les réfugiés."[210] Hence, dreaming of being a chameleon in order to vanish in various contexts is not always possible, because any shortage kindles antagonisms and reduces the possibilities of adaptation by the fact that the appropriative gesture—which is also a gesture of participating desire—is experienced as threatening.

Beyond the desire to control an object of desire that is difficult to reach in the context of the legitimacy of the geographic, paradigmatic, syntagmatic and symbolic displacements, the goal is often to be both from everywhere and from nowhere.[211] Vanishing in these contexts would be asserting oneself as omnicompetent and innovative during unforeseen situations where one has to be efficient at once. This means actively participating immediately in order to constantly become a *self-making man* or a *self-making woman*. This is the case of Piscine Patel or even of Moacyr Scliar's main character in *Max and the Cats*, facing the felines that accompany them in their respective rafts which they do not succeed to tame at once: "If he intended to start taming the beast, he would have to get down to work right away."[212] In this case, there is no second chance. Vanishing, also means to engage in relations established in the temporary of partial agreements, sometimes even ambiguous and through social links partially uncertain.

The complementary activity of the chameleon that penetrates all contexts and all discourses without agreeing with anyone is also able to leave discretely, once its participation has lasted long enough and brought it to develop its potential. Its playful and joyful side can often be seen in many works of fiction, for example in the work of the Quebec writer Louis Gauthier. His character delightfully enjoys his numerous travels that make his notion of house more like a transportable *home* than a rooted place: "Elle [Angela] était Sud-Américaine, Brésilienne d'origine allemande (ses premiers souvenirs d'enfance, des histoires de perroquets apprivoisés sur fond de forêt tropicale). Son père, aventurier, commerçant mais plus poète que commerçant, entraînait toute la famille dans ses nombreux déplacements. C'est ainsi qu'elle s'était trouvée successivement au Panama, au Honduras, au Belize, puis au Mexique et finalement aux États-Unis."[213]

The Popularity of the Chameleon Effect in the Media and Literary Discourses. In literature[214] there is a positive discussion about the chameleon. Recently, in the media, chameleonage is ironically appreciated. It infiltrates itself in a third space among the rigidity of binary paradigms. In *Modèle mental de l'altruisme*, Nik Lygeros speaks about "l'aspect protéiforme de l'intelligence, munie d'une structure de pensée complexe qui permet de créer des modèles mentaux qui simulent la réalité d'autrui. De cette manière, l'être s'approche si près de la nature d'autrui que ce dernier est persuadé d'être en face d'une personne semblable."[215] There are also many articles presenting the research on *biomimicry*[216] where we are informed about the fate of frogs that survive after having been frozen. We also learn about those who astonish us with the latest technological inventions. We are told about the imper illusion: "Fabriqué dans un matériau réfléchissant, ce manteau contient une caméra vidéo qui capte l'environnement immédiat de la personne qui le porte et en projette l'image sur le tissu, de façon à créer l'illusion qu'il est invisible. Conçu par Susumu Tachi de l'Université de Tokyo, ce vêtement ne sera toutefois pas sur le marché avant 2008."[217]

The word chameleon is used often nowadays because it glorifies the capacity to insert oneself in a transculturalism which is open to difference and the legitimacy of geographic displacements, linked to symbols that are everywhere and especially in magazines like *Géo*: "C'est le moment de se souvenir que l'exil, temporaire et choisi, n'est pas forcément un mal. Il amène avec lui une perte de repères, voire une perte d'identité et ceux-ci conduisent à une meilleure connaissance de l'autre, de sa langue, de ses modes de vie, de ses façons de raisonner."[218] Certainly, we understand from this sentence that it is about a temporary departure, and especially that the words used are still rather negative words like 'exile', but that they take positive colours, including the word loss. The discourse on mobility, much like the discourse on identity is thus changing rapidly. We shouldn't be astonished that the theme of the chameleon becomes a positive trend. "L'homme caméléon Desmond Richardson"[219] is an expression appreciating a media model like "Arnold Schwarzeneger: caméléon."[220] Let's also consider the cover of *Rotman Management* magazine featuring a colorful chameleon with the following title: "The Art of Change."[221] We must also highlight the role of story-telling: "He seems to have the two great gifts that are required to make a man a teller of tales [...] second, an ability to place himself, chameleon-like in any milieu of society, from the highest to the lowest."[222] Also, "le camélédion" highlighting that Stéphane Dion, leader of the Liberal party of Canada, "a réussi à transformer le prof d'université en politicien efficace"[223] (which didn't really materialize!). The invention of the multifunctional pieces of furniture also represent this shifting of forms: "Une chaise n'est pas une chaise. Les détournements de sens d'un objet commun offrent un antidote au spleen de février."[224] This chair reminds us that the binary semantic classifications can be transgressed when they are submitted to *design*. In a sense, the *design* asserts the playing capacity of the coordinating conjunction *mais* (like in poor but clean, or bourgeois but aesthete), in order to transform the story of our daily life by a playful aesthetics that pushes away the limits of the established. Design in its chameleonic function creates a wellness zone where everybody can dream their world and grow. Indeed, it is this dream that hotels suggest in the context of the promotion of the legitimation of the democratized symbolic and geographic displacements recycling the paradigm of sedentary lifestyle/nomadism evoked by Jacques Languirand in "Le Québec et l'Américanité."[225]

Statism and Dynamism: The Hotels

The Americas, as Fermin Toro noticed in Venezuela in 1839, encompassed movements and displacements in their cultural background from early on. Immigration is one of the founding characteristics of the appreciation of displacement, because it signifies both geographic and symbolic travel. These displacements are experienced negatively by those who hold on to a stable and euro-centered conception of identity, but positively by those who engage in the dynamics of the Americas, dynamics that are expanding in the contemporary context of globalization, highlighting the legitimacy of displacements.

This can be seen in the comments of both French-Canadian and Mexican thinkers of the 19th century and contemporary thinkers such as Pico Iyer as well as in many advertisements reconfiguring cultural anchors. At the end of the 19th century, Adolphe Basile Routhier from Montreal criticizes the American social, economic, spatial and ethnic mobility: "À proprement parler, les États-Unis ne sont pas une patrie pour la plus grande partie de leurs habitants. C'est une immense hôtellerie où de nombreuses caravanes de peuples sont venues prendre un billet de logement."[226] Like Sarmiento's famous expression "poor right now," describing poverty as a temporary situation of U.S. citizens, putting into perspective the attribution process for essentialist use and thus expressing the new logic that was put in place in the 19th century in the United States, Routhier is aware of the movement, dynamism, and the change of civilization, an epistemology that represents the United States. He is, however, in disagreement with this movement, the *melting pot* and the arrival of immigrants,[227] which soon went on to contribute to the economic development of the hotel that is for him the United States. For somebody who clings ideologically to the traditional definition of the nation as an entity based on the valorization of those who have roots, this mixture is unacceptable. It will remain so until the 1950s in popular literature as in *Zirska, immigrante inconnue* by Jean-Marie Carette.[228]

In Canada too hotels[229] see the day,[230] namely because the economy develops at the same rate as technology and exports. But for French-Canadian thinkers of the 19th century, they represent a threat, especially because they are the places where the American publications penetrate[231] as it is emphasized for instance by Chauveau in 1876.[232] In Routhier's perspective, with regards to the United States, the word homeland is no longer valid, because the multiplicity of origins is combined with the frenzy to succeed economically. This often occurs through spatial displacement as well as through the displacement of traditional paradigms for people who adapt to the modern business perspective within the United States' own democratic logic.

We find a similar attitude among Mexicans who travel to the United States in the same period. What shocks the most those who share their views in stories of their travels in the United States, is the movement related to progress and modernity. Already, in Manuel Balbotín, we are surprised by the fact that in boarding houses people do not quarrel with the cook if they find that the food doesn't suit their taste, they just leave.[233] The ease of travel surprises especially when it is related to an attitude where one does not enter into conflict. In this case, travelers simply go to another hotel. This aspect underlines that it is possible to move along easily because there is no shortage. The movement is also pointed out by Francisco Bulnes: "El Americano no puede vivir en un plano; tiene que imitar la Bolsa; ascender y descender; recibir en un piso, comer en otro, dormir más arriba, agitarse…"[234] These rather negative judgements in the perspective of the Mexican travelers, like Routhier already accustomed to a society aimed at stability, are coupled with the rhetoric stressing that the dominant religion in the United States is enormity. And the temples of enormity, in addition to the city of New York as a whole, are the hotels. Thus, it would seem that enormity and ease of displacement are the constituent elements of progress and that they have replaced the fundamental religious values and attachment to a community space. It is what Federico Gamboa highlights using the known image of oriental nomads to devalue hotels: "1903. EL HOTEL WALDORF-ASTORIA EN NUEVA YORK. *Caravansérail* según el diccionario francés, quiere decir: 'Parador público de Oriente, para alojar a las caravanas.' Enmiéndese la frase en el sentido de 'parador público del oriente de los EE.UU. para alojar viajeros presuntuosos y marcadamente *rastas*.'"[235]

These images are part of a rhetorical arsenal used by all those who live the barbarism/civilization dualism, and who apply the civilization pole to a certain model full of aspiration for stability or points of view inspired by the aristocratic world. These images show that these writers fail to support the new territorial dimensions (economic and cultural) of the American continent. They also fail to support its inhabitants who took part in the most important revolution of the 19th century by voting with their feet (meaning emigrating) to become owners participating in the growth of their world as well as of their individuality in a democratic context.

But Federico Gamboa does not merely use a rhetoric that is known because it is a dominant stereotype in the Mexican population. He says that the hotel converts into a symbol of the United States as a whole, sick of ostentation and full of new wealthy people. Travel represents evil, because it is coupled with social mobility and sociocultural transformations. Gamboa thus joins Routhier who wants people to remain attached to earth and simply be pleased with what they have. This is exactly why French-Canadian travelers such as Faucher de Saint-Maurice[236] will fight for the emperor Maximilian in Mexico during the invasion of that country by Napoléon III, because at first it seems that the poor Mexican peasants fighting for independence are the barbarians of a back-country in need of being civilized. Hence, it is necessary to establish an aristocratic basis of European origin south of the United States in order to contain the territorial, technological and financial expansion of this dynamic country, and control the fascination they exert on the poor, the outcast, and the ambitious of the planet.

Therefore, it is clear that Mexican travelers and thinkers share a type of rhetoric with Routhier. It is based on the rejection of movement, that is, the social mobility and the spatial mobility—both of which question the insistence on being rooted in a nation. This insistence merely recycles in a national setting the biblical myth, which claims that earth and meaning are inextricably linked, since man is born from clay. The traditional nationalism of these Canadian and Mexican thinkers cannot accept the democratization of mobility, even if it is at the basis of modernity and progress in the Americas. But there are also other more recent perspectives. In Max Apple's "The Oranging of America", an ironic text about the development of the hotel chain Howard Johnson, everything changes. Especially interesting is the fact that the positive organization of mobility depends on choice and ingenuity on the part of Mr. Johnson. He is always looking for places that will appeal to travelers by the aura that they give off. Howard and his assistant, Mildred, have travelled around the United States for decades in their limousine to find these places. She noted that Howard knew the country like the Indigenous peoples knew it.[237] This made him discover the places that would stop the travelers who wished to enjoy calmness and beauty. This insistence on beauty can be seen in both Tomson Highway's and Yvon Rivard's writings. However, it is not a true indigenous perspective on territory because for Indigenous people, territory is linked to ancestry and stories. Mildred grasps that businessmen of this genre are pioneers. During his visit in Israel, in the desert near Jericho, they feel complete serenity: "There was nothing there, absolutely nothing but pure bliss."[238] The places where these hotels are built are marked by the long period of history; that of people who passed by, as Jericho. In a way, like Jericho, they mark in an albeit ephemeral temporality, the locality linked to human migrations.

Nowadays, we capture the evolution of discourses in comparison to Routhier's perspective on mobility and to the judgements produced by Gamboa, both comparing the United States to a hotel rather than a place of settling. In addition to the remarks by Pico Iyer in *The Global Soul*, in order to understand the valorization of mobility today, we have to consider the many advertisements of hotel chains such as Four Seasons. In these ads, large hotels look all similar without any particular local specificity that would differentiate one country from another. Thus, the movement implied by hotels despite everything is controlled by an architectural structure, an administration, and similar services in any location on the planet. There is no effort to contextualize the hotel within a local architecture because a globalized class goes from one point to another in a pre-defined universe sponsored by a loyal and protective brand. The mobility is coupled with stability through the sharing of a place promoting temporary gatherings of members of a very large class, which escapes both the local and the national to engage in the regional or the global. This interconnected class is in constant transformation due to the fact that it can gain access to the planet and to countries formerly colonized, but now much richer than before. This connected class is also living in a precarious economic state because simultaneously, as Buffy Cram points out in *Radio Belly*, a part of the middle class in Western countries is facing economic slowdowns. A number of educated groups, artists, creators, intellectuals or professors are marginalized by the new class, the one that knows how to play the commercial and financial competition: "'You know they're calling them hybrid now?' I said. Then in my best newscaster voice: 'The New Hybrid Class'. I was the only one laughing. 'They're really quite educated' I added… 'Apparently they were once middle-class' I said."[239] It is interesting to note that here hybridity has a different meaning than in the texts devoted to intercultural relations often implicitly dividing the world between migrants and the settled. Here, hybridity mixes the richness of the cultural capital with economic insecurity, which can lead to urban migrancy since some of the members of these groups do not have a fixed address. This leads us to a new potentially interesting narrative based on the *mais* (but), such as educated but poor.

In any case, the coupling of mobility and stability of the hotel chain presented in the advertisement means that place as a word changes meaning.[240] It meets the concept of space produced by movement and operations. We refer here to the distinction Michel de Certeau makes between place and space in *L'Invention du quotidien*.[241] M. de Certeau follows the Saussurian distinction between language and speech, and sees language in place, whereas space is the expression of word. In our contemporary travels, this distinction tends to change, because *place* formerly seen as linked to 'roots' and 'appropriation' is displaced by space as a creativity stemming from pragmatic operations, and from specific assertions linked to acts of speech such as those that promise a place in the sun in *The Oranging of America* as told by Max Apple.

The Hotel as *Home*

In this dynamic, it is interesting to see that recently some advertisements seek to play the appropriative reterritorialization with a sense of humour that plays on the gap between *home* and hotel, because hotel invokes either antagonism or optimistic humour, since it embodies the important choices from the point of view of the paradigm interior/exterior, which in turn points to statism/movement. It must be understood that this gap is manifested only between the idea of the Anglo-Saxon *home*[242] (as an entity which can be carried somewhere else) and the notion of the hotel. In many non-Anglo-Saxon cultures, the link between the territory and the individual is very strong, and so the play on words would be more difficult. There is for example a French proverb that says: "On ne transporte pas sa terre natale à la semelle de ses souliers."[243] On the contrary, in most Anglo-Saxon cultures, the contradiction is not as strong because the *home* is, for many, a set of cultural and personal exportable structures.[244]

These differences in the meaning of words is clearly underlined in the half-fiction, half-documentary film *Home*, by the Québecoise director Phyllis Katrapani, screened on Tuesday August 27th 2002, at the 26th Montreal World Film Festival. The title of this French movie is in English, because, for the filmmaker, the word *home* cannot be translated: " 'Le mot anglais est chargé de sens', dit Phyllis Katrapani qui le traduit tout de même par chez-soi… 'Mais quand j'utilise le mot chez-soi, j'imagine quelqu'un qui est calé dans un sofa, avec un livre et un chat à ses côtés. Le concept du *home*, en anglais, est beaucoup plus vaste."[245]

The hotel expansion can therefore be seen as a postmodern expansion of this Anglo-Saxon conception, which developed in the colonial expansion of the empire and also in the extension of the *frontier*. Thus, appears the slogan "Is it possible TO BECOME HOMESICK for a hotel?"[246] This ad for the Four Seasons Hotels and Resorts marks at the same time the gap between stability and mobility and aims for customer loyalty. This fidelity is that of a female administrator or economist. Because of this, the stability centered on the *home* is transferred to a feeling of well-being linked to the place of convergence of economic exchange, the hotel. This transportable home (the hotel) is rarely displaying local features. In fact, the *home* is transportable, and the stamp of the *home* can spread globally.

However, some hotel chains play on a rooting that is not produced by the transportation of an environment specific to the international bourgeoisie in circulation, but takes into account the local aesthetics even if they are sanitized. These chains that are not of North American origin play a more marked differential local/global relation. "International Standards [...] Local Flavor" claims the Dutch owned chain of hotels, Golden Tulip, with photos of their hotels in Santiago, Miami, Trujillo (Peru) and Sao Paulo.[247] In the framework of this company, difference has a positive impact only if international standards are in place.[248] Thanks to these two examples, we see that companies decontextualize/recontextualize meaning by playing two complementary codes, a double coding which Jencks[249] speaks of, but in different ways that keep in mind the cultural differences of origin. In the case of the North American chain, there is a flow coming from a culture where *home* is mobile. In the case of the European chain, it is linked to a culture where the house is in part linked to a territory. It appears as a promise to a population in transit, which has, in part, lost its world. A new globalized city village. However, a hotel has more to do with an urban community than with a village, because it is thoroughly networked. Moreover, it is often more populous than a village. In these examples the different modalities of globalizing discourses are clearly marked. They do not tend, even for multinationals in support of the displacement, towards a homogenization, but rather to convergences where reconfigured differences are taken into account according to contemporary challenges.

A third advertisement plays in between these two dimensions. It comes from the Sheraton Argentina and caters to a good part of Latin America. By that we mean that it stems from a Latin American perspective on Latin America, but branched out to the United States and the world. We see the photo of two children smiling, accompanied by the following text: "Sí abuela, nosotros tambíen te extrañamos. Estar aquí es tan bueno como quedarse en tu casa."[250] Here (aquí) expresses both a reference to the intimate and the international. But the intimate is not defined as the Anglo-Saxon *home*. However, the text suggests that the Sheraton is as friendly as the home of grand-parents where the children are often more coddled than at the parents. There is an underlying process of cultural transfer, which tends to raise the idea that the hotel could also be a *home* and that, therefore, this friendly space is transportable. However, it is not possible to assert this directly in a society, which highly values family relationships and rootedness in a place. Consequently, the publicity is contextualized with an Argentinian cultural structure which demonstrates its willingness to displace the signification of *home*. It recognizes the stability of the home, without naming it. But it speaks to new generations and brings a new sense to the relationship between grandchildren and grandparent. It displaces the meanings in favor of enjoying an international public space, which becomes as attractive as grandmother's friendly place. The children already learn to be at home at the Sheraton, but without the grandmother, which is the first step. The second will be the structure of the immediate family. On the one hand, this advertisement plays on a semantics that recognizes the stability and the value of the local while moving some elements; on the other hand, it leads us to conceive of the house as a *home*, as a moving structure, which opens to a internationality in contact with the world. "Quién cuida de usted?" who is taking care of you, we ask ourselves beside the "S" logo of the Sheraton. Of course, it is Sheraton who is taking care of us.[251] Without going as far as to say that sometimes the results are contradictory, as James Bohman[252] thinks, there are still very strong familial and interpersonal ties which bind people together so that the house can't be easily displaced in the Argentinian concept and, therefore, the Four Seasons advertising analyzed above would be ineffective in a Latin American context.

In our networked technological world, when we want to present a place of passage as a permanently friendly space, the personal is mixed with the professional. This allows us to represent the hotel as a place where one feels at home, because at home we use the same technological tools, the same software, and we participate in the same activities. This is what happens in Novotel advertisements in Mexico, in particular the city of Monterrey where the culture is in some respects closest to that of the United States, which sees the hotel as the expression of the transportable *home*: "Novotel. Bienvenido — esta es su casa"[253], the ad claims by showing a father and son using a laptop to play together in the bedroom. The dynamics of networking are put in place, which marks accessibility. This is also highlighted by thinkers like Don Tapscott and Art Caston.[254] To the above examples, one can add the vision of Toronto as proposed by Pico Iyer in *Imagining Canada* when he was reading Ondaatje's novel *In the Skin of a Lion*. It tells the story of immigrants who, in the 19th century, built bridges in Toronto in order to facilitate the communication between the east and the west, the old and the new, and bring together different worlds that initially had little in common. Toronto represents the place where people feel better after all the horrors they have lived, whether it's the horrors of the Stalinist[255] regime or the Nazi horrors, not to mention the most recent horrors in the Middle East, Iran, Cambodia, Bosnia, Rwanda, etc. Toronto, for Pico Iyer, resembles: "A luxury hotel, an oasis of ease and abundance; and a hotel I think, is not such a terrible way of thinking about a society, all its inhabitants in their own separate, comfortable, well-serviced spaces, yet within common areas downstairs for dining, dancing and attending to civic responsibilities."[256]

From Routhier to Pico Iyer, we measure the change. The nation is represented by its urban centers, and those are full of hotels. But what was very negative became an oasis of luxury and comfort for all, because most travelers are techno-savy planetary nomads, maybe even waiting to migrate to Mars with the Mars One enterprise.[257] They are migrants who seek only to find a new place to settle. This dynamic of networking tends to transform the territory of the root into spaces of knowledge in travel. The spaces are very alive, like the hotel advertisement in Monterrey, and are felt like a *home* corresponding to the transportable office/home connected to their optic networks accessible by iPhone and Wi-Fi.

Notes

1. Joël Des Rosiers, *Théories caraïbes* (Montréal: Tryptique, 1996), 63. We translate: "The real birth place is one where we pose, for the first time, a foreign eye on ourselves: my first homelands have been foreign lands. I liked these strangely elusive, strangely intimate relations that exist between a man and the hot lands of which he is dispossessed in order to put all his efforts on promised lands, henceforth his object of desire."
2. Pico Iyer, *Imagining Canada: An Outsider's Hope for a Global Future* (Toronto: The Hart House Lecture, 2001), 16.
3. Charles Jencks, *The Language of Postmodern Architecture* (New York: Rizzoli, 1977).
4. Iyer, *Imagining Canada*, 17.
5. Lord Tweedsmuir (John Buchan), *Canadian Occasions* (Toronto: The Musson Book Company, 1941), 27.

6. Neil Bissoondath, *Selling Illusions: The Cult of Multiculturalism in Canada* (Toronto: Penguin, 1994).
7. Iyer, *Imagining Canada*, 29.
8. Lynn Diamond, *Leslie Muller ou le principe d'incertitude* (Montréal: Triptyque, 2011), 20. We translate: "What do you believe in, you, Minnie? — In ecstasy."
9. *Ibid.*, 200. We translate: "Minnie asked him what he believed in now. He replied: 'I believe that life is short.'"
10. Mark Kingwell, *The World We Want* (New York: Viking, 2000).
11. Nancy Huston, *Nord Perdu: suivi de Douze France* (Arles/Montréal: Actes Sud/Leméac, 1999).
12. Margaret Laurence, *Heart of a Stranger* (Toronto: McClelland and Stewart, 1976), 219.
13. Yvon Rivard, *Mort et naissance de Christophe Ulric* (Montréal: La Presse, 1976).
14. Octavio Paz, *Le singe grammairien* (Paris: Flammarion, 1972).
15. *Forbes*, May 15, 2000: 55.
16. Iyer, *Imagining Canada*, 29.
17. Édouard Glissant, *Introduction à une politique du divers* (Paris: Gallimard, 1996).
18. Diamond, *Leslie Muller ou le principe d'incertitude*, 200. We translate: "Lili had intervened with an ironic tone saying that the challenge of the 21st century would be to understand the link between cause and effect."
19. Pierre Teilhard De Chardin, *L'avenir de l'homme* (Paris: Seuil, 1969).
20. Tomson Highway, *Comparing Mythologies* (Ottawa: University of Ottawa Press, 2003), 46.
21. Étienne Parent, *Du travail chez l'homme* (23 septembre 1847), 75. We translate: "thou shalt work by the sweat of your brow" and "work is freedom."
22. "Et les sauvages ne restent sauvages que parce qu'ils ne développent pas assez la loi de la propriété." We translate : "And the savages remain savages because they do not sufficiently develop the law of property." Lamartine, *Le conseiller du peuple*, 1849–1851, vol. 1, p. 26.
23. Algirdas Julien Greimas, *Sémantique structurale* (Paris: Larousse, 1966).
24. Carlos Castaneda, *Journey to Ixtlan* (New York: Pocket Book, 1972).
25. On the walls and the foundation of the partially excavated ancient pyramid, a park for walking and a few restaurants that allow one to enjoy the view have just been built. The tourist attraction replaces the sacred space of the Lord.
26. Wang Hongyan, "Incorporer un contenu autochtone dans l'enseignement public : une façon d'améliorer les relations entre les autochtones et les immigrants anciens et nouveaux au Canada", in *Canadian Issues/Thèmes canadiens*, *Les relations autochtones immigrants aujourd'hui* (summer 2012): 55. We translate: "His measures include establishing a curriculum oriented towards their traditional lifestyle as it is defined by the *First Nations School* in Toronto, as well as the addition of courses on the Aboriginal history and perspectives within the curriculum."
27. Charles Taylor, *Multiculturalism: Examining the Politics of Recognition* (Princeton: Princeton University Press, 1994).
28. *Ibid.*
29. Gérard Bouchard, *L'Interculturalisme: un point de vue québécois* (Montréal: Boréal, 2012).
30. Will Kymlicka, *Multicultural Odysseys: Navigating the New International politics of Diversity* (Oxford: Oxford University Press, 2007).

31. Daniel Bonilla-Maldonado, *La Constitución multicultural* (Bogotá: Siglo del hombre editores, 2006).
32. Tariq Modood, *Multiculturalism* (Cambridge: Polity, 2007).
33. Ibid, 79.
34. Ibid, p. 80.
35. Ibid, 147.
36. Ibid, 151.
37. Robert Fulford, "Foreword" to Janis Kraulis (ed), *Canada: A Landscape Portrait* (Edmonton: Hurtig, 1982), 6.
38. Here is Gordon Brown's sentence: "When we look at history and at the values and ideas that shape British national identity, I would want to stress a belief in tolerance and liberty, a sense of civic duty, a sense of fair play, a sense of being open to the world." "Round table: Britain rediscovered", *Prospect*, 17 mars 2005, p.1. Here is the answer to this statement by Brown: "To get back to Tariq's broader point, I am not proposing some formulaic list of values that embody Britain for the next 200 years. Equally, I don't think it's good enough just to have all these ideas floating around and to say the debate is an end in itself." Modood, 6.
39. Modood, 152.
40. Michael Finkenthal, "Le sens des approches inter et multidisciplinaires pour l'étude du multiculturalisme comme problème complexe," in *Trans, multi, interculturalité, trans, multi, interdisciplinarité*, eds. Brigitte Fontille and Patrick Imbert (Québec: Presses de l'Université Laval, 2012): 19–34.
41. This sentence and the reference to Brown are not clear in Modood's book. Is it pronounced by Gordon Brown? No. Why is there then a reference to Brown? Let us note also that it is a round table and that Gordon Brown is only one of the numerous participants whose names follow: Neal Ascherson, Billy Bragg, Gordon Brown, Linda Colley, David Goodhart, Eric Kaufmann, David Lammy, Tariq Modood, Roger Scruton.
42. Fulford, 6.
43. René Girard, *Des choses cachées depuis la fondation du monde* (Paris: Livre de poche, 1978).
44. Stewart Bell, "Reflect Canadian values school told", *National Post* (Sunday, Nov. 10, 2012): A12.
45. Jack Jedwab, *The Multiculturalism Question: Debating Identity in 21st Century Canada* (Montreal/Kingston: McGill/Queen's University Press, 2014).
46. Rawi Hage, *Cockroach* (New York: Norton and Company, 2010), 11.
47. Iyer, *Imagining Canada*, 19.
48. Christian Bök, *Cristallography* (Toronto: Coach House Press, 1994), 12.
49. This insistence on the moment that lasts a long time is also found in recent advertisements: "One day can last a lifetime", states Bell Canada, which donates to mental health research, a research that will have an impact on the future generations, says the advertising. *Canada's Innovation Leaders, a RESEARCH infosource Inc. Publication* (Nov. 8th, 2013): 20.
50. Yvon Rivard, *Le siècle de Jeanne* (Montréal: Boréal, 2005), 288. We translate: "[…] I adamantly believed that the errors, the failures and the horrors of America do not proceed so much from the loss of memory or the collapse of the European culture than from the resist-

ance to this new culture of the moment, which is not devoid of memory, as it is thought so often, but which is on the contrary the greatest memory, more alive, that which, in every moment, makes me contemporary with the beginning and the end of the world."

51. Ibid, 293. We translate: "we must now start again, start again to see, to feel, to understand that this world and ourselves have no age since we are born together every moment and every moment is a mobile border where all the past and future centuries meet."
52. This link between beauty, risk of becoming self and freedom including the freedom to undertake is also noted in many contemporary works and in places where the influence of the Americas is mentioned. This is what we note in the work of the Indian writer Aravind Adiga. In his novel entitled *The White Tiger*, he is devoting himself to the passage from a traditional society to a society that takes partially its inspiration from a globalization for which the individualist, rich and technologic United States and North America are fascinating. He evokes the life of a poor farmer North of India who became a contractor in Bangalore, which reminds us of an article in the magazine *Wired* advocating for the success of the members of the minorities in India and finding their inspiration in the development of the United States: "Kar wanted to do something else. After earning his MBA from the University of Bombay in 1983, he set out to knock down the caste system's barriers, using technology as his battering ram. 'I concur strongly with Thomas Jefferson, he says. I am more interested in the dreams of the future than the history of the past. I am the first in my family to do his own things.'" *Wired*, March 2000: 158.
The character of Adiga says the following about those who are less organized than him: "*They remain slaves because they can't see what is beautiful in this world*". Aravind Adiga, *The White Tiger* (New Delhi: Harpercollins India, 2008), 40. See also p. 276: "Iqbal, that great poet, was so right. The moment you recognize what is beautiful in this world, you stop being a slave." On the subject of the North America fascination, see also Salman Rushdie, "The Firebird's Nest" *The New Yorker*, June 1997: 35: "America… My country (India) is just like yours (The United States), he'd said, flirting. Big, turbulent, and full of gods. We speak our kind of bad English and you speak yours. And before you became Romans, when you were just colonials, our masters were the same. You defeated them before we did. So now you have more money than we do. Otherwise, we're the same."
53. Jocelyne Saucier, *Il pleuvait des oiseaux* (Montréal: XYZ, 2011), 41. We translate: "We were installed in the slowness I like and he threw me, as if we had discussed the subject for hours: —an ideal place for what you are looking for."
54. Rivard, *Le siècle de Jeanne*, 317. We translate: "What is allowing us to be happy is not this thing in us that keeps us away from happiness and gives us the desire for happiness, which sees in all there is an image threatened by all there is?"
55. Ibid, 348. We translate: "The New World would have been perhaps possible only if we could perceive at once and simultaneously the beginning and the end of a world, and for that what wonderful exercise to hear on a deserted beach the steps of those who have passed and those who will come, like seeing in the middle of a crowd or the arms of a woman this empty space that nobody would ever fill, the fixed center of all movement, the wheel hub."
56. Ibid, 392.

57. Roméo Dallaire, *J'ai serré la main du diable: la faillite de l'humanité au Rwanda* (Outremont, Québec: Libre expression, 2003).
58. Gabriela Alejandra Karasik, *Cultura e identidad en el Noroeste argentino* (Buenos Aires: centro editor de América latina, 1994), 48. We translate : "The province of Jujuy and the Comisión de Homenaje to the archaeologists Juan B. Ambrosetti (1865–1917) and Salvador Debenedetti (1884–1930). From the millenary ashes of a dead people they exhumed the indigenous cultures and gave echo to the silence."
59. We can also see their access to the economic networks due to the new technologies: about twenty years ago, in Yavi, a young Indigenous Coya learned to use the computers and to connect to the Internet. On the one hand, he put all the village data on the computer and, on the other hand, he could access through the Internet information regarding the federal government in Buenos Aires such as subventions to vaccinate animals. This vaccination added to the Indigenous people's wealth and gave them access to new markets to sell their animals because they were vaccinated. Through his ability to capitalize a knowledge from the outside of the local territory of Jujuy blocked in the dualistic confrontations and its fights to retain the information, the new mayor transformed his community. He replaced the power of the traditional Indigenous elites. He accessed, thanks to the globalized medium of the Internet, information and funding from the federal and national governments. He succeeded in finding a third way, because he escaped the territorial logic and geographic, informative and symbolic boundaries. He escaped the belief that life is a zero-sum game, because, through the technological enrichment originating from the First World countries, he succeeded in obtaining economic advantages from the federal government in order to improve the fate of the Indigenous population at the local and provincial levels. The global, in this case, changed the dualist fixed power relations and allowed the local to experience a certain form of liberation. The global does not oppose to the local. The contemporary relations are more of the glocal type, that is of the global/local connections.
60. Glissant, *Introduction à une poétique du divers* (Paris : Gallimard, 1996), 117.
61. Ibid, 118. We translate: "It is not in the built works that we get our continuity, but paradoxically in the historical impossibility of the continuity." This paradox is linked to the capacity of not solving the contradictions, somewhat in the same way that multiculturalism leads to asserting the identity through the fact of having several that are complex in terms of a background where there are only minorities.
62. Ibid, 121.
63. Paul-Émile Borduas, *Refus Global; Projections libérantes* (Montréal: Parti Pris, 1974).
64. Elena Botchorichvili, *Seulement attendre et regarder* (Montréal: Boréal, 2012), 25. We translate: "Even if they had nothing in common, except their past, their execrated past. But can execration unite? Workers of the world, unite?"
65. Ibid, 47. We translate: "They? Us? Us is us, you is you? You is you, us is us?"
66. Ibid, 89. We translate: "Us is you…you is us …"
67. Nicolas Dickner, *Nikolski* (Québec: Alto, 2007), 222.
68. Diamond, 108. We translate: "To pay her studies, she (Anna) had reconstructed, for two years on behalf of a natural history museum, the full-sized skeleton of an Albertosaurus."

69. See nonetheless the observations of Ronald Wright on the Neanderthals and Cro-Magnons for a 10 000-year period. He reveals the genocidal struggles between these two groups. Ronald Wright, *A Short History of Progress* (Toronto: Anansi, 2004).
70. Robert Lepage, *La face cachée de la lune* (Québec: L'Instant même, 2007).
71. See also: Valérie Mandia, "Devant les silences de l'univers: des principes d'indétermination et d'incertitude chez Nancy Huston, Lynn Diamond et Isabel Allende", in *Rencontres multiculturelles: imprévus et coïncidences: Le Canada et les Amériques*, ed. P. Imbert (Ottawa: Chaire de recherche: "Canada: enjeux sociaux et culturels dans la société du savoir", 2013), 101–129.
72. Jean Rousset, *La littérature de l'âge baroque en France: Circé et le paon* (Paris: Corti, 1954).
73. This infinite black is not necessarily scary as we can see in the Keller Williams' publications. We can see in it a mathematical formula on an ink background above an astronaut whose visor reflects the spaceship. We can read the slogan: "One small step changes everything… We invite you to share our formula for success." *The Real Deal, New York Real Estate News*, vol. 9, no. 3, March 2011, back cover.
74. Dickner, 144.
75. *Ibid*. We translate: "As a general rule, the archaeologists are not interested that much in the nomads. The more a population travels, the less traces it leaves. We prefer to study the civilizations that settle down, build cities and produce lots of trash…—And the traditional territory in all this?—The Inuit had no idea what a dump was before the arrival of the Bay Hudson Company."
76. See also Daniel Castillo Durante, *Los vertederos de la postmodernidad* (Ottawa: Dovehouse Press, 2000).
77. Jacques Ferron, *La nuit* (Montréal: Parti pris, 1965), 12. We translate: "So, not really knowing where I was going, I didn't have cause for alarm."
78. Isabel Allende, *Hija de la fortuna* (Buenos Aires: Editorial Sudamericana, 1999), 385. We translate: "Here women can own land, buy and sell properties, and divorce if they really want to."
79. Ibid, 391. We translate: "You can't imagine what racism is, Lin, you have always lived among your people. Here, what I say or do matters to no one. For the Americans, I am just a pagan and disgusting Chinese and Eliza is scum. In the Chinese city I'm a renegade without tail and turned into a Yankee. I belong to no place."
80. Ibid, 282. We translate: "The American laws favour the individuals: each property is reduced to the space that everyone can exploit."
81. *Ibid*. We translate: "The Chilean companies turn the law by registering the rights in the name of each worker in order to control more territory."
82. Paulo Coelho, *Once Minutos* (Barcelona: Planeta, 2003), 153. We translate: "The encounters are waiting for us but, in most cases we avoid their success."
83. Coelho, *Once Minutos*, 153.
84. James Baldwin, *Giovanni's Room* (New York: The Dial Press, 1956), 242.
85. Eduardo Mendieta, *Global Fragments: Latin-Americanisms, Globalizations, and Critical Theory* (Albany: State University of New York Press, 2007), 185.
86. René Philoctète, *Massacre River* (New York: New Directions Publishing, 2005), 293.

87. Ibid, 292. This image is the opposite of the orange laughing roofs of the Howard Johnson hotels open to movements mentioned in Section: Statism and Dynamism.
88. Mendieta, *Global Fragments: Latin-Americanisms, Globalizations, and critical Theory*, 185.
89. Gérard Étienne, *Le Nègre crucifié* (Montréal: Nouvelle optique, 1974).
90. Gérard Étienne, *La pacotille* (Montréal: L'Hexagone, 1991).
91. Kim Thúy and Pascal Janovjak, *À toi* (Montréal: Libre expression, 2011), 75. We translate: "The professors gave me my diploma after three years, at the same time as the other students. But, contrary to the others, I was graded not according to my merit but to my determination. Twenty years later, I found myself again in front of them, unconditional of words, passionate about language, messengers of the imaginary, in order to share a moment of literature. So is everything possible?"
92. Walter Isaacson, *Steve Jobs* (New York: Simon and Schuster, 2011), 343.
93. *Ibid.*
94. Marshall McLuhan, *Notes on the Media as Art Form* (Corte Madera, CA: Gingko Press, 2005), 10.
95. Jamaica Kincaid, "Girl," in *At the Bottom of the River* (New York: Farrar, Strauss and Giroux, 1984), 72.
96. W. P. Kinsella, *Shoeless Joe Jackson comes to Iowa*, Dallas, Texas, Southern Methodist University Press, 1993.
97. Isaacson, *Steve Jobs*, 571.
98. Bök, *Cristallography*, 16.
99. Ibid, 63.
100. Robert Fulford, "Foreword" to Janis Kraulis, *Canada: A Landscape Portrait*, 8.
101. Joaquín Torres-García, *La ciudad sin nombre* (Montevideo: AAC, 1941). See also: Rosa Sarabia, "Manuscription in *La ciudad sin nombre* by Joaquín Torres-García", *Word and Image* (June 2010, 26: 3): 297–310.
102. Isabel Allende, *Hija de la fortuna*, 242. We translate: "It seemed that we have all come to look for something and we found something else."
103. Gabrielle Roy, *Un jardin au bout du monde* (Montréal, Boréal, 1994).
104. George Gilder, *Wealth and Poverty* (New York: Basic Books, 1981).
105. Tomson Highway, *Comparing Mythologies*, 49.
106. Éric Dupont, *La Logeuse* (Montréal: Marchand de feuilles, 2006), 15.
107. *Ibid.* We translate: "November 1st, 1987: comrade Madeleine Barachois, 55 years, Balance, was followed and savagely murdered screaming 'no! no! no!'. Proud owner of a Christmas cactus which, like magic, would always bloom a day before the December snowstorms, took the habit of prophesizing the worst blizzards. In this morning of November 1st, Madeleine bragged about her cactus blooming earlier that year. The inhabitants, exasperated by the idea of an early blizzard, reached the conclusion that the poor woman desired and induced these storms and, confounding causality and coincidence, gave birth to the second sister under a rain of stones."
108. Ibid, 218. We translate: "all signs are false."
109. Werner Heisenberg, *Le manuscrit de 1942* (Paris: Allia, 2003), 170. We translate: "We must remember before anything else that the political power is founded, over and over again, on crime."

110. "Diversity", *Forbes*, April 3, 2000: 191.
111. Yann Martel, *Life of Pi* (Toronto: Vintage, 2001), V.
112. Stephen Leacock, "Gertrude the Governess or, Simple Seventeen," in *Nonsense Novels* (Montreal: Publishers Press, 1911), 73.
113. Henri Laborit, *Éloge de la fuite* (Paris: Gallimard, 1976).
114. Basarab Nicolescu, "*In vitro* and *in vivo* Knowledge-Methodology of Transdisciplinarity", in *Transdisciplinarity: Theory and Practice*, ed. Basarab Nicolescu (Cresskill, New Jersey: Hampton Press, 2008).
115. Aided in this by the intertextual reference to the Brazilian author Moacyr Scilar who has also written, in *Max and the Cats* (New York, Ballantine, 1990), the story of a castaway with a wild cat in his escape from Nazi Berlin to Brazil.
116. Fulford, 8.
117. Maria Salomon, *Social Capital Outcomes of Adult Learning and Literacy Initiatives*, The Centre for Literacy/Le centre d'alphabétisation (Québec, August 2010), 2.
118. Ibid, 19. This novel is thus very different from Rawi Hage's *Cockroach*, manifesting a constant daily violence in the social interactions nourished by resentment.
119. Madeleine Thien, *Do Not Say We Have Nothing* (Toronto: Vintage, 2016), 458.
120. Nicolescu, 5.
121. Martel, *Life of Pi*, 356.
122. Ibid, 357.
123. Ibid, 352.
124. Greimas, *Sémantique structurale*.
125. Edwige Danticat, *Create Dangerously* (Princeton: Princeton University Press, 2010), 15.
126. *Ibid*. There are no immigrant artists in this era of globalization.
127. We find Andrée Firretti's text entitled "Dany Laferrière: le modèle parfait de l'anti-Québécois" completely unfounded from the point of view of the literary canon theme, in addition to being the least excluding. See *indépendantes.org* December 13, 2013.
128. We also see this regional integration in New Orleans in John Kennedy Toole's novel *A Confederacy of dunces* (Bâton-rouge: Louisiana State University, 1980). The character of Ignatius Reilly is confronted with the antagonism of the fools allied against him, much like the author himself whose novel was refused by many publishers. The book would be published only after his suicide and become a bestseller. Here too, for the character as for the author, the regional combines with exclusion dynamics widespread on the planet.
129. Patrick Imbert, *Les Amériques transculturelles: Les stéréotypes du jeu à somme nulle* (Québec: Les Presses de l'Université Laval, 2013).
130. This is also underscored by Ulrich Beck in his book *World at Risk* (Cambridge: Polity Press, 2009).
131. Pico Iyer, *The Global Soul* (New York: Vintage, 2000), 229.
132. Charles Sanders Peirce, *Writings of C.S. Peirce* (Bloomington: Bloomington University Press, 1982).
133. Greimas, *Sémantique structurale*.
134. Algirdas Julien Greimas, *Maupassant* (Paris: Seuil, 1980).

135. See also René Girard's use of the analysis of the Québécois cinema: Étienne Beaulieu, *Sang et lumière: la communauté du sacré dans le cinéma québécois* (Québec: L'instant même, 2007).
136. Michael Penny, *Outside, Inside* (Montreal: McGill/Queen's University Press, 2014).
137. For us, stereotypes are anchored in paradigms, while clichés, as for Riffaterre, are anchored in syntagmatic developments. Michel Riffaterre, *Essais de stylistique structurale* (Paris: Flammarion, 1972).
138. Alberto Moravia, *Desideria* (Paris: Flammarion, 1978), 361. We translate: "The house of a proletarian is modest, simple, even poor but clean like the face of an honest woman."
139. Isabel Allende, *Retrato en Sepia* (Buenos Aires: Ed. Sudamericana, 2000), 49. We translate: "They entered a little house, without ventilation, but clean and orderly."
140. Fiodor Dostoïevsky, *Les Frères Karamazov* (Paris: Livre de poche, 1972), 402. We translate: "The room he occupied was poor but clean."
141. Agatha Christie, *The ABC Murders* (New York: The Berkeley Books, 1963), 25.
142. Hector Charbonneau, *Gabriel et Geneviève* (Moncton: éditions d'Acadie, 1974), 18. We translate: "Cleanliness is the ornament of the poor; he who dons it is adorned with beautiful clothes."
143. Daniel Castillo Durante, *Ce feu si lent de l'exil* (Montréal: XYZ, 2009), 242. We translate: "The building was antiquated but well maintained."
144. See J.-P. Braud, *L'Affaire de la main volée* (Paris: Seuil, 1993), notably the passage entitled "Le corps laborieux dans son environnement industriel" (166).
145. "Boomtown Slum", *The Economist* (December 22, 2012): 74.
146. For the development of poor but honest, see: Samuel Smiles, *Self-Help with Illustrations of Character, Conduct, and Perseverance* (New York: Harper and Brothers, 1874).
147. Jean-Marie Pontaut, *Demi-Lune* (Paris: Fayard, 2005), 11. We translate: "A young baker from Bordeaux, poor but honest as it is said in the stories of uncle Paul."
148. Nathalie Petrowski, "J'habite chez ma sœur," *La Presse*, Montréal, Friday November 15, 1996: A 5. When we know that the journalist speaks about Richard Therrien, one of the participants in the revolutionary cell of the Quebec Liberation Front, we see that the march towards a better future may, henceforth, pass through devious ways, especially if they value exactly the interior/exterior paradigm as it is about to advance Quebec's independence. We translate: "They are poor, it's true, but they are proud."
149. Domingo Faustino Sarmiento, *Sarmiento's Travels in The United States in 1847*, translated in English by M. A. Rockland, (Princeton, Princeton University Press, 1970).
150. Anyelick Campos Zamora and Larissa Tristan Jimenez, *Nicaragüenses en las noticias* (San José, Costa Rica: Universidad de Costa Rica, 2010), 37. The citation is found in the book by R. Soto, "El discurso sobre la inmigración a principios del siglo XX: una estrategia nacionalista de selección autovalorativa", *Revista de Historia*, 40, p. 79–97. We translate: "A wave of healthy immigration, both from a moral and physical point of view, exclusively workers or even better, families of workers whose blood would be like the magnificent blood of our people, and their customs like ours: Spanish, Italian, German, French, Irish farmers…"
151. Carlos Sandoval García, *Otros amenazantes: los nicaragüenses y la formación de identidades nacionales en Costa Rica*, San José (Costa Rica): Universidad de Costa Rica, 2002), p. 48.

152. Anyelick Campos Zamora and Larissa Tristan Jimenez, *op. cit.*, p. 44. The citation is found in the book by Carlos Sandoval García, *Otros amenazantes : los nicaragüenses y la formación de identidades nacionales en Costa Rica* (San José: Editorial Universidad de Costa Rica, 2002), 50. We translate: "In this context there are certain oppositions that are repeated: lawfulness versus unlawfulness is the narrative context that prevails in the case of the 'immigrants', cleanliness versus contagious prevails when diseases are the main subject…"
153. Anyelick Campos Zamora and Larissa Tristan Jimenez, 37. Evidently, egalitarian means egalitarian for the Costaricains descended from Europeans, because the others are strongly excluded. We translate: "They are dark-skinned and poor, while the opposite would be whiteness and an egalitarian nation of middle class."
154. Vladimir Propp, *Morphologie du conte* (Paris: Seuil, 1972).
155. Don Delillo, "Videotape," *Harper's Magazine*, December 1, 1994: 17
156. Gabriel García Márquez, *Cent ans de solitude* (Paris: Seuil, 1968).
157. Jacques Stephen Alexis, *Compère général soleil* (Paris: Gallimard, 1982).
158. Augusto Roa Bastos, *La veille de l'amiral* (Paris: Seuil, 1994).
159. Rafael Lucas, "Préface," *in* Franketienne, *Mûr à crever* (Bordeaux: Ana éditions, 2004), 9. We translate: "there really is a narrative thread, but it is stripped of its habitual status of main theme."
160. Homi Bhabha, "Of Mimicry and Man: The Ambivalence of Colonial Discourse", *October*, no. 28 (1984): 125–133.
161. Tom Robbins, *Wild Ducks Flying Backward* (New York: Bantam, 2005), 255.
162. Isaacson, 527.
163. John Murphy, Manuel J. Caro and Jung Choi, "Estética Cuántica: A New Approach to Culture" [Online] <www.gradnet.de/papers/.pomo01.paper/ Choi01.htm>
164. Kim Thúy, *Rú* (Montréal: Libre expression, 2009), 86. We translate: "This American dream gave assertiveness to my voice, determination to my gestures, precision to my desires, speed to my gait and force to my eyes."
165. John Dewey, "Escape from Peril", in *The Quest for Certainty* (London: George Allen & Unwin, 1929), 112–113.
166. Charles Sanders Peirce, "How to Make Our Ideas Clear", in *Popular Sciences Monthly*, January 1878, vol. 12: 293.
167. John Gribbin, *In Search of Schrödinger's Cat: Quantum Physics and Reality* (New York: Bantam, 1988), 164.
168. Rafael Catala, "Literatura y ciencia en las culturas de habla Española", in *La torre: revista de la Universidad de Puerto Rico*, Special volume on Hispanic Literature and Science, ed. Rivero-Potter (vol. 3, no. 9, 1998): 525. We translate: "The quantic physics and the theory of relativity with the humanities and the religion."
169. José Vasconcelos, "Tratado de metafisica", *Obras completas*, vol III (Mexico: Libros mexicanos unidos, 1959), 493.
170. Ernesto Cardenal, *Cántico cósmico* (Managua: Nueva Nicaragua, 1989).
171. Ibid, 585. We translate: "The number is hardly the sign of the moments where alternates the rhythm of the movement."
172. Ibid, 589. We translate: "They are manifesting, in any case, since forever different ways of understanding the character of the synthesis."

173. Let us not forget the 1960s' practice of linking oriental philosophies and scientific theories related to relativity, which is a process already latent with Vasconcelos in "Tratado de metafisica" (592). We translate: "The flow is made and unmade. We could say Ying and Yang, the progression and the regression of Taoism, the oriental equivalent of the Heraclitus' perpetual flow. We think, in relation to these discursive hybridisations, of *Tao of Physics* by Fritjof Capra or even of publications like *The Last Whole Earth Catalog* (New York, Random House, 1972) quoted especially by Steve Jobs as source of a new culture that revolutionizes the United States, the Americas and the planet. This is what is underlined nowadays almost everywhere and especially in advertisings that aim to transform the philosophic-cultural perspectives of the population. This is the case of Keller Williams of New York: "deltav=ve 1n mo/m1. The formula that initiated the launch of a 4.5-million-pound space shuttle to reach its destination. One small step changes everything." *The Real Deal, New York Real Estate News*, vol. 9, no. 3, March 2011, back cover.
174. Alicia Rivero, "Heisenberg's Uncertainty Principle in Contemporary Spanish American Fiction" in *Science and the Creative Imagination in Latin America*, eds. Evelyn Fishburn and Eduardo L. Ortiz (London: Institute for the Study of the Americas, 2005): 251–273.
175. Stephen Leacock, "Common Sense and the Universe," in *Last Leaves* (Toronto: McClelland and Stewart, 1945), 50.
176. Isabel Allende, *The House of the Spirits* (New York: Bantam, 1985).
177. Modood, *Multiculturalism*, 27.
178. William H. Harrison, *In Praise of Mixed Religion* (Montreal/Kingston: McGill/Queen's University, 2014).
179. Abla Fahroud, *Le Bonheur à la queue glissante* (Montréal : L'Hexagone, 1998), 46. We translate: "One day he had the idea to go see the rabbi or the priest or the imam, in order to ask for his help."
180. Linda Hutcheon, *As Canadian as possible…under the Circumstances* (Toronto: ECW Press/York University, 1990), 43.
181. Douglas Coupland, *The Gum Thief* (Toronto: Random House, 2007), 7.
182. Ronald Wright, *A Short History of Progress*.
183. Édouard Glissant, *Poétique de la relation* (Paris: Gallimard, 1990), 61. We translate: "The generalization inspired by Christ was relayed in that moment by the one suggested by Darwin, both of them being in opposition at first. In both cases it was about transcending the ancient mythical filiation, linked to the future of a community, to surpass it in a generalizing conception, which would have kept however the force of the linearity principle and which would have 'included' and motivated history."
184. Ibid, 62. We translate: "There is thus in the Myth a hidden violence, that gets caught in the mesh of the filiation and challenges absolutely the existence of the Other as element of relation."
185. Ying Chen, *Quatre mille marches* (Montréal: Boréal, 2004), 12. We translate: "My true country is where I become what I want to be."
186. Bridget Hayden, *Salvadoreños en Costa Rica: vidas desplazadas* (San José: Universidad de Costa Rica, 2005), 173. We translate: "Antonio… said that the place where someone happened to be was not really important. A person can adapt to any country."

187. Jean-Philippe Rossignol, *Vie éclectique* (Paris: Gallimard, 2011), 33. We translate: "It gives under its feather of chameleon."
188. Sergio Kokis, *Le pavillon des miroirs* (Montréal: XYZ, 1994), 40. We translate: "always was a stranger everywhere."
189. Ibid, 18. We translate: "I am pleased now to go unnoticed, to avoid requests, to play the chameleon, to not take too seriously the enthusiasm of my fellow beings. The solitude, behind the appearance of a puppet, is the only comfortable position in my case."
190. Eugène Ionesco, *Les chaises* followed by *L'impromptu de l'Alma ou le caméléon du berger* (Paris: Gallimard, 1973), 101. We translate: "If you want, I am still the shepherd, the theatre being the chameleon because I embraced the theatrical career, and the theatre changes, of course, because the theatre is life. It changes like life...The chameleon too is life."
191. Nando Michaud, *Les montres sont molles mais les temps sont durs* (Montréal: Pierre Tisseyre, 1988), 9.
192. Bill Schermbrucker, *Chameleon* (Vancouver: Talon Books, 1983), 147.
193. *Ibid.*
194. James Naughtie on Doris Lessing on the subject of *The Grass is Singing*, BBC, Sept. 2001.
195. Schermbrucker, 124.
196. The Manpower Group's ad features a multicoloured-eye chameleon that sees more: "Seeing the unseen is humanly possible. True vision is seeing people's full potential. When a global technology company needed keen eyes for visual inspections, ManpowerGroup recruitment experts saw an unconventional solution. We hired hearing-impaired workers whose eyesight was more acute, boosting productivity by 25%. For innovative Workforce Solutions and a more insightful look into your business, visit manpowergroup.com" (*The Economist*, Feb. 2, 2013: 8). [On line] [manpowergroup.com].
197. Schermbrucker, 110.
198. Ibid, 12.
199. Ibid, 152.
200. Gloria Anzaldúa, *Borderland/La frontera*: The New Mestiza, San Francisco, Aunt Lute Books, 1999, p. 80.
201. In Nuevo Léon (Mexico), in particular in its capital city Monterrey, one often dreams of mixing a Mexican approach and the Protestant ethic, and the goal to succeed following the model on the other side of the border.
202. Truman Capote, "A Day's Work", in *Music for Chameleons* (New York: Random, 1980), 112.
203. Yann Martel, *Self* (Toronto: Knopf, 1996), 238. For a critique of the concept of hybridity, see Amaryll Chanady, "Entre hybridité et interculture: de nouveaux paradigmes identitaires à la fin du deuxième millénaire," in *L'interculturel au cœur des Amériques*, eds. D. Castillo Durante and P. Imbert (Ottawa/Winnipeg: Université d'Ottawa/Université du Manitoba/Legas, 2003): 21–34.
204. George Rodrigue and Tom Brokaw, *Blue Dog Man* (New York: Stewart, Tabori and Chang, 1999), 21.
205. Lorrie Moore, *Anagrams* (New York: Knopf, 1986).

206. Kim Thúy and Pascal Janovjak, *À toi*, 31. We translate: "For weeks I thought that Pi-r was a Vietnamese name from the mountainous regions meaning maybe 'renewal' or 'source' or even 'whistling wind'. But it was only Pierre, pronounced by a Vietnamese woman glued day and night to her sewing machine, hoping that her son will have a face as common as this name."
207. Ibid, 104. We translate: "to avoid the conflicts, to breath without existing, to melt in the background… I learnt really quickly to be invisible and useful at the same time, so that nobody could blame me, so that nobody gets to me."
208. Will Kymlicka, *Multicultural Citizenship: A Liberal Theory of Minority Rights* (Oxford: Clarendon Press, 1995), 18.
209. Seema Ahluwalia, "Exploiter la générosité et entretenir l'ignorance : Ô Canada, terre de nos aïeux", in *Canadian Issues/Thèmes canadiens*, *Les relations autochtones immigrants aujourd'hui* (summer 2012): 48.
210. Lucia Madariaga-Vignudo, "Les réfugiés africains vus par les Autochtones urbains: une étude de cas du centre-ville de Winnipeg", in *Canadian Issues/Thèmes canadiens*, *les relations autochtones immigrants aujourd'hui*, (summer 2012): 18. We translate: "Several participants underlined that the access to work is one of the fields where the Indigenous people have the impression of being in close competition with the refugees."
211. This is what is implicitly criticized in the following sentence by Andrée Ferretti, "Dany Laferrière: le modèle parfait de l'anti-québécois", *Indépendantes.org*, 13 December 2013: "From his natal Haïti, between Florida and France, Dany Laferrière has only been passing in Quebec." As if it was not normal to travel like Michel Tremblay who also appreciates Key West in Florida, without forgetting the politicians like Parizeau who would stay for a long time in France. Is James Baldwin less American because he also lived in France between the two world wars? And Marguerite Yourcenar in the East coast of the United States?
212. Moacyr Scliar, 47.
213. Louis Gauthier, *Souvenirs du San Chiquita* (Montréal: VLB, 1978), 72. We translate: "She [Angela] was South-American, Brazilian of German origin (her first childhood memories, stories of tamed parrots against a tropical forest background). Her father, adventurer, merchant but more poet than merchant, used to take the whole family in his numerous travels. In this way she found herself successively in Panama, Honduras, Belize, then in Mexico and finally in the United-States."
214. Let us also not forget that the publisher Howard Halliday runs the Chameleon publishing house in William Kotzwinkl's novel *Midnight Examiner* (New York: Marlowe and Company, 1989).
215. Nik Lygeros, "Effet caméléon," in *Modèle mental de l'Altruisme*, 2000: 1. [On line] [www.megafoundation.org/ubiquity/march00/altruismefr. html].
216. Kate Barrette, "Mother Nature, industrial designer," *The Globe and Mail*, Tuesday, 4 April, 2006: B 11.
217. *L'actualité*, February 2004: 104. We translate: "Manufactured in a reflexive material, this coat contains a video camera capturing the immediate environment of the person who wears it and projects its image on the tissue in such a way that the illusion of invisibility is created. Conceived by Shusumu Tachi of Tokyo University, this piece of clothing cannot

be found in the market before 2008." All these occurrences are linked to the rational cultural or to the techno-cultural. However, another fascinating work would necessitate another research especially because the existing work mixes scientific and essayistic discourse in a hybridity that makes the rational lose its stability. It is the one proposed by Wade Davis in *The Serpent and the Rainbow* (New York: Simon and Schuster, 1985), 251. He is looking through the voodoo and the zombie to explore the world of the passage from the living to the dead and to the living through the knowledge of poisons, incantations and the Caribbean knowledge of African origin leading to an esoteric appreciation of the change and of a form of reincarnation: "That's why we say 'learn to change'. We are in the world and we can change in the world. Everyone says that the Shapwel changes people into pigs but we say this only because it teaches that everything is relative."

218. Éric Meyer, "Pourquoi il faut partir de France", *Géo*, no. 414, August 2013: 5. We translate: "This is the moment to remember that the exile, temporary and chosen, is not necessarily evil. It brings about a loss of landmarks, that is a loss of identity and those lead to a better knowledge of the other, of his language, of his lifestyles, of his ways of reasoning."
219. Dominique Simonnet, "Desmond Richarson: 'Je danse ma vie,' " *L'Express*, 14 September, 2006: 72.
220. Nicolas Bérubé, "Arnold Schwarzenegger: caméléon." *La Presse* (Montréal, Tuesday, 7 November, 2006): A 6.
221. *Rotman Management* (Toronto: The University of Toronto, Spring 2019), Cover.
222. Mark Le Fanu, *Evening Standard*, quoted on the back of the cover of the Ben Okri's book, *The Famished Road* (London: Jonathan Cape, 1991).
223. Vincent Marissal, "Le camélédion," *La Presse*, Montréal, lundi Dec. 4, 2006: A 5. We translate: "succeeded in transforming the university professor into an efficient politician."
224. *En route*, February 2003, p. 15. We translate: "A chair is not a chair. The diversions of meaning of a common object offer an antidote to the February spleen."
225. Jacques Languirand, *Klondyke* suivi de *Le Québec et l'Américanité* (Montréal: Cercle du livre de France, 1971).
226. Adolphe-Basile Routhier, *Causeries du dimanche* (Montréal: Beauchemin et Valois, 1871), 86. We translate: "Strictly speaking, the United States is not a country for the majority of their inhabitants. It is a vast hotel where many caravans with people have come to take a housing ticket."
227. A certain number of immigrants settle however in Lower-Canada. Some are continental voyagers: "Maisonnette (near Québec) inhabited by a French family that has already travelled through Brazil and the West Indies without finding fortune...rolling stone doesn't gather moss." (Vicomte de Basteret, *De Québec à Lima* (Paris, Hachette,1860), 43). However, this moderate monarchist viscount is indeed the representative of a society that rejects the movement and the American dynamism by the fact that he uses a sedentary proverb glorifying the seigneurial regime. We should note that for Europeans the proverb means not succeeding in capitalizing, while for the North-Americans, it means not gathering futile or harmful elements.
228. Jean-Marie Carette, *Zirska, immigrante inconnue* (Montréal: Serge Brousseau, 1947).

229. See on the subject of the great American hotels: Thomas Mueller, "Hotelgeschichte und Hotelgeschichten," in *Natur, Räume, Landschaften*, eds. B. Krause and U. Scheck (München: Judicium Verlag, 1998): 189–198.
230. "There is a superabundance of hotels in the neighbourhood of the Falls of Niagara." James Stuart, *Three Years in North America* (Edinburgh: R. Cadell, 1833), 158.
231. This theme of the influence of the American media that undermine Canadian culture and destroy the identity of its populations will be a constant in the English Canadian cultural landscape as well as in the French Canadian. From regulations to deregulations, various approaches will appear depending on whether it is about a protectionist policy or not. These media are the privileged vehicles of a culture where the popular and the specialized are mixing. This suits the populations that wish to refer to certain known myths, yet transformed by modern technology. This popular/specialized culture is what the thinkers influenced by Europe call mass culture. However, mass culture is much more present in Stalinist Soviet Union and in Nazi Europe, as it was about bureaucratic, centralized political regimes submitted to repression that voluntarily sought to transform the people into masses submitted to the chief and to the party.
232. Pierre-J. Olivier Chauveau, *L'instruction publique au Canada* (Québec: A. Core, 1876), 314. European visitors are also fascinated by the Montreal hotels: "The most beautiful hotels are lost among the secondary houses." Théodore Pavie, *Souvenirs atlantiques* (Paris: Robert, 1838), 157.
233. See Manuel Balbotín's (1824–1894), *Un día del mes de enero a los 40 grados de latitud norte* (1873), a fragment of which is quoted in a collection of texts: Emmanuel Carballo, *¿Qué pais es éste ? Los Estados Unidos y los gringos vistos por escritores mexicanos de los siglos XIX y XX* (México: Consejo Nacional para la Cultura y las Artes, 1996), 120.
234. See Francisco Bulnes (1847–1924), *Sobre el hemisferio norte, 11, 000 leguas. Impresiones de viaje a Cuba, los Estados unidos, Japón, China, Egipto y Europ* (1871). A fragment of which is quoted in a collection of texts: Emmanuel Carballo, 151. We translate: "The American cannot live according to a plan; he has to copy the Exchange, going up and down, receiving on one floor, eating on another and sleeping higher, agitating…"
235. See Federico Gamboa (1864–1939) with an extract from his diary (1907–1938) entitled *Diario* quoted in a collection of texts: Emmanuel Carballo, 179. We translate: "1903. WALDORF-ASTORIA HOTEL IN NEW YORK. A caravanserai. According to the French dictionaries, this means: public inn of the Orient to house the caravans. The sentence may also mean inn in the East of the United States to house the presumptuous travellers and particularly the Rastafari…"
236. Faucher de Saint-Maurice, *De Québec à Mexico* (Montréal: Duvernay, 1874). See on this subject: Roger Le Moine, "L'Aventure mexicaine de quelques Québécois: 1864–1867", in *Les discours du Nouveau Monde au Canada français et en Amérique latine au XIXe siècle/Los discursos del Nuevo Mundo en el Canadá francófono y en América latina en el siglo XIX*, eds. Marie Couillard and Patrick Imbert (Ottawa: Legas, 1995): 253–262
237. Max Apple, *The Oranging of America and other Stories* (New York: Viking/Penguin, 1974), 178.
238. Ibid, 182.
239. Buffy Cram, *Radio Belly* (Vancouver: Douglas and McIntyre, 2012), 51.

240. Patrick Imbert and Adriana Rizzo, "Las bases del sistema territorial nacional frente a lo global en las Américas," *Revista Cronía*, Facultad de Ciencias Humanas. Universidad Nacional de Río Cuarto. Nro. 3, 2001.
241. Michel de Certeau, *L'invention du quotidien* (Paris: UGE, 1980), 208.
242. "Home is the only thing you do not leave home without." This is what Anton Shammas states in a conference in 1994 (quoted by Walter Mignolo, "Human understanding and (Latin) American Interests—The Politics and Sensibilities of Geohistorical Locations," in *A Companion to Postcolonial Studies*, eds. H. Schwartz and S. Ray (Oxford: Blackwell, 1999), 182).
243. We can translate *homesick* which means "avoir le mal du pays" not as having images from one's family but rather of the community and the territory, of the village hidden in the hollow of the valley, etc. We translate: "One does not carry one's homeland on the sole of one's shoes."
244. This does not mean that the rooting is not appreciated but rather that it does not prevent the travel. Ansi Mary Tolan, Global Managing Director of Accenture Resources, states that she loved, as a child, travelling with her father who knew how to appreciate the local culture of the Black-Forest in Germany. She underlines however that her family has a property on Michigan Lake since 1914 (*Continental*, August 2002: 33).
245. *La Presse*, Tuesday August 27, 2002: C3. We translate: " 'The English word is full of meaning' says Phillis Katrapani who translates it, however, as 'at home'..." "But when I use the words at home, I imagine somebody settled on a couch, with a book and a cat by their side. The concept of *home* in English is much more comprehensive."
246. *Forbes*, 15 May, 2000: 55.
247. *American Way*, 15 May, 2000: 39.
248. Same thing for the Taj chain of India: "She has international business facilities, but her hospitality is distinctly Indian" (*Forbes*, 21 August 2000: 113).
249. Charles Jencks, *The Language of Postmodern Architecture*.
250. *En Vuelo* (Aerolineas Argentinas), Nov. 2000: 49. Our translation: "Yes grandma, we miss you too. Being here, it's like staying in your home." See also the Marriott's advertisement where it shows a family with two children in the first plan but without insisting like in the Sheraton advertisement on the destruction of the links between children and grand-parents (*Ìcaro*, August 2002, p. 27).
251. We discover a similar dynamic in a daily newspaper like *La Nación* which publishes an economic section entitled *The Wall Street Journal Americas*. We discover, for example, world and more local news regarding Venezuela, Brazil, Uruguay in Spanish and under identical format as in the United States': See, for example, *La Nación*, Buenos Aires, viernes 10 de Noviembre de 2000, sección 2: 7, *The Wall Street Journal Americas*.
252. James Bohman, "The Globalization of the Public Sphere", *Philosophy and Social Criticism*, vol. 24, no. 2/3 April 1998: 203.
253. *Escala* (Aeromexico), Nov. 2002: 93. We translate: "Novotel. Welcome, here is your house."
254. Don Tapscott and Art Caston, *Paradigm Shift* (New York: McGraw Hill, 1995).
255. Figes, Orlando, *The Whisperers: Private Life in Stalin's Russia*. London: Allen Lane, 2007.
256. Pico Iyer, *Imagining Canada*, 25.
257. [On line] [www.mars-one.com/mission].

Bibliography

Adiga, Aravind. *The White Tiger*. New Delhi: HarperCollins, 2008.

Ahluwalia, Seema. "Exploiter la générosité et entretenir l'ignorance : Ô Canada, terre de nos aïeux." In *Canadian Issues/Thèmes canadiens, Les relations autochtones immigrants aujourd'hui*. Summer 2012: 46–52.

Alexis, Jacques Stephen. *Compère général soleil*. Paris: Gallimard, 1982.

Allende, Isabel. *Hija de la fortuna*. Buenos Aires: Ed. Sudamericana, 1999.

———. *Retrato en Sepia*. Buenos Aires: Ed. Sudamericana, 2000.

———. *The House of the Spirits*. New York: Bantam Books, 1985.

American Way. 15 May, 2000: 39.

Anzaldúa, Gloria. *Borderland/La frontera: The New Mestiza*. San Francisco: Aunt Lute Books, 1999.

Apple, Max. *The Oranging of America and Other Stories*. New York: Viking/Penguin, 1974.

Baldwin, James. *Giovanni's Room*. New York: The Delta Books, 1956.

Barrette, Kate. "Mother Nature, industrial designer." *The Globe and Mail*, Tuesday, 4 April, 2006: B 11.

Beck, Ulrich. *World at Risk*. Cambridge: Polity Press, 2009.

Bertrand, Karine. Étienne Beaulieu. *Sang et lumière: la communauté du sacré dans le cinéma québécois*. Québec: L'instant même, 2007.

Bérubé, Nicolas. "Arnold Schwarzenegger: caméléon." *La Presse* (Montréal, Tuesday, 7 November 2006): A6.

Bohman, James. "The Globalization of the Public Sphere." *Philosophy and Social Criticism*, vol. 24, no. 2/3 (April 1998): 199–216.

"Boomtown Slum." *The Economist*, December 22, 2012: 72–35.

Braud, J.-P. *L'Affaire de la main volée*. Paris: Seuil, 1993.

Bell, Stewart. "Reflect Canadian values school told." *National Post*, Sunday, Nov. 10, 2012: A12.

Bhabha, Homi. "Of Mimicry and Man: The Ambivalence of Colonial Discourse." *October*, no. 28, 1984: 125–33.

Bissoondath, Neil. *Selling Illusions: The Cult of Multiculturalism in Canada*. Toronto: Penguin, 1994.

Bök, Christian. *Cristallography*. Toronto: Coach House Press, 1994.

Bonilla-Maldonado, Daniel. *La Constitución multicultural*. Bogotá: Siglo del Hombre Editores, 2006.

Borduas, Paul-Émile. *Refus Global; Projections libérantes*. Montréal: Parti pris, 1974.

Botchorichvili, Elena. *Seulement attendre et regarder*. Montréal: Boréal, 2012.

Bouchard, Gérard. *L'Interculturalisme: un point de vue québécois*. Montréal: Boréal, 2012.

Campos Zamora, Anyelick and Larissa Tristán Jiménez. *Nicaragüenses en las noticias*. San José (Costa Rica): Universidad de Costa Rica, 2009.

Capote, Truman. "A Day's Work." In *Music for Chameleons*. New York: Random, 1980.

Capra, Fritjof. *The Tao of Physics: An Exploration of the Parallels Between Modern Physics and Eastern Mysticism*. Boulder/New York: Shambhala/Random House, 1983.
Carballo, Emmanuel. *¿Qué país es éste? Los estados Unidos y los gringos vistos por escritores mexicanos de los siglos XIX y XX*. México: Consejo Nacional para la Cultura y las Artes, 1996.
Cardenal, Ernesto. *Cántico cósmico*. Managua: Nueva Nicaragua, 1989.
Carette, Jean-Marie. *Zirska, immigrante inconnue*. Montréal: Serge Brousseau, 1947.
Castaneda, Carlos. *Journey to Ixtlan*. New York: Washington Square Press, 1972.
Castillo Durante, Daniel. *Ce feu si lent de l'exil*. Montréal: XYZ, 2009.
Castillo Durante, Daniel. *Los vertederos de la postmodernidad*. Ottawa: Dovehouse Press, 2000.
Catala, Rafael. "Literatura y ciencia en las culturas de habla Espanola." In *La torre: revista de la Universidad de Puerto Rico*. Special volume on Hispanic literature and Science. Ed. Rivero-Potter. Vol. 3, no. 9, 1998: 66–75.
Certeau, Michel de. *L'Invention du quotidien*. Paris: UGE, 1980.
Chanady, Amaryll. "Entre hybridité et interculture: de nouveaux paradigmes identitaires à la fin du deuxième millénaire." In *L'interculturel au cœur des Amériques*. Eds. D. Castillo Durante and P. Imbert. Ottawa/Winnipeg: Université d'Ottawa/Université du Manitoba/Legas, 2003: 21–34.
Charbonneau, Hector. *Gabriel et Geneviève*. Moncton: éditions d'Acadie, 1974.
Chauveau, Pierre-J. Olivier. *L'instruction publique au Canada*. Québec: A. Côté, 1876.
Chen, Ying. *Quatre mille marches*. Montréal: Boréal, 2004.
Christie, Agatha. *The ABC Murders*. New York: The Berkeley Books, 1963.
Coelho, Paulo. *Once Minutos*. Barcelona: Planeta, 2003.
Continental, August 2002: 33.
Coupland, Douglas. *The Gum Thief*. Toronto: Random House, 2007.
Cram, Buffy. *Radio Belly*. Vancouver: Douglas and McIntyre, 2012.
Dallaire, Roméo. *J'ai serré la main du diable: La faillite de l'humanité au Rwanda*. Outremont, Québec: Libre express, 2003.
Danticat, Edwige. *Create Dangerously*. Princeton: Princeton University Press, 2010.
Davis, Wade. *The Serpent and the Rainbow*. New York: Simon and Schuster, 1985.
Delillo, Don. "Videotape." *Harper's Magazine*, December 1, 1994: 17.
Des Rosiers, Joël. *Théories caraïbes*. Montréal, Tryptique, 1996.
Dewey, John. "Escape from Peril." In *The Quest for Certainty: A Study of the Relation of Knowledge and Action*. London: George Allen & Unwin, 1929.
Diamond, Lynn. *Leslie Muller ou le principe d'incertitude*. Montréal: Triptyque, 2011.
Dickner, Nicolas. *Nikolski*. Québec: Alto, 2007.
"Diversity." *Forbes*, April 3, 2000: 191.
Dostoïevsky, Fiodor. *Les Frères Karamazov*. Paris: Livre de poche, 1972.
Dupont, Éric. *La logeuse*. Montréal: Marchand de feuilles, 2006.
En Vuelo (Aerolineas Argentinas). Noviembre 2000: 49.
En route. February 2003: 15.
Escala (Aeromexico). Noviembre 2002: 93.
Étienne, Gérard. *Le Nègre crucifié*. Montréal: Nouvelle optique, 1974.
Étienne, Gérard. *La pacotille*. Montréal: L'Hexagone, 1991.

Fahroud, Abla. *Le Bonheur à la queue glissante*. Montréal: L'Hexagone, 1998.
Faucher de Saint-Maurice. *De Québec à Mexico*. Montréal: Duvernay, 1874.
Ferretti, Andrée. "Dany Laferrière: le modèle parfait de l'anti-québécois." *Indépendantes.org* (13 December 2013).
Ferron, Jacques. *La Nuit*. Montréal: Parti pris, 1965.
Figes, Orlando. *The Whisperers: Private Life in Stalin's Russia*. London: Allen Lane, 2007.
Finkenthal, Michael. "Le sens des approches inter et multidisciplinaires pour l'étude du multiculturalisme comme problème complexe." In *Trans, multi, interculturalité, trans, multi, interdisciplinarité*, eds. Brigitte Fontille and Patrick Imbert. Québec: Presses de l'Université Laval, 2012 : 19–34.
Fulford, Robert. "Foreword" to Janis Kraulis (ed). *Canada: A Landscape Portrait*. Edmonton: Hurtig, 1982.
Forbes, August 21, 2000: 113
Forbes, May 15, 2000: 55.
García, Carlos Sandoval. *Otros amenazantes: Los nicaragüenses y la formación de identidades nacionales en Costa Rica*. San José: Editorial Universidad de Costa Rica, 2002.
García Márquez, Gabriel. *Cent ans de solitude*. Paris: Seuil, 1968.
Gauthier, Louis. *Souvenirs du San Chiquita*. Montréal: VLB, 1978.
Gilder, George. *Wealth and Poverty*. New York: Basic Books, 1981.
Girard, René. *Des choses cachées depuis la fondation du monde*. Paris: Livre de poche, 1978.
Glissant, Édouard. *Introduction à une poétique du divers*. Paris: Gallimard, 1996.
Glissant, Édouard. *Poétique de la relation*. Paris: Gallimard, 1990.
Greimas, Algirdas Julien. *Maupassant*. Paris: Seuil, 1980.
Greimas, Algirdas Julien. *Sémantique structurale*. Paris: Larousse, 1966.
Gribbin, John. *In Search of Schrödinger's Cat: Quantum Physics and Reality*. New York: Bantam, 1988.
Hage, Rawi. *Cockroach*. New York: Norton and Company, 2010.
Harrison, William H. *In Praise of Mixed Religion*. Montreal/Kingston: McGill/Queen's University, 2014.
Hayden, Bridget. *Salvadoreños en Costa Rica: vidas desplazadas*. San José: Universidad de Costa Rica, 2005.
Heisenberg, Werner. *Le manuscrit de 1942*. Paris: Allia, 2003.
Highway, Tomson. *Comparing Mythologies*. Ottawa: University of Ottawa Press, 2003.
Hongyan, Wang. "Incorporer un contenu autochtone dans l'enseignement public : une façon d'améliorer les relations entre les autochtones et les immigrants anciens et nouveaux au Canada." In *Canadian Issues/Thèmes canadiens, Les relations autochtones immigrants aujourd'hui* (Summer 2012): 53–57.
Huston, Nancy. *Nord Perdu: suivi de Douze France*. Arles/Montréal: Actes Sud/Leméac, 1999.
Hutcheon, Linda. *As Canadian as possible…under the Circumstances*. Toronto: ECW Press/York University, 1990.
Ìcaro. August 2002: 27.
Imbert, Patrick. *Les Amériques transculturelles: Les stéréotypes du jeu à somme nulle*. Québec: Les Presses de l'Université Laval, 2013.

Imbert, Patrick and Adriana Rizzo. "Las bases del sistema territorial nacional frente a lo global en las Américas." *Revista Cronía*, Facultad de Ciencias Humanas. Universidad Nacional de Río Cuarto. Nro. 3, 2001.
Ionesco, Eugène. *Les chaises*, followed by *L'impromptu de l'Alma ou le Caméléon du berger*. Paris: Gallimard, 1973.
Isaacson, Walter. *Steve Jobs*. New York: Simon and Schuster, 2011.
Iyer, Pico. *The Global Soul*. New York: Vintage, 2000.
Iyer, Pico. *Imagining Canada: An Outsider's Hope for a Global Future*. Toronto: The Hart House, 2001.
Jedwab, Jack. *The Multiculturalism Question: Debating Identity in 21st Century Canada*. Montreal/Kingston: McGill/Queen's University Press, 2014.
Jencks, Charles. *The Language of Postmodern Architecture*. New York: Rizzoli, 1977.
Karasik, Gabriela Alejandra. *Cultura e identidad en el Noroeste argentine*. Buenos Aires: Centro editor de América Latina, 1994.
Kymlicka, Will. *Multicultural Citizenship: A Liberal Theory of Minority Rights*. Oxford, Clarendon Press, 1995.
Kincaid, Jamaica. "Girl." In *At the Bottom of the River*. New York: Farrar, Strauss and Giroux, 1984.
Kinsella, W. P. *Shoeless Joe Jackson Comes to Iowa*. Dallas, Texas: Southern Methodist University Press, 1993.
Kingwell, Mark. *The World We Want*. New York: Viking, 2000.
Kokis, Sergio. *Le Pavillon des miroirs*. Montréal: XYZ, 1994.
Kotzwinkle, William. *Midnight Examiner*. New York: Marlowe and Company, 1989.
Kymlicka, Will. *Multicultural Odysseys: Navigating the New International Politics of Diversity*. Oxford: Oxford University Press, 2007.
Laborit, Henri. *Éloge de la fuite*. Paris: Gallimard, 1976.
La Nación. Buenos Aires, viernes 10 de Noviembre de 2000, sección 2: 7 (Extracted from *The Wall Street Journal Americas*).
Languirand, Jacques. *Klondyke* suivi de *Le Québec et l'Américanité*. Montréal: Cercle du livre de France, 1971.
La Presse, Tuesday August 27, 2002: C3.
Laurence, Margaret. *Heart of a Stranger*. Toronto: McClelland and Stewart, 1976.
Leacock, Stephen. "Common Sense and the Universe." In *Last Leaves*. Toronto: McClelland and Stewart, 1945: 35–51.
Leacock, Stephen. "Gertrude the Governess or, Simple Seventeen." In *Nonsense Novels*. Montreal: Publishers Press, 1911.
Le Fanu, Mark. *Evening Standard*. (Quoted on the back cover of Ben Okri's book, *The Famished Road*. London: Jonathan Cape, 1991).
Le Moine, Roger. "L'Aventure mexicaine de quelques Québécois: 1864–1867." In *Les discours du Nouveau Monde au Canada français et en Amérique latine au XIXe siècle/Los discursos del Nuevo Mundo en el Canadá francófono y en América latina en el siglo XIX*. Eds. Marie Couillard and Patrick Imbert. Ottawa: Legas, 1995: 253–262.
Lepage, Robert. *La face cachée de la lune*. Québec: L'Instant même, 2007.

Lord Tweedsmuir (John Buchan). *Canadian Occasions*. Toronto: The Musson Book Company, 1941.
Lucas, Rafael. "Préface." *In* Franketienne, *Mûr à crever*. Bordeaux: Ana éditions, 2004.
Lygeros, Nik. "Effet caméléon." In *Modèle mental de l'Altruisme*, 2000: 1. [On line] [www.megafoundation.org/ubiquity/march00/altruismefr.html].
Madariaga-Vignudo, Lucia. "Les réfugiés africains vus par les Autochtones urbains : une étude de cas du centre-ville de Winnipeg." In *Canadian Issues/Thèmes canadiens, les relations autochtones immigrants aujourd'hui*. Summer 2012: 15–18.
Mandia, Valérie. "Devant les silences de l'univers: des principes d'indétermination et d'incertitude chez Nancy Huston, Lynn Diamond et Isabel Allende." In *Rencontres multiculturelles: imprévus et coïncidences: Le Canada et les Amériques*, ed. P. Imbert. Ottawa: Chaire de recherche: "Canada: enjeux sociaux et culturels dans la société du savoir", 2013: 101–29.
Marissal, Vincent. "Le camélédion." *La Presse* (Montréal, Monday Dec. 4, 2006): A 5.
Martel, Yann. *Life of Pi*. Toronto: Vintage, 2001.
Martel, Yann. *Self*. Toronto: Knopf, 1996.
McLuhan, Marshall. *Notes on the Media as Art Form*. Corte Madera, CA: Gingko Press, 2005.
Michaud, Nando. *Les montres sont molles mais les temps sont durs*. Montréal: Pierre Tisseyre, 1988.
Mignolo, Walter. "Human understanding and (Latin) American Interests—The Politics and Sensibilities of Geohistorical Locations." In *A Companion to Postcolonial Studies*. Eds. H. Schwartz and S. Ray. Oxford: Blackwell, 1999.
Mendieta, Eduardo. *Global Fragments: Latin-Americanisms, Globalizations, and critical Theory*. Albany: State University of New York Press, 2007.
Meyer, Éric. "Pourquoi il faut partir de France." *Géo*, no. 414, August 2013.
Moore, Lorrie. *Anagrams*. New York: Knopf, 1986.
Moravia, Alberto. *Desideria*. Paris: Flammarion, 1978.
Mueller, Thomas. "Hotelgeschichte und Hotelgeschichten." In *Natur, Räume, Landschaften*. Eds. B. Krause and U. Scheck. München: Judicium Verlag, 1998: 189–98.
Murphy, John, Manuel J. Caro and Jung Choi, "Estética Cuántica : A New Approach to Culture", www.gradnet.de/papers/ppmp01.paper/Choi01.htm (consulted December 2013)
Nicolescu, Basarab. "*In vitro* and *in vivo* Knowledge-Methodology of Transdisciplinarity." In *Transdisciplinarity: Theory and Practice*. Ed. Basarab Nicolescu. Cresskill, New Jersey: Hampton Press, 2008.
Pavie, Théodore. *Souvenirs atlantiques*. Paris: Robert, 1838.
Paz, Octavio. *Le singe grammairien*. Paris: Flammarion, 1972.
Peirce, Charles Sanders. "How to Make Our Ideas Clear." In *Popular Sciences Monthly*, January 1878, vol. 12: 286–302.
Peirce, Charles Sanders. *Writings of C.S. Peirce*. Bloomington: Bloomington University Press, 1982.
Penny, Michael. *Outside, Inside*. Montreal: McGill/Queen's University Press, 2014.
Petrowski, Nathalie. "J'habite chez ma sœur." *La Presse*, Montréal, Friday November 15, 1996: A 5.
Philoctète, René. *Massacre River*. New York: New Directions Publishing, 2005.
Pontaut, Jean-Marie. *Demi-Lune*. Paris: Fayard, 2005.

Propp, Vladimir. *Morphologie du conte*. Paris: Seuil, 1972.
RESEARCH infosource Inc. Publication. Canada's Innovation Leaders (Nov. 8th 2013): 20.
Riffaterre, Michel. *Essais de stylistique structurale*. Paris: Flammarion, 1972.
Rivard, Yvon. *Le siècle de Jeanne*. Montréal: Boréal, 2005.
Rivard, Yvon. *Mort et naissance de Christophe Ulric*. Montréal: La Presse, 1976.
Rivero, Alicia. "Heisenberg's Uncertainty Principle in Contemporary Spanish American Fiction." In *Science and the Creative Imagination in Latin America*. Eds. Evelyn Fishburn and Eduardo L. Ortiz. London: Institute for the Study of the Americas, 2005: 251–73.
Roa Bastos, Augusto. *La veille de l'amiral*. Paris: Seuil, 1994.
Robbins, Tom. *Wild Ducks Flying Backward*. New York: Bantam, 2005.
Rodrigue, George and Tom Brokaw. *Blue Dog Man*. New York: Stewart, Tabori and Chang, 1999.
Rossignol, Jean-Philippe. *Vie éclectique*. Paris: Gallimard, 2011.
Rotman Management. Toronto: The University of Toronto. Spring 2019.
Rousset, Jean. *La littérature de l'âge baroque en France: Circé et le paon*. Paris: Corti, 1954.
Routhier, Adolphe-Basile. *Causeries du dimanche*. Montréal: Beauchemin et Valois, 1871.
Roy, Gabrielle. *Un jardin au bout du monde*. Montréal: Boréal, 1994.
Rushdie, Salman. "*The Firebird's Nest*". *The New Yorker*, June 1997: 33–37.
Salomon, Maria. *Social Capital Outcomes of Adult Learning and Literacy Initiatives*. The Centre for Literacy/le centre d'alphabétisation. Québec, August 2010.
Sarabia, Rosa. "Manuscription in *La ciudad sin nombre* by JoaquínTorres-García." *Word and Image* (June 2010, 26: 3): 297–310.
Sarmiento, Domingo Faustino. *Sarmiento's Travels in The United States in 1847*. Translated in English by M.A. Rockland. Princeton: Princeton University Press, 1970.
Saucier, Jocelyne. *Il pleuvait des oiseaux*. Montréal: XYZ, 2011.
Schermbrucker, Bill. *Chameleon*. Vancouver: Talon Books, 1983.
Scliar, Moacyr. *Max and the Cats*. New York: Ballantine, 1990.
Simonnet, Dominique. "Desmond Richardson: 'Je danse ma vie.'" *L'Express*, 14 septembre 2006: 72.
Smiles, Samuel. *Self-Help with Illustrations of Character, Conduct, and Perseverance*. New York: Harper and Brothers, 1874.
Stuart, James. *Three Years in North America*. Edinburgh: R. Cadell, 1833.
Tapscott, Don and Art Caston. *Paradigm Shift*. New York: McGraw Hill, 1995.
Taylor, Charles. *Multiculturalism: Examining the Politics of Recognition*. Princeton: Princeton University Press, 1994.
Teilhard De Chardin, Pierre. *L'avenir de l'homme*. Paris: Seuil, 1959.
The Economist, February 2, 2013: 8.
The Last Whole Earth Catalog. New York: Random House, 1972.
The Real Deal, New York Real Estate News, vol. 9, no. 3, March 2011, back of cover.
Thien, Madeleine. *Do Not Say We Have Nothing*. Toronto: Vintage, 2016.
Thúy, Kim and Pascal Janovjak. *À toi*. Montréal: Libre expression, 2011.
Thúy, Kim. *Rú*. Montréal: Libre expression, 2009.
Toole, John Kennedy. *A Confederacy of Dunces*. Bâton-rouge: Louisiana State University, 1980.

Torres-García, Joaquín. *La ciudad sin nombre*. Montevideo: AAC, 1941.
Vasconcelos, José. "Tratado de metafisica." *Obras completas*: vol III. Mexico: Libros mexicanos unidos, 1959.
Vicomte de Basteret *De Québec à Lima*. Paris: Hachette, 1860.
Wired, March 2000: 158.
Wright, Ronald. *A Short History of Progress*. Toronto: Anansi, 2004.

CONCLUSION

The Surplus of Knowledge

> The re-invention of the Americas, however, abandons such binary relations between centre and periphery, between European and aboriginal…in favour of transversal or horizontal relations…[1]

In the contemporary world, we have shown that binary relations do not help to effectively manage social and cultural relations. These dualistic semantic paradigms like most paradigms are communicated through stereotypes and metaphors, narratives, *a priori* arguments and general cultural and theoretical considerations. They have defined the development of identities to foster cultural homogenization based on and aimed at exclusion in the 19th and 20th century Americas, in line with national characteristics based on European models. We have explored their recontextualization and increased fluidity in the context of globalization and the postmodern/postcolonial/inter-multi-trans-cultural era, which has led to an analysis of multiple self-images going beyond the initial dualism and open to the included third and to otherness. We started with dualism and determinism, which developed into a particular type of Americas, cut into nation-states like 19th century Europe, but without access to an already globalized colonial wealth, meaning that smaller countries struggled to build a big enough economic and socio-cultural market. This was followed by an era of liberal globalization linked to interculturalism, multiculturalism and transculturalism and to the development of new relations amidst confronting multiple self-images. These are henceforth connected to "glocalization" and to américanités / americanidad / americanidade[2], influenced by Americanization but not to be confused with it.

It is important to keep in mind that from a transcultural perspective, culture is not a set of elements connected to the past. Instead, in contemporary Canadian literature, culture is perceived as facilitating communication among groups and individuals. It allows a general exchange of knowledge through the networking of a global human brain that, moreover, gravitates towards dreams powered by technology and galactic expansion escaping natural constraints. This is very well put in a poem by Christian Bök, where the natural aspects of crystallography acquire aesthetic, scientific and techno-galactic dimensions, which allow the encounter between nature and knowledge in a renewed ecological world. This knowledge is perceived as expanding almost infinitely, as reflected in some fascinating images from the film *Life of Pi*, where the ocean and the sky meet. It can be compared with a text written by Christian Bök: "[…] stars and bubbles of air/ rising through an infinite/depth: we rise with them/through this dark, slow/motion snowfall in reverse."[3] This strongly syncretic scientific, techno-galactic dimension resulting from discursive encounters between the psychedelic hippie questioning of digital technology and indigenous and Zen influences is eloquently expressed by Steve Jobs (Apple's former boss), and is strongly embodied in the splendid work of art by renowned indigenous Colombian painter Jacanamijoy. His works are displayed in museums worldwide. He stresses that "Indigenism is a dangerous label and I doubt my work can be explained solely in this way … True art, on the contrary, is there to destroy stereotypes, paradigms, and clichés."[4]

Since then, not forgetting language, history, and customs (which are all the manifestation of notable or forgotten encounters), culture in knowledge societies is strongly linked to the economy, technology, translation[5] and aesthetics and marked by them with a force that can be qualified as gravitational.[6] Complementing its chameleon-like efficiency in seeking out encounters, culture aims for expansion. It is founded on the accumulation of knowledge recognized through diplomas and degrees, on *know-how* evidenced by experience, on efficient access to technological tools allowing the manipulation and management of knowledge, and on the ability to imagine and invent the possible in the chaotic and complex opacity of the world. The continuous link between access to knowledge and the economy within cultural and aesthetic transformations is the engine of democratic dynamics in individuals and groups growing in a cognitive and creative frontier open to talent. This means that cities, and not "empty spaces," are now the new frontier in particular what is called the smart city, which will soon be overflowing with data-analytics services, sensors and algorithms such as the Sidewalk Labs project in Toronto. A city like Toronto is now populated with hundreds of thousands of educated immigrants and foreign students. From this perspective, multiculturalism takes another specific form. It is linked to the idea of the recognition of differences, which produces differences, according to Gregory Bateson[7]; differences, it can even be said, that are often unforeseen, as Glissant reminds us (regarding creolité). The inter, multi and transcultural are, then, the expression of the desire of self-belonging within encounters with others, who are also eager to self-belong.[8] Self-belonging, rather than belonging to an institution, to a state, or to economic-professional functionality, as criticized by Yvon Rivard in all his books and deplored by Simon Nadeau in *L'Autre modernité*: "Étrange sentiment de ne plus s'appartenir… ne plus être dignes de ce qu'il y a de meilleur en nous… la conscience de cette existence absolue qui est la nôtre, sentiment de notre irréductibilité à tout ce qui est gage de la plus grande des libertés, la liberté intérieure?"[9] This desire to self-belong, which implies empowerment, can be seen in the texts of Glissant and Tomson Highway, for example, but it is a desire that inspires dreams in the majority of groups and individuals, especially in new generations connected to the planet who aim to live a practical multiculturalism in an economic dynamic allowing them to achieve their potential. This desire, which is expressed in the management of chameleonization, leads contemporary individualities to try to build a world where self-expansion is developed through the accumulation of knowledge and the multiplication of networks, linked to institutions but not immutably dependent on them in a hierarchical way. This is what the creators of access to knowledge have dreamt of; people like Steve Jobs, Bill Gates, Mark Zuckerberg, George Gilder, and many others. It is also what those who leave the countryside dream of, settling in difficult conditions in the *Arrival cities* referred to by Doug Saunders. Cities which are places of ferment and transition towards more comfortable neighbourhoods and the hope of achieving all human creative potential.

Consequently, transamerican transcultural comparisons help clarify how the different regions of the Americas have developed and how they continue daily to invent and reinvent themselves. They pass from essentialized identities to polycultural relational identities where everyone aims to share what is best in human beings, from pedagogic or technological creativity to spiritual transcendence, as shown by Piscine on the raft with the tiger. As Eduardo Mendieta[10], Abril Trigo[11] and Yvon Rivard[12] underline, the Americas still represent an unfinished project, like any society, of course, but more so than others, because they are based on the legitimacy of displacement, permanent transition and the promotion of change.

In order to live in contexts that allow victory without harming others—to live a life that is not a zero-sum game where one loses and the other wins—it is necessary to access many fields of knowledge, discourses, languages and cultures, developing their originality in new combinations open to permanent social and cultural innovation. These dynamics are underlined by Simon Nadeau in *L'Autre Modernité*. Nadeau evokes the "solitaires d'aujourd'hui et de demain qui ne peuvent se résoudre à rentrer sous la tente des cultures nationales, mais qui refusent tout aussi bien de se fondre dans le vide et l'insignifiance de la culture de masse postnationale."[13] He distances himself from "deux principaux écueils culturels contemporains: soit l'intégrisme culturel, qui condamne sommairement l'individualisme contemporain au nom d'un retour, sous une forme ou une autre, à la 'pensée commune;' et la *nigauderie contemporaine*, qui caractérise le badaud de la culture…"[14] The omnipresent surplus of knowledge is therefore no longer disabling, as is the *not quite*, the inadequate, precursor to the other modernity, that of the 21st century world, according to Nadeau. The continuous expansion of the surplus of knowledge works to overrun the dichotomy between tradition, modernity and colonial logic based on dominance and the imposition of the zero-sum game. This surplus is no longer disabling for the bilingual Francophones of Canada who faced exclusion in the past, trapped within the English dominance of the Nation-State's, and therefore in dualist power relations. The surplus of knowledge is now positive because instead of leading to a status of *not quite*, "like" or inadequate in the eyes of the powerful that impose their monolingualism and monoculture rooted in a limited territory called the Nation-State,—being bi or multilingual and bi or multicultural, becomes an advantage in the context of globalization. Indeed, it is important to understand the others and to speak their language in order to be competitive. Now Canadian Francophones who have graduated and have acquired a specialization in a specific field have an important advantage, because they are at least bicultural and bilingual in two international languages, which help them to become contextualized within the diversity of globalized encounters. This is what leads to the targeting of multiple issues within the dynamics leading to the development of a global brain, networked in the sense understood by Pierre Lévy, who invites us to study his IEML system: *Information Economy Meta-Language*.[15] This would allow the organization of data independent of cultural constraints, therefore providing increased and efficient access to the management of knowledge.

These innovations and dreams do not equal a loss of self. Quite the contrary. The loss of self takes place when it becomes necessary to protect the self in order to face the exclusive dominance of the other, controlling the centers of power and manipulating the dynamics of exclusion, burying the excluded in invisibility while they were already marked by difference. Looking forward, the possibilities of success are multiplying and favouring self-realization. Indeed, in the logic of the knowledge-based society, encounters are numerous and leave positive marks on others and on the self. Arturo Islas, quoted by Iain Chambers, highlights this: "To live elsewhere, means to continually find yourself involved in a conversation in which different identities are recognized, exchanged and mixed, but do not vanish."[16] Chambers' comment concurs with the ideas of numerous thinkers already quoted, to whom we add Kim Butler: "Narratives of diaspora once focused on oppression and displacement; today they focus on diaspora as a potential strategy of empowerment."[17] This connects well with Spillers' conception of diaspora literacy, which in 1991 aimed at analyzing oppression and displacement and finding strategies for empowerment mostly in a corpus of Afro-Caribbean texts.[18] However, it can be maintained that an emphasis on victimization without simultaneously analyzing the dynamics—which can help to escape from a marginalized location—confines the excluded subject to a discourse of resentment. Analyzing exclusion should also consider people to be privileged managers of their knowledge and lives.

Transnational space (especially transnational artistic and literary space), has not been deterritorialized, as it is not concerned with loss, as Pico Iyer highlights in his humorous novel *The Global Soul*. More accurately, the transnational is marked by the exponential increase in global technological and cultural access on a local level, and by the global diffusion of localities: Peruvian hats are sold in the artisan markets of Seoul, Ottawa and Berlin. Spaces, like identities, are more and more relational and can no longer be considered as independent entities.

We are still measuring these dynamics, in initiatives across the planet, spreading global education as proposed by the International Baccalaureate organization. In this case, during the tests for the exams, it is important to consider different value systems when choosing texts to analyze that do not require too many explanatory notes or cause negative reactions from moral or other points of view. It is also important to choose texts that are open to diverse perspectives (different from exclusively local ones), which will open students' perspectives to the world through their challenges. It is also important to understand that the students engaged in international programs want to really live them as international programs. This means that the students' work should not be corrected by local teachers, whose readings would be similar to those they did for national exams and who might impose their stereotypes on textual interpretation aiming to break away from ingrained readings. The reader's place, as we saw earlier, has some significance, and varies as a function of the meanings, which are sought.[19] Encounters and access to the new and the multiple are stimulating. They are no longer the New World's privilege, though the New World stimulates desire through its artistic productions, like *Le cirque du soleil* established by Montrealer Guy Laliberté, or by its universally accessible technology, like the Internet and the tools to access it such as the iPhone, iPad and other systems leading to Artificial intelligence, deep learning or the Blockchain. Encounters and access require us, however, to reject certain habits, which are prisons, as with all protection and stereotyped cultural productions, as E.T. Hall stated in 1959 in *The Silent Language*.[20]

The focus of reflections on meanings and narratives is no longer on solving contradictions in a mythical, fluid, rationally structured and Hegelian synthesis. The goal is now to compile all the possibilities and all the knowledge in a dynamic of the included third, escaping the ignorance programmed by the limits and the prohibitions imposed by state, national and religious allegiances. "The enemy is ignorance" states American Greg Mortenson[21], creator of schools for girls in northern Pakistan and Afghanistan based on his ideal of cross-cultural democracy allowing the *empowerment* of relevant groups, especially of women and young girls. In his case, his practical cross-culturalism had an important impact: Jahan, a young Pakistan girl, was able to expand her knowledge of her culture, language, Muslim religion as well as the sciences and the English language in a school founded by Greg Mortenson. She arrived in a village meeting presided by him, asking for financial help, as she was ready to study medicine in order to help the population of the valley:

> Here comes this teenage girl, in the center of a conservative Islamic village, waltzing in front of a circle of men, breaking through sixteen layers of traditions at once. She had graduated from school and was the first educated woman in a valley of three thousand people. She didn't defer to anyone, sat down right in front of Greg, and handed him the product of the revolutionary skills she'd acquired—a proposal, in English, to better herself, and improve the life of her village.[22]

The cross-cultural dimension involves the recognition of the other in the one, and of the one in the other, in the face of an uncertain future in which a personal and societal development project opens to multiculturalism and to *affirmative action*[23] process, both helping quickly make up for lost time. Encounters require a strengthening of the democratic context to escape discourses obsessed with violent orthodoxy and reinstating state religion, like in Hugo Chavez's Venezuela. In this country, one can see murals showing the Virgin Mary holding the baby Jesus and a Kalashnikov.[24] In order to strengthen democracy, education is the key. Not through the contemplation of heritage[25], but by the study of current encounters (and those to rediscover), through a critical perspective, familiarity with systems of semiotic meaning and training allowing for multiple meanings linked to multiple contexts and the promotion of perspectives favouring dynamics linked to the included third. These dynamics can give a voice to the excluded in a somewhat relative context in the face of orthodoxy. These new perspectives are also based on the acknowledgement (hence the "somewhat") of what is undeniable—although negated—by the arbitrary of the absolute, extolled by countless dictators, despots, fundamentalists and terrorists, hiding murders either by discourse alluding to disappearances or by the promise of eternity. What is undeniable is the fact that people who were alive are now dead, bringing to mind the *testimonies* opposing state terrorism. Keep in mind also the various Truth and Reconciliation Commissions in Central and South America, and the one devoted to reform schools for Indigenous peoples in Canada, where a number of children died from abuse. These dynamics allow us to bear witness by showing that the lynchers (those who have developed a historic and mythical discourse stating that the victim is inadequate, barbaric or guilty of dividing the community), are ignorant and/or liars. This is the moment to point out the lyncher's lie, which sacrifices lives in the name of a truth diffused by a monopoly of historic-archival, orthodox-religious purveyors of media-disinformation. Indeed, if a human being cannot recognize the truth, and cannot know it, and even less impose it (only God can), he can point out the lie. He can point out the lie of those who imprison others in the role of scapegoats, denying them the possibility of development, through genocide, oppression and fatwa (as in the case of Salman Rushdie and many others), or by refusing them access to economic, cultural, social, and educational systems.

This is what nowadays places artists, writers, thinkers and intellectuals against terrorists. This is an image not associated with artists and their ideological colleagues until the seventies when intellectuals were often idealizing revolutionary movements. It is important not to forget the various manifestos produced by the surrealists, by Philippe Sollers championing Maoist China[26] (forgetting the massacres of millions and the deadly re-education camps)[27], and by Michel Foucault presenting, with complete certainty, that Iranian Islamist Mollah's plan was completely transparent:

> Pour les libertés, elles seront respectées dans la mesure où leur usage ne nuira pas à autrui; les minorités seront protégées et libres de vivre à leur guise à condition de ne pas porter dommage à la majorité. Entre l'homme et la femme, il n'y aura pas inégalité de droits, mais différence, puisqu'il y a différence de nature.[28]

In fact, it was the author of *L'Ordre du discours* who published the text! Here he summarizes the disheartening and restrictive perspectives of Iranian religious fundamentalists, as his reasoning relies on a perfunctory interior/exterior dualism. For Michel Foucault, the negative interior is the West while the anti-west exterior is positive. When caught up in interior/exterior dualism, all narratives, even those constructed using approaches completely contrary to scientific ones, are presented as legitimate. Intellectuals too fail in the face of this omnipresent paradigm that always resolves itself in the monism of exclusionary and violent orthodoxy. As if the minorities caused harm to the majority, and not often the opposite (as stressed by Kymlicka and Taylor), and as if there was a difference in nature between man and woman; meaning an essentialization of roles frozen forever. Many intellectuals valued the cause of the dominated, but they resumed the *a priori* of deadly and excluding discourses (which they refused to see as such), or else they borrowed the lines of State disinformation and kept silent about the gulags, because like many intellectuals, especially in Europe in the fifties, sixties and seventies, they were looking for clear solutions, clear definitions, and narratives that would win support and allegiances. On the other hand, current writers, artists and intellectuals tend to recognize the "continuity between peace and human freedom" as Vaclav Havel[29] reminds us. This continuity is complementary to the policies of a social democracy that knows how to engage in liberal competition, as in the policies of affirmative action. These policies are linked to multicultural guidelines and to their practice, according to principles that allow the widest possible extension for groups in non-dominant positions with respect to Human Rights. It is important to remember, however, that this extension exists in a context where the groups that are singled out (by those that consider themselves to be representative of the norm) are not all focused exclusively on racial and ethnic questions. In the 1950s, Franz Boas' student and United-States writer Zora Neale Hurston, stresses: "It is urgent to realize that minorities do think, and think about something other than the race problem."[30] This must also be qualified by the fact that these minorities are sometimes obliged to react to the way people who consider themselves normal see them. However, what preoccupies minorities is being able to participate actively in their economic, scientific, cultural and social development in a new context. This means having access to professions that match their abilities and their diplomas and degrees and having access to services, including health and education. It furthermore means giving them the opportunity to grow, to capitalize on knowledge and to actively participate in the socio-cultural and economic dynamics that allow the appropriation of assets in order to develop them further and to innovate constantly, without losing sight of their evolving cultural baggage.

Notes

1. Barbara Godard, "Relational Logics: Of Linguistic and Other Transactions in the Americas," in *Perspectivas Transnacionais*, ed. Sandra R. G. Almeida (Belo Horizonte: ABECAN/UFMG, 2005), 243.
2. Marcio Bahia, "Americanidad: Towards the Mapping of a Concept," in *Americas World and the World's Americas/Les mondes des Amériques et les Amériques du monde*, eds. Amaryll Chanady, George Handley and Patrick Imbert (Ottawa: Legas, 2006), 23–36.
3. Christian Bök, *Cristallography* (Toronto: Coach House Press, 1994), 67.
4. *Panorama of the Americas*, "La vuelta al día de Jacanamijoy/A day in the life of Jacanamijoy," Official Magazine of Copa Airlines (December 2013), 120.
5. *Translation Effects: The Shaping of Modern Canadian Culture*, eds. Kathy Mezei, Sherry Simon and Luise von Flotow (Montréal/Kingston: McGill-Queen's University Press, 2014).
6. A force already understood by Jules Supervielle, who was inspired by vast Uruguayan spaces in his collection of poems entitled *Gravitations* (Paris: Gallimard, 1925).
7. Gregory Bateson, *Steps to an Ecology of Mind* (New York: Ballantine, 1972).
8. Beyond domination and propaganda, a trend that nourished the thinkers of the 19th and 20th centuries, as highlighted by Julien Benda (quoting Renan): "Man belongs neither to his language nor to his race; he belongs only to himself, for he is a free being, that is, a moral being." Julien Benda, *The Treason of the Intellectuals* (introduction by Roger Kimball) (New Brunswick (USA): Transaction Publisher, 2007), 64.
9. Simon Nadeau, *L'Autre Modernité* (Montréal: Boréal, 2013), 173–74. Our translation: "Strange feeling to no longer belong…to no longer be worthy of what is best inside of us…our conscience of this absolute existence, the feeling of our own *irreducibility*; that is a gauge of the greatest freedom, inner freedom?"
10. Eduardo Mendieta, *Global Fragments: Latin-Americanisms, Globalizations, and Critical Theory* (Albany: State University of New York Press, 2007).

11. Abril Trigo, *¿Cultura uruguaya, culturas linyeras?* (Montevideo: Vintén, 1997).
12. Yvon Rivard, *Le siècle de Jeanne* (Montréal: Boréal, 2005).
13. Nadeau, 232. Our translation: "loners of today and tomorrow who cannot bring themselves to return to the umbrella of national culture, but who refuse as well to blend into the vacuum and the insignificance of post-national mass culture."
14. Nadeau, 233. Our translation: "the two main contemporary cultural pitfalls: either cultural fundamentalism, which summarily condemns contemporary individualism in the name of a return, in one form or another, to the 'common mind', and 'contemporary silliness', that characterizes the cultural spectator..."
15. Pierre Lévy, *La sphère sémantique 1: Computation, cognition, économie de l'information* (Paris: Lavoisier, 2011).
16. Iain Chambers, *Migrancy, Culture, Identity* (London-New York: Routledge, 1993), 18–19.
17. Kim D. Butler, "Multilayered Politics in the African Diaspora: the Metadiaspora Concept and Minidiaspora Realities," in *Opportunity Structures in Diaspora Relations: Comparisons in Contemporary Multilevel Politics of Diaspora and Transnational Identities*, ed. Gloria P. Totoricagüena (Reno: University of Nevada, 2007), 19.
18. Hortense J. Spillers, "Introduction: Who Cuts the Border? Some Readings on 'America'", in *Comparative American Identities: Race, Sex and Nationality in the Modern Text*, ed. Hortense J. Spillers (New York: Routledge, 1991), 1–25.
19. Catherine Doherty, "Local Time, Glocal Space and Glocal Identities in Transnational Education," in *Teaching in Transnational Higher Education* (2008): 160–74.
20. E. T. Hall, *The Silent Language* (New York: Doubleday, 1959), 187.
21. Greg Mortenson and David Oliver Relin, *Three Cups of Tea* (Toronto: Penguin, 2006), 298.
22. *Ibid*.
23. Fidel Tubino, "Las ambivalencias de las acciones afirmativas" in Juan Ansion *et al.*, *Educar en ciudadania intercultural* (Lima: Pontificia Universidad Católica del Perú, 2007), 91–109.
24. Isaac Nahon-Serfaty, "La construction du néo-mythe : discours et production de sens en Amérique latine," in *Trans, multi, interculturalité, trans, multi, interdisciplinarité*, eds. Brigitte Fontille and Patrick Imbert (Québec: Les Presses de l'Université Laval, 2012), 181–201.
25. Patrick Imbert, "Patrimônios e comparações transamericanas," in *Patrimônio Artistico: Caminhos, Memorias e preservaçao*, eds. Nadia Maria Weber Santos and Zila Bernd (Canoas, Brésil: Université UniLaSalle, 2012), 81–91.
26. Philippe Sollers, "Quelques thèses," in *En Chine, Tel Quel* (fall 1974, no. 59): 10–11.
27. About this historical situation, see: Madeleine Thien, *Do not Say We Have Nothing* (Toronto: Vintage, 2017).
28. Daniel Defert and François Ewalt, *Michel Foucault, Dits et écrits*, 1979, "À quoi rêvent les Iraniens ?", (Paris: Gallimard, vol. IV, 1984): 692. Our translation: "Regarding freedom, it will be respected to the extent that it does not harm others; minorities will be protected and free to live as they please, provided they do not harm the majority. Between man and woman, there will be no inequality of rights, but difference, since there is a difference of nature."
29. Vaclav Havel, *Living in Truth* (London/Boston: Faber and Faber, 1989), 188.
30. Quoted in Ann Charters, *The Story and Its Writers* (Boston/New York: Bedford/St Martin's, 1999), 669.

Bibliography

Bahia, Marcio. "Americanidad: Towards the Mapping of a Concept." In *Americas World and the World's Americas/Les mondes des Amériques et les Amériques du monde*. Eds. Amaryll Chanady, George Handley, and Patrick Imbert. Ottawa: Legas, 2006. 23–36.

Bateson, Gregory. *Steps to an Ecology of Mind*. New York: Ballantine, 1972.

Benda, Julien. *The Treason of the Intellectuals*. Introduction by Roger Kimball. New Brunswick, USA: Transaction Publisher, 2007.

Bök, Christian. *Crystallography*. Toronto: Coach House Press, 1994.

Butler, Kim D. "Multilayered Politics in the African Diaspora: The Metadiaspora Concept and Minidiaspora Realities." In *Opportunity Structures in Diaspora Relations: Comparisons in Contemporary Multilevel Politics of Diaspora and Transnational Identities*. Ed. Gloria P. Totoricagüena. Reno: University of Nevada, 2007.

Chambers, Iain. *Migrancy, Culture, Identity*. London/New York: Routledge, 1993.

Charters, Ann. *The Story and Its Writers*. Boston/New York: Bedford/St Martin's, 1999.

Defert, Daniel, and François Ewalt. *Michel Foucault, Dits et écrits*, 1979, "À quoi rêvent les Iraniens?" Paris: Gallimard, vol. IV, 1984.

Doherty, Catherine. "Local Time, Global Space and Global Identities in Transnational Education." In *Teaching in Transnational Higher Education*. Eds. Lee Dunn and Michelle Wallace, 2008. 160–74.

Godard, Barbara. "Relational Logics: Of Linguistic and Other Transactions in the Americas." In *Perspectivas Transnacionais*. Ed. Sandra R. G. Almeida. Belo Horizonte: ABECAN/UFMG, 2005. 241–73.

Hall, E. T. *The Silent Language*. New York: Doubleday, 1959.

Havel, Vaclav. *Living in Truth*. London/Boston: Faber and Faber, 1989.

Imbert, Patrick. "Patrimônios e comparações transamericanas." In *Patrimônio Artistico: Caminhos, Memorias e preservaçao*. Eds. Nadia Maria Weber Santos and Zila Bernd. Canoas, Brésil: Université UnilaSalle, 2012. 81–91.

Lévy, Pierre. *La sphère sémantique 1: Computation, cognition, économie de l'information*. Paris: Lavoisier, 2011.

Mendieta, Eduardo. *Global Fragments: Latin-Americanisms, Globalizations, and critical Theory*. Albany: State University of New York Press, 2007.

Mortenson, Greg, and David Oliver Relin. *Three Cups of Tea*. Toronto: Penguin, 2006.

Nadeau, Simon. *L'Autre Modernité*. Montréal: Boréal, 2013.

Nahon-Serfaty, Isaac. "La construction du néo-mythe: discours et production de sens en Amérique latine." In *Trans, multi, interculturalité, trans, multi, interdisciplinarité*. Eds. Brigitte Fontille and Patrick Imbert. Québec: Les Presses de l'Université Laval, 2012. 181–201.

Panorama of the Americas. "La vuelta al día de Jacanamijoy/A Day in the Life of Jacanamijoy." Official Magazine of Copa Airlines (December 2013): 120.

Rivard, Yvon. *Le siècle de Jeanne*. Montréal: Boréal, 2005.

Sollers, Philippe. "Quelques thèses." In *En Chine, Tel Quel* (Fall 1974, no. 59): 10–11.

Spillers, Hortense J. "Introduction: Who Cuts the Border? Some Readings on 'America.'" In *Comparative American Identities: Race, Sex and Nationality in the Modern Text*. Ed. Hortense J. Spillers. New York: Routledge, 1991. 1–25.

Supervielle, Jules. *Gravitations*. Paris: Gallimard, 1925.

Thien, Madeleine. *Do not Say We Have Nothing*. Toronto: Vintage, 2017.

Translation Effects: The Shaping of Modern Canadian Culture. Eds. Kathy Mezei, Sherry Simon, and Luise von Flotow. Montréal/Kingston: McGill-Queen's University Press, 2014.

Trigo, Abril. *¿Cultura uruguaya, culturas linyeras?* Montevideo: Vintén, 1997.

Tubino, Fidel. "Las ambivalencias de las acciones afirmativas." In Juan Ansion *et al. Educar en ciudadania intercultural*. Lima: Pontificia Universidad Católica del Perú, 2007. 91–109.

www.ingramcontent.com/pod-product-compliance
Ingram Content Group UK Ltd.
Pitfield, Milton Keynes, MK11 3LW, UK
UKHW021837100926
8556IPUK00004B/403

9 781433 172137